T0326585

Austerity and the
Labor Movement

Austerity and the Labor Movement

MICHAEL SCHIAVONE

SUNY PRESS

Published by State University of New York Press, Albany

For information, contact State University of New York Press, Albany, NY
www.sunypress.edu

Production, Eileen Nizer
Marketing, Michael Campochiaro

Library of Congress Cataloging-in-Publication Data

Names: Schiavone, Michael, author.
Title: Austerity and the labor movement / Michael Schiavone.
Description: Albany : State University of New York Press, [2016] | Includes
    bibliographical references and index.
Identifiers: LCCN 2016007687 (print) | LCCN 2016015174 (ebook) | ISBN
    9781438462936 (hardcover : alk. paper) | ISBN 9781438462950 (e-book)
Subjects: LCSH: Labor movement. | Neoliberalism. | Economic policy. |
    Economic stabilization.
Classification: LCC HD4855.S35 2016 (print) | LCC HD4855 (ebook) | DDC
    331.88—dc23
LC record available at https://lccn.loc.gov/2016007687

10 9 8 7 6 5 4 3 2 1

For Su Lan and Valentina

Contents

Acknowledgments

I would like to thank the anonymous reviewers for SUNY Press who offered important recommendations on how to improve the manuscript. Moreover, one reviewer read the original draft and the revised version. This reader offered so many useful suggestions and criticisms that I cannot thank him or her enough. If every reviewer was like this person, academia would be a much better place.

Likewise, Michael Rinella, senior editor at SUNY Press, was great throughout. This was the second time I worked with Michael, and I cannot say enough positive things about him. As I wrote in the acknowledgments of *Sports and Labor in the United States*: "Every author should have an editor like him."

As always, I would like to thank my wife Su Lan and our daughter Valentina. My wife is an inspiration and brings me so much happiness every single day. Without her, this book would have never seen the light of day. As the book was nearing completion, our daughter Valentina came into our lives. She is an incredibly smart and beautiful baby who can always make me smile. I dedicate the book to them.

Chapter 1

Austerity and the Labor Movement

Austerity is the new "buzz word" in advanced industrialized democracies in academia and the media, and more importantly in the lexicon of politicians from both the Left and the Right. Nowadays it is practically impossible to read a newspaper or watch the news without seeing or hearing the term. Austerity policies have become the new norm throughout both the developed and developing world. In 2009, the soon-to-be United Kingdom Prime Minister, David Cameron, infamously declared that the UK was entering an "age of austerity." Austerity policies are now almost a given throughout parts of Europe and are the key component of International Monetary Fund's structural adjustment programs. The United States government adopted austerity measures almost by stealth, whereas following its election in 2013, the Australian Liberal government attempted to introduce a range of austerity measures despite the relatively good health of the Australian economy. Austerity is now seemingly the rule rather than the exception, irrespective of the state of a country's economy.

As to what austerity is and what it entails, the best definition comes from political economist Mark Blyth, who defines austerity as a

> form of voluntary deflation in which the economy adjusts through the reduction of wages, prices, and public spending to restore competitiveness, which is (supposedly) best achieved by cutting the state's budget, debts, and deficits. Doing so, its advocates believe, will inspire "business confidence" since the government will neither be "crowding-out" the market for

investment by sucking up all the available capital through the issuance of debt, nor adding to the nation's already "too big" debt.

Blyth goes on to quote University of Chicago academic and austerity supporter, John Cochrane:

> Every dollar of increased government spending must correspond to one less dollar of private spending. Jobs created by stimulus spending are offset by jobs lost from the decline in private spending. We can build roads instead of factories, but fiscal stimulus can't help us to build more of both.[1]

However, what austerity entails can vary from country to country. *The Economist* claims that "A government can impose an austerity programme and still spend far more than it receives in the form of taxes; indeed the British coalition government had a deficit of 9.3% of GDP in the first year of austerity, a very high figure by peacetime standards. But because this was less than the 11% of GDP in the year before, it counts as austerity."[2] Nevertheless, at its heart, austerity advocates believe that a government should intervene as little as possible in the workings of the market. In other words, austerity goes hand in hand with neoliberalism. But it is important to note that under austerity measures governments have generally been raising taxes on individuals. Tax increases are not normally associated with neoliberalism. While governments have been raising taxes, primarily personal taxes, they have also been lowering business taxes. It is the general public who must endure tax increases, not business.

While there is a plethora of news stories and the like regarding austerity, one area that is neglected is the labor movement's response to austerity worldwide. This book will primarily examine the UK and US labor movement's efforts against austerity. As we shall see, the labor movement is seemingly powerless in the UK and the US to prevent or even mitigate austerity policies. This has been a major detriment to the lives of the majority of people in both countries. While the focus will be on the UK and the US, the book will also provide an overview and analyze the labor movement's attempt to overturn austerity in Greece, Spain, and Ireland. The common theme throughout is that, despite mass protests (though these are rare in the US), austerity has continued largely unabated in Greece, Spain, Ireland, the UK, and the US, and has caused much human suffering, while having a limited impact, even on the most optimistic account, on improving the economic well-being of each country.

Neoliberalism and Austerity

What led to the rise of austerity? For us to answer that question we first must understand neoliberalism. Neoliberalism, which is the ideology behind the latest rise of austerity, is a revival of laissez-faire liberalism. The proponents of neoliberalism argue that by removing government involvement from almost all aspects of managing the economy, and allowing the market to perform its "natural" role, this will result in economic prosperity for a country and its citizens. Thus, governments should privatize all public enterprises, slay the inflation dragon, liberalize trade and finance, and embrace austerity policies. Neoliberalism has become such a dominant political ideology that political parties all across the ideological spectrum have adopted neoliberal reforms in both developed and developing countries. Arguably the best analysis of what led to neoliberalism comes from Stephen Gill, who identifies four essential initiators of the neoliberal order: multinational companies, the transnational financial network, transnational elite networks, and the major capitalist countries, such as the US.

Gill argues that multinationals (MNCs) have the power to play off one country against another, and are thus able to get the best deal for their operations. They can do this because they have the power to decide the geographical location of production. They can shift funds from one country to another, or even open a production plant in one country while closing a production factory performing the same task in another. Furthermore, MNCs "through pricing and intra-firm trade, minimize tax liabilities and maximize global profits, implying a narrower tax base for governments than would be the case if production were organized along national lines."[3] In other words, by threatening a government's tax base, MNCs give governments an excuse to cut back on health and welfare services and thus please the international elites.

The second initiator of neoliberalism that Gill identifies is the transnational financial network. He argues that due to the mobility of capital, the "investment climate of one country will be judged by business with reference to the climate which prevails elsewhere." This leads to governments being "pressured into providing an investment climate judged attractive by global standards." In addition, the mobility of capital makes it easier for MNCs to play off one government against another, and even different regions in the same country, to obtain the best deal for themselves.[4] Of course, MNCs consider that the structuring of the "best deals" is often along neoliberal lines.

The third main initiator of neoliberal globalization, according to Gill, are the "organic intellectuals" in transnational elite networks. Gill claims these transnational elites are located in unofficial bodies like the Trilateral Commission, Bilderberg conferences, and official bodies such as the IMF and OECD. Regarding the Trilateral Commission, Gill claims that it cultivates politicians and future leaders, thus further strengthening the neoliberal ideology in political circles. He also emphasizes the role that some British and American universities play in educating the proponents of IMF austerity packages and the "best and brightest" of the Third World, thus extending and strengthening neoliberalism. Furthermore, these transnational elite networks are "well-served by a range of international periodicals, such as . . . *The Economist, Far Eastern Economic Review*, and *The Wall Street Journal*."[5]

Thus, through transnational elite networks, there is a strengthening of the neoliberal agenda, increasing pressure on states to conform to the globalization project. However, it is not just MNCs and transnational financial and elite networks that have been at the forefront of the neoliberal agenda, according to Gill. He also argues that major capitalist states, especially the US, have been a crucial part of the globalization project. Beginning with the second Reagan administration, Gill argues that the US led the push for a new world order. This involved the "liberalizing of the more dynamic sectors of the international economy, as well as liberalizing labour and capital markets within the United States, in ways which benefit the strongest American corporations."[6]

As I shall demonstrate in the following chapters, the transnational financial networks, the transnational elite, and the major capitalist countries have all been at the forefront of the austerity agenda. For them, "simple" neoliberalism was not enough. Neoliberal advocates wanted further reform. Gill argues that "[w]hat has emerged is a consensus on the part of conservative, liberal and social democratic parties on the need for deeper neo-liberal reforms to flexibilize and further weaken organized labor and socialist forces, and thereby to deepen disciplinary neo-liberalism by means of policies of austerity stretching well into the future to pay for the gigantic bailouts of capital."[7] Thus, part of the austerity agenda is an attempt to dramatically undermine the power of the labor movement because this will allow even more neoliberal "reforms" in the future. Quite simply, without organized labor being a bulwark against neoliberalism, right-wing policies can be even more easily enacted.

Gill claims that these initiators of neoliberalism are trying to form a "new constitutionalism," which he defines as "the political project of attempting to make transnational liberalism, and if possible liberal democratic capitalism, the sole model for future development." New constitutionalism does not rely on ideology and market power alone for the restructuring of the world economy along neoliberal lines; there is also an emphasis on strengthening the surveillance mechanisms of the WTO, IMF, and private bond-rating agencies. The increase in surveillance techniques "helps to sustain the legal and political conditions for transnational capital" by locking countries in to the neoliberal project, regardless of changes in government. For example, Gill claims that new constitutionalist thinking lies behind the EU's Maastricht agreement. Within its legal framework, governments are forced to implement neoliberal reforms regardless of their citizens' wishes.[8] This has led to a convergence of government economic thinking among EU states. Thus, there is a reduction in citizens' democratic choice, as government and opposition parties resemble each other in their economic policies. Moreover, in this era of austerity, this legal framework locks countries into the austerity agenda. Thus, irrespective of the controlling political party, countries are forced to embrace austerity to some extent.

It is important to note that while austerity follows on from the logic of neoliberalism, and as Gill alludes to and I shall demonstrate in the following chapters, the current rise of austerity is arguably without precedent—it is neoliberalism taken to the nth degree. I will highlight that neoliberalism and, more specifically for the purposes of this book, austerity have been detrimental not only to the economic and general well-being of working people and the lower socioeconomic classes in the US and the UK but to the *majority* of the population in both countries. The book also demonstrates that this holds true in Greece, Spain, and Ireland, as well. Moreover, I shall argue that, as Gill notes, the rise of austerity has indeed weakened organized labor in many countries. However, a key theme throughout the following chapters is that in many cases organized labor has accepted a level of austerity due to self-interest and/or underestimating the drive by politicians and international organizations to implement austerity. Therefore, organized labor has played a role in its own decline as well as accepting the rise of austerity across the globe.

One must ask, however, if austerity has been so detrimental to the majority of people in a variety of countries why politicians have continued with such economic policies. Is it rational for a wide variety of politicians to embrace austerity? A potential answer is that with the rise of neoliberalism in the early 1980s politicians from both the Left and the Right have become beholden to such economic policies. Thus, following the world economic crisis of 2007–2008 and the perceived failure of economic stimulus packages in a number of countries to solve the problem (see Chapters 2, 3, and 4), politicians returned to their ideological roots. As such, it was necessary for countries to adopt austerity policies to stave off an even greater economic collapse. Moreover, austerity policies were seen as leading to economic booms in Australia, Denmark, Ireland, and Sweden in the 1980s and early 1990s. It is beyond the scope of this book to determine whether austerity did indeed benefit these countries, but the perception was that austerity led to economic prosperity. And, as is often the case, perception became reality: austerity works. Another potential reason why politicians continue to advocate for austerity is that such economic policies have not been detrimental to all segments of the population. The so-called "one percenters" and the rich more generally have largely benefited from austerity. Indeed, as we shall see, there has been rising economic inequality in the majority of countries where austerity has been implemented. Now whether politicians have embraced austerity and neoliberalism more generally to benefit the wealthy is open to considerable debate—one that is beyond the scope of this book. However, even though austerity has caused immense suffering to the working class, poor, and vulnerable, and seems not to have helped the economy at large, politicians still believe wholeheartedly in austerity. Thus, whether the so-called elites (politicians as well as the mainstream media, who generally favor austerity) in many countries are austerity ideologues, or believe that austerity will eventually benefit the majority, or favor the wealthy is uncertain, but what is beyond dispute is austerity is *the* dominant economic policy in Greece, Spain, Ireland, the UK, and the US and has had adverse effects on the working class, the poor, and the vulnerable in each of these countries.

As we shall see, the rise of austerity is in part due to the ideological agenda of the organic intellectuals to remake the world along neoliberal lines. At the same time, the rise of austerity is also due in part to an attempt to solve the world's economic problems that came to the fore during the global financial crisis. While the current version of austerity is in many ways unprecedented, this is not to claim that austerity has not been implemented in the past. We now turn to a brief history of austerity in the US and UK.

Austerity in the United States and the United Kingdom: 1920–1930s

The early part of the twentieth century saw many countries across the globe struggling economically. The US and the UK, among others, decided the best course of action was to reduce government spending. These countries' respective governments decided that austerity was the cure to economic woes.

The US, unlike most other countries, emerged from World War I in reasonably good financial shape—there were high levels of investment and public spending. However, despite the flourishing stock market, unemployment began to increase and agricultural prices were decreasing. This came to a head in 1929, when the stock market crashed. The crash led to a fear that—just as the UK had done earlier—the US would abandon the gold standard. This resulted in a flow of money leaving the country, which in turn led to a rise in interest rates, a weakened economy and, more important, people suffering even further. In response to the crisis, the Hoover administration initially increased public spending; by 1931 public spending was up a third from 1929. However, state spending as a percentage of GDP declined. Moreover, the budget was in deficit as taxes declined and spending increased. This led President Hoover to attempt to balance the budget.[9]

In 1931 Hoover infamously declared that under his watch the US could not "squander itself to prosperity on the ruin of its taxpayers." Taxes were thus raised across the board to the tune of $900 million, and there was a reduction in public spending. Rather than help the economy, these austerity policies made things significantly worse. The economy went into a depression, with GDP declining by 12.9 percent, unemployment increasing from 8 percent in 1930 to 23 percent in 1932, and imports being greatly reduced. The latter had the effect of hindering other countries' attempts to export their way out of financial hardship. It was a lose-lose situation for all concerned. The incoming Roosevelt administration upon gaining power dramatically increased public spending; in 1934 spending was increased by 10.7 percent. This helped the economy, and unemployment decreased to 17 percent in 1936, with GDP increasing by 12.9 percent. As a result, adjusted for inflation, GDP increased to the same level it was in 1929. However, austerity was soon to roar back when, following the advice of treasury secretary Henry Morgenthau, Roosevelt implemented new social security taxes and monetary tightening in an attempt to balance the budget. This led to an increase in unemployment and dragged the economy back into recession in 1938, with GDP declining by 3.3 percent for the year and 5.5 percent since 1936. It was not until the Roosevelt administration fully embraced the New Deal, which was according to H.W. Arndt the "most spectacular attempt that was made after the Great Depression to promote recovery by means of a deliberate expansionist policy as the chief stimulus of economic activity, and without recourse to totalitarian control of the economic system," and US entry into World War II (which led to massive public spending) that the economy began to recover. By 1944, unemployment was only 1.2 percent and the New Deal and the War led to successive years of GDP growth above 8 percent.[10]

In other words, it was Keynesianism and its policy of increased government spending during an economic downturn, and not austerity, that led the US out of the Great Depression. In repudiating austerity, Roosevelt astutely claimed, "Let us unanimously recognize . . . that the federal debt, whether it be twenty-five billions or forty billions can only be paid if the nation obtains a vastly increased citizen income."[11] The UK also adopted austerity policies to combat its economic downturn in the 1920s. As in the US, these policies only made things worse.

Following World War I, the UK was struggling economically. The war had taken a heavy toll. The UK government and treasury of the 1920s and 1930s believed in unfettered capitalism; the government should not intervene, or intervene as little as possible, in the workings of the market. This position was summed up by the Chancellor of the Exchequer, Stanley Baldwin, in 1922: "Money taken for government purposes is money taken away from trade, and borrowing will thus tend to depress trade and increase unemployment." Likewise, the treasury economist Ralph Hawtrey stated: "The original contention that the public works themselves give additional employment is radically fallacious. When employment is improved, this is the result of some reaction on credit, and the true remedy for unemployment is to be found in a direct regulation of credit on sound lines."[12]

While the treasury would not intervene to spend money to "buy" the country's way out of the economic malaise, the government attempted to pay back its loans taken out during the war, and in 1925 the government returned to the gold standard. Such a strategy benefited not the economy, but finance profits. The austerity policies led to unemployment increasing to 22.1 percent in 1932, compared to 10.4 percent in 1929, while GDP declined by 1.63 percent in 1930, 6.47 percent in 1931, and 2.17 percent in 1932. It was not only Conservative governments in the UK that embraced austerity—a Labour government also followed similar economic policies. Under the Labour minority, government austerity policies remained in place, the economy and, more importantly, people were still suffering, and there was still a budget deficit. However, following the downfall of the Labour government, the incoming Conservatives made things even worse. In an attempt to receive a loan of $200 million from J.P. Morgan and Company, an attempt that was to prove successful, the government cut spending while increasing taxes. These policies led to the UK abandoning the gold standard in 1931. This resulted in a decline of unemployment to 15.5 percent in 1935, but real economic output in 1938 was only slightly above 1918 levels. Moreover, austerity policies were not even successful in reducing the deficit; the debt to GDP ratio increased from 170 percent in 1930 to 190 percent in 1933.[13]

Overall, the thinking by governments of both the Left and Right during the period in the United Kingdom was summed up by Winston Churchill in 1929:

> Let us, first of all, by way of preliminary digression, address ourselves to the burning question of whether national prosperity can be restored or enhanced by the Government borrowing money and spending it on making more work. The orthodox Treasury view . . . is that when the Government borrow[s] in the money market it becomes a new competitor with industry and engrosses to itself resources which would otherwise have been employed by private enterprise, and in the process it raises the rent of money to all who have need of it. This orthodox view holds, therefore, that a special, even perhaps a double, responsibility rests upon the State when it decides to enter the money market as a rival to the ordinary life and trade of the country. The onus is laid upon the Government to prove either that the need is paramount as in the case of national safety being in danger; or that the work is necessary, and would not be otherwise undertaken; or that the spending of the money by the Government would produce more beneficial results than if it had been left available for trade and industry.[14]

However, in the end, the UK economy only recovered due to increased spending on the military in the lead-up to World War II, as well as a housing boom that was due largely to short-term interest rates being near zero percent and an expansionary monetary policy. In other words, the UK economy recovered not through austerity and unfettered capitalism, but through Keynesianism.[15] Thus, in both the US and the UK in the 1920s and 1930s, austerity did not help their economies—it made them worse.

Of course, whether an even more left-wing economic policy would have produced a better result is open to debate. What is not debatable is that partly as a result of the success of Keynesianism in the US and UK, governments across the political spectrum in the West began to embrace Keynesianism. As such, Keynesianism for a long time was considered economic orthodoxy. This orthodoxy was not to last, however, as Keynesianism was considered by an increasing number of economists and politicians as being unable to deal with stagflation: a depressed economy and high inflation. This led in part to neoliberalism (which is basically a new name for unfettered capitalism) and austerity once again coming back in vogue. Austerity was used in the 1980s and early 1990s in Australia, Denmark, Ireland, and Sweden, among other countries (see Chapter 2 for a discussion on whether austerity was the main cause of Ireland's economic boom). However, for the purposes of this book, we will examine when austerity was next used in the US, more specifically in New York City.

Austerity in New York City in the 1970s

In 1974 it was becoming clear that New York City was mired in a severe financial crisis; approximately 20 percent of the city's operating funds went to paying off debt. The crisis reached a peak in March 1975 when the US's major investment bank refused to "underwrite or buy more New York City notes or bonds." In response, an austerity "government" was formed. This was not a democratically elected government, but one imposed upon the city. The "government" was comprised of a number of bodies with wide-ranging powers, the most important and powerful being the Emergency Financial Control Body (EFCB). The EFCB membership compromised the "governor, the mayor, the state comptroller, the city comptroller, and three appointees of the governor from the private sector." The "government" cut social services to the poor, attacked unionized workers' rights, and offered "incentives to its wealthy financial class." Mayor Abraham Bearne announced that forty thousand jobs would be lost and there would be spending cuts to the city's public hospitals, the City University of New York, and a range of other social services. Offering incentives to the rich was ironic considering that the banks played a role in the financial crisis in the first place.[16]

Richard Seymour outlines how the banks contributed to the crisis and then in turn profited from it:

> The first stage of this was encouraging the city—through the Technical Debt Management Committee and the Board of Directors of the Citizen Budget Commission on which the banks were well represented—to get further and further into debt. The banks profited from this. The second was protecting their own profit margins when the debt became obviously unsustainable. They unloaded their own investments in the city's precarious debts, selling them off while the price was reasonably high. Simultaneously, they advised their small investor clients to purchase large amounts of this precarious debt. The third was insisting that in the event of the city's bankruptcy, the financial system should have first lien on the city's funds—which meant, of course, placing their needs above those of residents. The fourth was identifying the source of the problem as union militancy and social programmes, and devising a 'rescue' plan predicated on austerity. Fifth, the banks began to establish institutional mechanisms to convey their demands for austerity to the city's authorities, beginning with the Financial Community Liaison Group. Finally, and with aplomb, they gained effective control over the city's politics and finances through a series of institutions, above all the EFCB."[17]

Thus, the banks partly caused the crisis, a crisis that led to tens of thousands of public sector workers losing their jobs, and the poor suffering a greater burden due to spending cuts aimed at them, while the banks profited from it.

Considering the range of spending cuts and proposed job losses, it was not a surprise that workers mobilized for protest in an attempt to get the austerity measures overturned. The teachers' union went on strike for eight days; the union went on strike even though its leadership was against such a strategy. Likewise, sanitation workers engaged in a two-day wildcat strike. Following the announced public sector layoffs, hundreds of policemen blocked Brooklyn Bridge and protested in front of City Hall.

These were not authorized protests; rank-and-file workers were engaging in protest action in an attempt to protect their wages, conditions, and jobs. However, soon the municipal union leadership would undermine the militancy of the rank-and-file. Believing that the austerity policies were inevitable, and any protest action would be pointless, the municipal unions' leadership cut a deal with City Hall. The unions supported the Emergency Financial Control Act, which came into existence in September 1975, which among other measures included a year-long wage freeze for city employees that could be extended until June 1978. Not surprisingly, the media, banks, and politicians praised the unions' stance. Quite simply, the union leadership did not care about the wider community; it was only trying to minimize the damage to its members. In return for supporting austerity measures, in 1977 the New York state legislature allowed the municipal unions to "agency shop." Agency shop is where nonunion employees of a company, which also has union employees, have to pay a fee to cover the union's costs involved in collective bargaining. The municipal unions had been attempting to get the legislature to allow them to agency shop since the 1960s. Thus, in this regard it was a benefit to the union. Nonetheless, the decision to support austerity policies led to workers suffering financial hardship. In 1975, twenty-five thousand municipal employees were fired; by 1980 the municipal workforce declined by another forty thousand due to natural attrition. Those workers lucky enough to keep their jobs were forced to work harder because of a decreased workforce, were subject to a wage freeze until 1978, and brought home lower net incomes due to higher taxes; also, any worker employed after 1976 had a greatly reduced pension plan.[18]

That the union leadership only cared about narrow self-interest greatly reduced the strength of the anti-austerity protest movement compromised of community groups and students. New York City's municipal unions previously had a long history of mass mobilization to support workers' rights and the community. The union leadership ensured that this would not happen in the fight against austerity. Whether the anti-austerity movement would have been successful to stave off the austerity policies is uncertain, but by striking a deal with City Hall the union leadership doomed the protest movement.[19]

As we shall see in the following chapters, unions putting their own interests above other unions, workers, and the wider community is a common theme when organized labor is confronted by governments intent on implementing austerity measures. They would rather cut deals with the government, even when it means lower wages and job losses for their members, in the belief that if they do not do so the government will impose even harsher measures. Under this scenario unions believe they are defending their members' interests by accepting job losses, lower wages, and worse working conditions. Quite simply, organized labor has failed to learn from the past, and thus has been doomed to repeat it.

In addition to condemning the protest movement, the sell-out by the New York municipal unions' leadership had negative consequences for workers across the country. Indeed, unions and workers are not simply victims of austerity and neoliberalism, but by agreeing to austerity measures they make large segments of the population suffer. As the powerful municipal unions in New York City were forced to accept concessions, this inspired mayors across the country to demand similar concessions from their unionized workforce. As Michael Spear claims, "[f]rom San Francisco, to Cleveland, and to Atlanta, mayors began to increasingly insist upon concessions from their municipal unions. Perhaps the clearest example of this demand for concessions after New York City is when Mayor Maynard Jackson (the first African American mayor of Atlanta) fired thousands of striking Atlanta sanitation workers (most of whom were African American) in 1977." Moreover, since then a majority of municipal unions in New York have focused on their own self-interest to the detriment of workers as a whole. In mayoral elections, there have been numerous instances in which the unions have remained neutral or supported right-wing candidates, such as Edward Koch, Rudolph Giuliani, and Michael Bloomberg. The unions also embraced a top-down approach and generally disdained rank-and-file involvement; it was the leadership that decided policy, not the rank-and-file.[20] There was also two other major consequences of the municipal unions supporting austerity policies and agreeing to concessions; namely, it signaled the end of the social contract and heralded the era of concession bargaining, an era that continues to this day.

The social contract was "characterized by management's willingness to live with the labor movement where it was already organized and its continued resistance to and avoidance of unions outside labor's well-organized core sectors. Unions . . . accepted managerial prerogatives that conceded control over production, the labor process, and technology, as well as other strategic business decisions. They also accepted productivity bargaining. . . . Both parties accepted (or tolerated) substantially greater government intrusion into what had been the private sphere of labor-management relations."[21] While business unionism was relatively successful during the boom period of American capitalism (1947–1973), it could not cope with the attack on unionism from the government and employers following the abandonment of the social contract in the late 1970s. However, once the social contract was assigned to history, unions that adopted a self-interested approach were unable to stop or even slow the attacks upon it by the government and business. This is because by concentrating on the existing membership and on "bread and butter" issues such as wages and working conditions, unions were not a major part of people's lives. Business unions embrace the "servicing model" of unionism. As the name implies, its primary purpose is to service the needs of its members, and business unions are not concerned about organizing workers not belonging to a union. What happens to other workers and the wider community is a concern only to business unions if it is related to them and their members. Consequently, most people in the wider community did not really care that the labor movement was under attack. Thus, unions could not rely on community support and, as happened with the New York City municipal unions, an increasing number of unions from that point forward agreed to concessions even if it meant others suffered. As Richard Hurd argues, "[o]nce concessionary bargaining had taken hold, it proved difficult for unions to halt the trend especially given economic pressures which persisted."[22]

Today, in almost every industry imaginable, employers demand that unions engage in concession bargaining: "From the makers of agricultural implements, aluminum, automobiles, buildings, glass, newspapers, oil, processed meats, rubber, steel, to airlines, mine owners, supermarket chains, trucking companies, to local and regional governments and school districts, came demands for wage cuts, wage and pension freezes, reduction or elimination of automatic cost-of-living adjustments, and the establishment of permanently lower pay scales for newly hired workers." Concession bargaining has even extended to the sporting arena as unions in the National Basketball Association, the National Football League, and the National Hockey League have been forced to accept substandard contracts.[23]

Employers demand concessions irrespective if the company is profitable or not—they just want increased profits. Although companies demand concessions from their ordinary workforce, they often have no hesitation in paying management large bonuses. Thus the sell-out by the leadership of the New York City municipal unions had far-reaching consequences. At the same time this was occurring in the US, the idea of austerity policies as an economic policy throughout the world was gaining credence through the efforts of the International Monetary Fund.

Neoliberalism, the IMF, and Structural Adjustment Policies

As noted above, during the New York City financial crisis, much of the Western world was trying to deal with stagflation and the seemingly inability of Keynesianism to overcome the problem. This led many politicians to embrace neoliberalism. Milton Friedman's ideas became very popular, especially his theory of monetarism. Monetarist policy argues that "by making money scarce, inflation can be combated effectively and sound micro-economic reasoning can be forced upon the state as a whole." The US Treasury "pushed for the 1984 decision to abolish the US withholding tax on foreign holdings of US bonds as this increased the attractiveness of US financial assets to foreign investors." This successfully encouraged Japanese financial liberalization, and resulted in Japanese investors becoming the major foreign funding contributor of US deficits in the 1980s. In addition, in the UK, the Thatcher government embraced neoliberalism, and this resulted in the UK's decision in 1979 to abandon exchange controls. Likewise neoliberal treasurers Paul Keating and Roger Douglas had a large role in Australia's and New Zealand's decisions to abolish their respective capital controls. In relation to financial markets, the US abandoned a range of capital controls in 1974 in an attempt to enhance the attractiveness of New York City as a financial capital market. And the UK's decision to eliminate its capital controls in 1979 was partly due to attempting to retain London's competitiveness compared to New York. This pattern continued throughout the 1980s; the US decision to abolish withholding tax on foreign holdings of US securities in 1984 led to West Germany implementing the same policy. This was West Germany's first major deregulatory move in the 1980s.[24] Quite simply, as Gill argues, the developed world began to embrace neoliberalism in a large part due to major capitalist countries. Whether Keynesianism was able to deal with stagflation or a more left-wing economic policy would have been more successful is open to debate, but what is beyond debate is that an increasing number of politicians around the world became advocates of neoliberalism. Neoliberalism became the dominant political ideology.

Furthermore, corresponding with the actions of various Western governments was the formulation of the Washington Consensus by economist John Williamson in 1989. This led to neoliberalism being "exported" to the developing world. According to Williamson,

> [t]he first written usage was in my background paper for a conference that the Institute for International Economics

convened in order to examine the extent to which the old ideas
of development economics that had governed Latin American
economic policy since the 1950s were being swept aside by
the set of ideas that had long been accepted as appropriate
within the OECD. In order to try and ensure that the back-
ground papers for that conference dealt with a common set
of issues, I made a list of ten policies that I thought more or
less everyone in Washington would agree were needed more
or less everywhere in Latin America, and labeled this the
"Washington Consensus."[25]

The ten policies are fiscal discipline, reordering public expenditure priorities (which "suggested switching expenditure in a progrowth and pro-poor
way, from things like nonmerit subsidies to basic health and education
and infrastructure"), tax reform, liberalizing interest rates, a competitive
exchange rate, trade liberalization, liberalization of inward foreign direct
investment, privatization, deregulation, and property rights. Williamson
claims that such policy "ideas . . . had long been accepted as appropriate
within the OECD," but in reality, as Blyth claims, apart from the liberalization of foreign direct investment and countries ensuring a competitive
exchange rate, none of these policies were used to any great extent by
developed countries across the world during this timeframe.[26]

Nonetheless, while such policies were not used as a complete economic package by developed countries, as noted above, the groundwork
was put into place across the developed world by Reagan, Thatcher, and
other neoliberal politicians. Moreover, the Washington Consensus was
soon to be tested by the International Monetary Fund (IMF) and the
World Bank in developing countries that were struggling economically.
It was the transnational elite network within the IMF and the World
Bank that pushed for austerity policies. As was the case in the US and
UK in the 1920s and 1930s, austerity policies under the guise of the
Washington Consensus were not anymore successful in the developing
world. As Blyth notes: "As a recent survey of the results of IMF and World
Bank reforms in Latin America shows, after the crises of the 1990s, the
region's reform index was basically flat in the 2000s. What seemed to be
generated instead of growth were large financial crises, as capital accounts
were opened up and controls on inflows were abolished—a uniquely IMF
addition to the Washington Consensus checklist—and banking systems
were liberalized. For Latin America in particular, the 1990s compounded
the losses of the debt crisis decade of the 1980s." Instead of leading to

growth, austerity policies in Latin America led to economies contracting. In addition, these economies performed better in the 2000s when many countries either abandoned austerity policies or greatly reduced their size and impact. Austerity did not lead to growth; it led to economies declining in size. Furthermore, many countries had higher debt levels after the IMF "reforms." For example, Mexico owed $100 billion in 1985. Mexico paid $160 billion against its debt from 1985–1994. But at the end of that period, Mexico still owed $140 billion. By 2000, Mexico's debt exceeded $160 billion. Currently, Mexico's total foreign debt is $211 billion, while its current total debt is $462 billion. Likewise, Brazil paid off $216 billion in interest from 1989 to 1997, but still owes $398 billion. Its current total debt is $1.1 trillion dollars.[27]

Thus, structural adjustment programs in Latin American countries like Mexico and Brazil did not solve the debt problem and economic crises in these countries—they made the problems worse. The failure of the IMF and the World Bank to help developing countries economically led the World Bank to move away from austerity and the Washington Consensus. However, the IMF not only failed to question why such polices failed in developing countries—they soon began to implement them in struggling developed countries. As in the developing world, austerity did not make things better; it arguably made the crisis much worse.

Due to the economic crisis consuming many countries and considering the arguably negative impact austerity has had on developed countries, it is not surprising that there have been mass protests against such policies and the ideology behind them around the world. Arguably the most famous recent protest movement has been the Occupy Wall Street Movement, now renamed the Occupy Movement. However, for decades it was the labor movement that protected employees' rights and engaged in mass protests against policies that adversely affected all working people, their families, and the community. Without the labor movement it is very doubtful that workers would have the "eight-hour workday, five-day workweek, paid vacations, retirement and health-care benefits, safety regulations, bans on sweatshops or child labor, protections against employment discrimination, and other workplace advances now taken for granted. . . . [These] were the result of struggles—invariably protected, often bloody, and sometimes even deadly—by workers and their unions."[28] Quite simply, unions have helped *all* workers and their families lead a better life than would have otherwise been the case. However, the labor movement is in a major decline in both the US and the UK. Nonetheless, workers are not simply victims of austerity and neoliberalism more generally. They have the power to make positive change to society. Like-wise, as we shall see in the following chapters, when organized labor failed to confront neoliberalism and austerity, the end result was that almost all segments of the population suffered.

Unionism in the United States

While there have been many explanations of what led to labor's decline in the US, undoubtedly business unionism had a major role. Business unionism is concerned only with narrowly defined so-called "bread and butter" issues, such as union members' wages and working conditions. The best definition of business unionism is provided by Robert Hoxie:

> [It is e]ssentially trade-conscious rather than class-con-scious . . . it expresses the viewpoints and interests of the workers in craft or industry rather than those of the working class as a whole. It aims chiefly at more, here and now, for the organized workers of the craft or industry, in terms of mainly higher wages, shorter hours, and better working conditions, regardless for the most part of the welfare of the workers outside the particular organic group, and regardless in general of political and social considerations, except in so far as these bear directly upon its own economic ends.[29]

Former AFL-CIO president George Meany was an advocate of this type of business unionism. He believed the role of unions is to intervene where management decisions affect workers directly, but unions should not care about anything that does not directly influence union members.[30] While business unionism was relatively successful during the "golden years" of American capitalism (1947–1973), it could not cope with the attack on unionism from the government and employers following the abandon-ment of the social contract in the late 1970s. From that point in time, the union movement was on a dramatic downward trend. At first, it tried to ignore the problem, hoping that a change in government would cure all of labor's woes. Eventually, realizing something had to be done, the AFL-CIO made organizing its top priority. However, as recent figures suggest, the union movement has not been successful. Union membership has declined from its peak of 34.8 percent in 1954. It fell to 26 percent in

1973, more than halved to 12.6 percent by 2000, and fell even further to 11.1 percent in 2014, its lowest level since the 1930s. Contrasting business unionism, Chapter 5 provides an overview and analysis of a type of unionism that has been successful around the world in organizing new members, in achieving higher wages and better working conditions for union members, and in helping communities on the whole—namely, social movement unionism. Social movement unions are democratic, with the rank-and-file playing a crucial role in all affairs of the union; they are militant in collective bargaining, and they have alliances with social movements and community groups because they realize that the health of communities and the health of unions are intertwined. A key defining aspect of social movement unions is that they are not self-interested; they believe that an injury to one is an injury to all. Obviously, social movement unions want their members to have good wages and working conditions, but they also want a vibrant healthy community where everyone benefits, not just a select few. As such, social movement unions fight for all matters that affect working people, not just better wages and working conditions.

One might argue that unions once had a place in society, but in this day and age such policies as paid holidays and bans on sweatshops are never going to be revoked. Thus, the argument might go, the labor movement is no longer relevant in this globalized era, at least in the developed world. Such an argument is badly mistaken. As I stated in *Unions in Crisis?*, "[w]eekly wages of nonsupervisory private sector workers today are lower in real terms (adjusted for inflation) than in the early 1960s, and they are 17 percent lower than their peak in 1972. During this time, productivity has increased by 80 percent. In other words, people are working harder for a lot less money." At the same time, the rich are getting richer:

> In the early 1970s, European countries had greater wealth inequality than America. Since then, however, inequality in America has skyrocketed. Today, 5 percent of the American population owns 59 percent of the wealth, with CEOs receiving, on average, 245 times the amount that an average worker receives; in 1980 this figure was 42 to 1. A full-time job does not guarantee a person a good income: 58.4 percent of the working poor work full time. The situation is not just confined to the current generation. A group headed by a member of the Federal Reserve Bank of Chicago claims that approximately

60 percent of a person's wage is based on the income level of their father.[31]

Unions are important for all workers. In 2014, American union members' median weekly income was $970, compared to $763 for non-union workers. The situation is even more pronounced for women and minorities: women who are union members earn $904, compared to $687 for women who do not belong to a union; African American union members earn an extra 32.5 percent compared to nonunion African Americans ($810 to $611); Latino union members earn 41.5 percent more than other Latinos ($811 to $573); and Asian American union members earn 4.5 percent more than their nonunion counterparts ($979 to $937).[32]

Indeed, apart from a few high-end jobs, in every occupational category union members receive higher salaries than nonunion workers. For example, in sales and office occupations, union members receive an extra 20.5 percent over nonunion workers; in natural resources, construction, and maintenance occupations, the difference rises to over 52.6 percent—and it is an astonishing 58.1 percent in service occupations.[33]

In relation to pension benefits and sick days, union members are also better off. Eighty-six percent of union workers participate in pension plans, compared to 48 percent of nonunion workers. Moreover, as the AFL-CIO notes, "[s]eventy-seven percent of union workers have guaranteed pensions, compared with 17 percent of nonunion workers." Likewise, 83 percent of union members have paid sick leave, compared to 62 percent of nonunion workers.[34] Guaranteed pensions are better than defined-contribution plans because they are federally insured and, as the name implies, guarantee a monthly amount. In contrast, for defined-contribution plans, the monthly pension amount depends on how well the investment is doing.

The benefit for workers of unions is clearly illustrated in so-called right-to-work states. Twenty-four states have passed laws that make it very difficult for unions to gain a presence. Right-to-work laws outlaw all union security provisions in collective bargaining agreements. Such provisions can include new employees being able to join the union after a certain time period and employers deducting union dues from employees' wages. The laws also force unions to represent all employees, irrespective if they pay dues or not. Such laws have a negative effect on union organizing drives. For instance, why would an employee want to join a union if he or she does not have to join and pay dues and yet will receive the same rewards as a unionized employee? The so-called right-to-work laws adversely affect all employees. On average, employees in right-to-work states earn 3.1 percent less a year ($1,558) than employees in non–right-to-work states. Workplace deaths are 52.9 percent higher in right-to-work states. In addition, right-to-work states "spend $2,671 less per pupil on elementary and secondary education than free-bargaining states."[35] In other words, right-to-work states are bad for employees and their families.

For low-wage workers, unions are a godsend. In all low-wage occupations in which workers are straddling the poverty line, union members receive substantially higher wages than their nonunion counterparts. For example, in 2014, unionized employees in health care occupations earned an extra 15.4 percent compared to nonunion workers; this figure increased to 23.5 percent for food preparation and serving-related occupations. Building and grounds cleaning and maintenance workers who belong to a union earned 41.2 percent more than nonunion workers in the same industry.[36]

Likewise, unions are essential for helping workers rise above the poverty line and toward middle-class status. For example, nonunion workers in installation, maintenance, and repair occupations earn $782 per week, while their union counterparts earn $1,064 per week (a difference of 36 percent). Nonunion workers in transportation and material-moving occupations earn $608 per week, compared to $850 for union members (a difference of 39.8 percent). Workers in construction and extraction occupations who do not belong to a union earn $697 per week, compared to union members in the same industries who earn $1,095 (a difference of 57.1 percent). These figures clearly indicate that in certain industries the pay disparity between a unionized job and a nonunionized job means the difference in workers hovering just above the poverty line and the struggles that come from that, and workers living a relatively comfortable life. Union membership also helps those in professional occupations; nonunion workers in community and social service occupations earn $822 per week, compared to $1,017 for union members (a difference of 23.7 percent). Nonunion education, training, and library occupation workers earn $851 per year, while union members in the same industry earn $1,077 (a difference of 26.5 percent).[37]

Despite the above statistics that indisputability demonstrate that union members are clearly much better off than there nonunion counterparts, unions are in trouble. As we shall see in Chapter 4, this is a problem not only for union members, but for nearly all segments of the US population, due to austerity and neoliberalism.

Unionism in the United Kingdom

As in the US, the decline of the labor movement has been steady in the UK since the 1980s. Union membership in the late 1960s was nearly 44 percent, a level similar to the war-time peak of the 1940s. Rather than decline, as happened in the US, union membership actually began to grow. One reason for the growth is that the labor movement was "caught up" in the rebellion of the 1960s. Social movements of that time helped revitalize unions. Unions became involved in antiwar marches, campaigns for nuclear disarmament, environmental protests, and anti-Pinochet campaigns, among numerous other causes. The spirit of rebellion reverberated around the workplace. Lowell Turner claims that social movements "revitalized labor in the American public sector and throughout the British economy by way of young, radicalized employees, demanding a better workplace and not afraid to speak out, by way of the contagious effects of activism, as workers saw what others had achieved (be they workers in other areas, university students or peace demonstrators), and by creating a broad social fabric of mobilization, in which labor struggles could be sure to find new allies and supporters." This sense of rebellion led to a number of wildcat strikes in the 1960s and 1970s. Moreover, the alliance with social movements and fighting for everything that affects people in the workplace and in the community paid dividends. Organized labor was part of the fabric of society. By 1979, union membership stood at 55.4 percent, with thirteen million Britons belonging to a trade union, compared to an average of nine to ten million between 1951 and 1960. There was also a dramatic increase in women members; the number of women belonging to unions increased from two million in 1960 to almost four million by 1979.[38] However, the incoming conservative government led by Margaret Thatcher posed a significant challenge to the labor movement—a challenge it was unable to overcome.

Almost immediately following her election as British Prime Minister, Margaret Thatcher would target unions. Between 1980 and 1993 (Thatcher was removed as Prime Minister in 1990 and replaced by her Tory Party colleague John Major) there were six Acts of Parliament that severely curtailed the power of the labor movement. The Acts of Parliament led to a ban on sympathy strikes; postal ballots were needed for industrial action to occur; there could be High Court injunctions from employers to stop strikes if even a modicum of doubt existed about the legality of strike action ("if unions persisted they could be charged with contempt of court and fined or even have their assets seized"); and the

Commissioner for the Rights of Trade Union Members was formed to "encourage members to pursue complaints against their unions." Although the Labour Party regained office in 1997, the majority of the antiunion laws remained in place (see Chapter 3 for a critique of organized labor's ties with the Labour Party).[39]

Aiding the sense of doom within the UK labor movement during this time was that throughout the 1980s there were a number of high-profile failed strikes. These included the miners' strike of 1984–1985 in which unions tried to prevent the closure of five government-owned pits earmarked for closure. During the strike, 11,291 people were arrested, and the strike's failure led to many more pits being closed and the remaining ones being privatized. Another defeat was the Transport and General Workers' Union being fined £200,000 (approximately £590,000 in 2014 currency) in 1984 for contempt of court for continuing a strike against Austin Rover, as the union did not fully comply with balloting laws. The heavy fine and the threat that workers would be fired led to the strike withering away. The series of failed strikes led to a sense of defeatism within the labor movement. It was incapable of dealing with the new antiunion agenda by the Conservative government. As Turner argues, "[t]he existing regulation of industrial relations in the workplace gave them [unions] little if any protection when, for example, an emboldened employer decided to ignore the union, or play one union off against the other, or co-opt workers into a house union friendly to the company and hostile to other unions. Weak institutionalization left British unions dependent upon their own ability to mobilize, upon their own organized power. When that power collapsed in the face of severe economic and political conditions, British unionists had no platform upon which to stand."[40]

Thus, by the time a "friendly" Labour Party returned to power in 1997, union membership had declined to 30.9 percent. However, the Labour government did very little to help the labor movement, and unions seemed almost willing to accept their decline. The labor movement was no longer militant and largely agreed to the neoliberal agenda of the Labour Party. As a result, union membership continued to decline. In 2013, union membership in the UK was 6.5 million (23 percent of the workforce), with public sector membership at 3.8 million (55.4 percent of the public sector workforce) and private sector membership at 2.6 million (14.4 percent of the private sector workforce).While US unions, for instance, would be ecstatic if almost a quarter of the workforce was unionized, union membership in the UK is on a long and seemingly unstoppable downward trend.

Despite this downward trend, unions in the UK, as in the US, are still important for workers. Unionized private sector workers earn 8.1 percent more than nonunionized workers. This increases to 21.6 percent for unionized public sector workers compared to their nonunionized counterparts. Union membership is especially beneficial to sixteen- to twenty-four-year-olds; union members in this age group earn an extra 38.8 percent over their nonunion counterparts. Full-time union members also receive an extra 3.8 days of paid leave, while part-time union members receive an extra 5.5 days of paid leave compared to their nonunion colleagues. Unions also lead to more workers receiving pay increases; in 2011, public sector unions secured a raise for workers 55 percent of the time that they were involved in bargaining. This declines to 35 percent when unions did not bargain on behalf of employees. Union workplaces also have fewer accidents, and unions have been important in increasing the number of workplaces that have formal written policies covering diversity.[41]

Quite simply, as in the US, unions are very beneficial to workers and their families. Despite unions being important to all workers, as in the US, the UK's union movement's influence and power are at one of its lowest ebbs in history. The decline in the strength of unions has hurt all workers and their families. As I shall demonstrate in Chapter 3, this is clearly seen with the rise of austerity policies. Chapter 3 will also highlight that unions accepting austerity policies has caused even more suffering.

Chapter Structure

While the main focus of the book is the impact of austerity policies and the response by organized labor in the UK and the US, Chapter 2 will provide an analysis on what has happened in Greece, Spain, and Ireland. In many ways, the response of the labor movement in these three countries is eerily similar to the situation in the UK and the US. In Spain and Ireland, the economies were buoyant before running into major turbulence. In comparison, Greece was struggling after entering a recession in 2009. What all three had in common, though, was that each country was forced to seek a European Union–International Monetary Fund bailout package and in return forced to adopt harsh austerity measures. In each instance, austerity did not improve the economic well-being of the country, but arguably made things worse. This had a major negative impact on almost all segments of each country's population. Furthermore, the labor movement in each country staged mass strikes and protests (although less so in Ireland). However, the labor movement was almost completely ineffectual in overturning austerity or even mitigating its harshest effects. I shall argue that organized labor underestimated the austerity agenda by politicians, the EU, and the IMF, and sections of it were self-interested and put their own agenda ahead of what would benefit the entire society. This undermined the anti-austerity protests almost immediately, and thus the protests were doomed to fail.

In Chapter 3 we will look at the impact of austerity policies in the UK. The UK economy ran into trouble, like most countries around the world, due to the global economic crisis. The incoming Conservative government led by David Cameron was beholden to the austerity ideology. His government implemented an "age of austerity," which has, on the most optimistic analysis, only marginally improved the economy, while making the majority of people worse off. The labor movement despite staging numerous protests has been totally ineffectual in forcing the government to abandon or even modify the austerity policies without agreeing to major concessions. This is because at the height of mass action against austerity a number of unions cut deals with the government and accepted austerity. They put their own self-interest above that of the wider community. Moreover, the labor movement largely relied on an electoral strategy to elect the Labour Party to government. However, the Labour Party accepted austerity and the belief that there is no alternative.

In Chapter 4 we will examine the impact on austerity in the US. Unlike the other countries analyzed in this book, austerity in the US has happened almost by stealth. Nonetheless, the decline in federal spending is almost unsurpassed in American history. The impact of this has led to rising inequality across the US. Unlike in the other countries discussed, there have been no major labor movement protests nationally in the US. The battle against austerity has been occurring at the state and local level. In Wisconsin, the incoming governor implemented austerity policies and draconian antiunion laws. After initially showing immense power in mass mobilization, the labor movement put its interests ahead of others and also relied on an electoral strategy to overturn the laws—a strategy that spectacularly failed. In contrast, in Chicago, the Chicago Teachers' Union's social movement unionism ideology utilized the rank-and-file and has ties with the local community. Unlike any other labor movement I examine around the world, the CTU managed to partly overturn austerity policies because it was militant and refused to "sell out" its allies in the community by accepting a deal that would not have benefited all concerned.

Chapter 5, which serves as a conclusion as well as an in-depth chapter in-itself, looks at what can be done to overcome austerity. The chapter analyzes the potential of social movements, such as the Occupy Movement, to lead the fight against austerity. I argue that while such movements are important and beneficial, they alone are unlikely to overcome austerity. Likewise, in this chapter I argue that the rise of anti-austerity parties in Greece and Spain should be welcomed, but as is often the case there is a gulf between what politicians promise and what they can actually deliver. However, in the UK and the US (more so in the latter), the likelihood that left-wing political parties will gain mass support is unlikely largely due to the nature of electoral politics in each country. Thus, I conclude the chapter and the book by arguing that the labor movement needs to make major changes if it is going to stop austerity policies from continuing; halt its own decline; and, most important, help *all* workers, their families, and their communities. I argue that the labor movement in the UK and the US needs to embrace, as the Chicago Teachers' Unions did, social movement unionism. Whether unions will embrace social movement unionism is uncertain, but quite simply the labor movement must do something different compared to its current trajectory because it has been almost totally ineffectual in the fight against austerity and neoliberalism more generally. As a result, the people in the UK, the US, and around the world have suffered greatly. It is a sad state of affairs indeed.

Chapter 2

Austerity in Modern-Day Europe

Despite the far from perfect record of austerity in the developed and the developing world prior to the global economic crisis, the idea of austerity being able to solve economic crises once again gained traction in the twenty-first century. It gained such traction that for a while austerity became the accepted norm. It was the only policy a country should turn to if it ran into economic, and especially debt, problems. Austerity policies were used (and still are) throughout Europe when countries experienced economic malaise due to the global economic crisis. It is important to note that the basis for austerity that swept throughout Europe in the 2010s was in part due to Germany's push in the late 1990s to ensure that European Union members who used the euro maintain fiscal responsibility. Under the Stability and Growth Pact of 1997, those countries wishing to join the euro must have national debt below 60 percent of GDP, and at worst an annual budget deficit no more than 3 percent of GDP. The Stability and Growth Pact is a clear example of Gill's new constitutionalism; governments are forced to implement neoliberal reforms, in this case if they want to be part of the Euro, regardless of their citizens' wishes. The idea of high sovereign debt was already viewed as a negative well before austerity reared back to life. Thus, this combined with the perceived success of austerity in the 1980s in some European countries, and the continued embrace of neoliberalism, it was only "logical" that governments throughout Europe began to consider austerity as the de facto economic policy.

This chapter will look at three examples of austerity in practice in Europe—in Greece, Spain, and Ireland. In each of these examples, the country went from an economic boom (less so in Greece) to a major economic downturn in seemingly a blink of an eye. Austerity policies were used in an attempt to improve the situation; they did not. Austerity resulted in hardship across each country and, at best, having only a very limited effect in improving the economic well-being of the country after years of misery. Furthermore, the labor movement in each country was seemingly unable to prevent austerity from occurring or even forcing the government to modify the policies without agreeing to major concessions. This chapter provides a general overview of what happened in each of these countries and the negative impact austerity had on large segments of the population. The chapter also demonstrates that the labor movement in each country put their own and their members' self-interest ahead of the general public. This is a theme that will be especially prevalent when the book moves to organized labor's response to austerity in the UK and the US. This self-interest stymied protests, resulted in the protests not being as effective as they could have been, and made it easier for the governments in Greece, Spain, and Ireland to implement further austerity policies.

Austerity and Greece

The poster child for austerity and the damage it causes is Greece. Before it ran into trouble, Greece's economy was not performing that badly. From 1996 to 2004 the Greek economy grew largely because of increased public spending (in part due to the costs of hosting the 2004 Summer Olympics), investment from the European Union (EU), and lower costs in the capital markets as the market assumed that the European Central Bank "would back all outstanding debt issued by member states since it was all in the 'same' new euro currency." By way of comparison, in 1992 Germany borrowed money at 8 percent, while the Greeks did so at 24 percent. Once Greece joined the EU, the borrowing rate dropped dramatically. For example, ten-year borrowing costs for Germany in 2007 were 4.02 percent, while for Greece they were only 4.29 percent. Despite the myth of Greek workers being lazy, in this period labor productivity increased by 30 percent and was one of the highest in the world. Productivity continued to increase until the 2008–2009 worldwide economic crisis. The real average retirement age in Greece is 60.9 years for women and 62.4 for men, which are higher than in Germany. Beginning in 2004 GDP per worker began declining; this was caused by employees becoming lazy or unproductive. Instead it was due to contractionary policies implemented by the government; reducing the debt level became the top priority. Previously, successive Greek governments more often than not viewed expansionary policies as the top priority. As a result, in 2004 the debt to GDP ratio reached 100 percent, and even this high figure would eventually increase dramatically because of the global economic crisis. Moreover, as is relatively well known, there is a large black market economy in operation, and successive Greek governments have never been politically motivated to enforce taxation. Also, Greek governments engaged in practices that were not exactly faultless. As Neil Irwin notes, the Greek government engaged in a "series of currency swaps arranged with the assistance of Goldman Sachs in the early 2000s that essentially allowed the Greek government to borrow money without issuing debt that would show up in official statistics. Less widely known were such tricks as underreporting how much the nation was spending on its military (a particularly large expense given perennially tense relations with Turkey) and the failure to account for debts owed to hospitals."[1]

All of these matters came to a head in October 2009 when it was revealed that the fiscal deficit was not the previously reported 6.5 percent of GDP, but almost 13 percent. Indeed, the budget deficit was 15.9 percent of the entire economy—the highest level in the world. This led to increased costs on Greek debt and borrowing, and rating agencies downgraded Greek bonds from A (a level they should never have been) to BBB–. The consequence of these actions saw debt rise dramatically and GDP decline. Quite simply, the Greek economy collapsed. However, the economy was still potentially salvageable; as Blyth argues, "[t]he ideal policy back in 2009 would have cost around 50 billion euros. It would have required either the ECB, or Germany as its major creditor, to buy the secondary-market Greek debt that was subject to near-term rollover risk, bury it somewhere deep in its balance sheet, and walk away." Such a policy was not undertaken because of electoral politics in Germany (it was easier to blame the Greek people for the country's economic woes), and the European Central Bank forbids one country from bailing out another, except in situations such as natural disasters. In February and March 2010 the Greek government announced a range of measures to help solve the debt crisis. It implemented a 10 percent reduction in salaried bonuses, and the central government implemented a hiring ban, a 2 percent increase of the Value-Added Tax (VAT) to 21 percent, a tax on petrol, alcohol, and tobacco, and a reduction in government spending.[2] In other words, the government introduced a range of austerity measures before the first bailout imposed austerity on the Greek people. Austerity was not simply forced on the country by the EU and the IMF. However, the austerity measures did little to ease the fears of the market; thus, the situation spiraled out of control.

The European Union initially suggested that there would be no bail-out of Greece; the country would be left to solve its problems by itself. However, pressure began to mount that a bailout was needed—a bailout with austerity strings attached. The impetus for the change in thinking came in early February 2010 when at one of their regularly scheduled summits, the Group of Seven finance ministers came to a consensus that the global economy had recovered from the 2008–2009 economic crisis. As such, governments should move away from stimulus policies. There was one problem with such a move: by most measures the world economy was far from healed. The major economies were still struggling, inflation was a long way from being an issue, and short-term interest rates were near zero. In this regard, one might wonder why the finance ministers would want to move away from stimulus policies so soon after the finan-cial crisis. The answer is in part that, as argued in the previous chapter, the majority of the world political establishment advocates for neoliberalism. Stimulus policies cut against the current economic orthodoxy. For the Group of Seven finance ministers, austerity was the better approach for struggling economies with debt problems. It was the "transnational elite" and major capitalist countries that pushed the austerity agenda. As Paul Krugman claims: "The German political and intellectual establishment has never had much use for Keynesian economics; neither has much of the Republican Party in the United States. In the heat of an acute economic crisis—as in the autumn of 2008 and the winter of 2009—these dissent-ing voices could to some extent be shouted down; but once things had calmed they began pushing back hard." If a country required a bailout, the entire economy would have to be reformed along neoliberal lines.[3] It was transnational elite network and major capitalist countries that wanted to move away from economic stimulus packages in the Keynesianism tradi-tion and move toward neoliberalism and austerity. Likewise, the trans-national financial network led Greece to the path of austerity by severely downgrading Greek bonds.

The other main reason that finance ministers wanted to move away from economic stimulus packages is that sovereign debt was now per-ceived to be an issue. As Philip Lane argues, in late 2009, "a number of countries reported larger-than-expected increases in deficit/GDP ratios. For example, fiscal revenues in Ireland and Spain fell much more quickly than GDP, as a result of the high sensitivity of tax revenues to declines in construction activity and asset prices. In addition, the scale of the recession and rising estimates of prospective banking-sector losses on bad loans in a number of countries also had a negative indirect impact on sovereign bond values, since investors recognized that a deteriorating banking sector posed fiscal risks." The problems of Ireland and Spain (see below) were compounded by, as noted above, a massive increase in Greece's debt level for the previous year, plus there were revisions to previous years' debt figures that led to them being worse than what was initially reported. This helped frame the debt crisis as a problem caused by "fiscal irresponsibility of the peripheral nations."[4] Debt was now considered a major hindrance to the economic well-being of the world economy; more to the point, it was a problem caused by so-called lesser countries.

The notion that a high debt to GDP ratio was a problem that required immediate attention received considerable impetus from a January 2010 working paper by Carmen Reinhart and Kenneth Rogoff in the *National Bureau of Economic Research*. The intellectual elite were pushing the idea that sovereign debt must be severely curtailed. The paper in part argued that a country will struggle to maintain growth if the debt to GDP ratio is above 90 percent. Indeed, Reinhart and Rogoff claimed that the overall growth average of twenty countries with debt at or above the 90 percent level between 1945 and 2009 was –0.1 percent. In addition, GDP growth is 1 percent lower than it would be otherwise when the debt to GDP ratio is 90 percent or above. As such, reducing debt should be prioritized if a country is to grow. There was a growing consensus that austerity was needed in a large measure to help countries such as Greece. However, in 2013 it was revealed that an Excel blunder resulted in Reinhart and Rogoff's findings to be in error, and countries with a debt to GDP ratio at 90 percent or above actually grew by 0.2 percent (which further increased to 0.5 percent when new data became available). In addition, the "difference in median economic growth rates was only 0.4 percentage points between countries whose public-debt-to-G.D.P. ratio was between 60 percent and 90 percent, and those where the ratio was over 90 percent (2.9 percent median growth, versus 2.5 percent)." But it would take three more years for the error to be revealed. In the meantime, conservative politicians and austerity advocates jumped on the findings and argued that austerity measures were essential in debt-ridden countries. Reducing a country's debt level became top priority.[5]

In March 2010, European leaders promised they would not allow Greece to go bankrupt and that the IMF would provide money to the country. It was a vague declaration, basically stating that "while the nations of the eurozone would stand behind their weaker members, they would do so reluctantly, only when they had absolutely no other choice, with huge procedural obstacles, and on a scale inadequate to the size of the problem." The financial markets realized this; Greece's cost of borrowing declined only slightly following the meeting and increased dramatically in April. Greece had bonds worth €8.5 billion due in May, and it became apparent that the country would not be able to find a new buyer for the bonds at a realistic rate. The country required an international bailout or it would be bankrupt. On April 23, Greece Prime Minister Papandreou implored the international community for €45 billion in emergency loans. He stated that "[i]t is a national and imperative need to officially ask our partners in the EU for the activation of the support mechanism. . . . All of us—the present government and the Greek people—have inherited a ship that is about to sink. . . . We are on a difficult course, a new Odyssey for Hellenism. But we now know the way to Ithaca and have charted our route." By April 27 the cost of borrowing for Greece reached 9.7 percent and the country had few if any markets to borrow from. For Greece, a bailout was seemingly the only course of action.[6]

In May 2010, Greece negotiated a €110 billion (approximately US $146.2 billion) bailout from the IMF (contributing €30 billion) and the European Union (contributing €80 billion). In return for the bailout, the Greek government agreed to a range of austerity measures. Thus, in addition to the transnational elite who wanted Greece to adopt austerity measures, so did the transnational financial network and the major capitalist countries. The measures included higher property taxes; raising the VAT by another 2 percent to 23 percent; a further 10 percent tax increase on alcohol, petrol, and tobacco; public sector wages and pensions being frozen for at least three years; public sector workers no longer receiving annual bonuses (equivalent to two months' pay); public sector workers retirement age increasing from 61 to 65; a reduction of state-owned companies from 6,000 to 2,000; and, in a show of "solidarity," politicians' bonuses also were eliminated. The last measure was little comfort to ordinary Greeks who now had to deal with fewer government services, lower wages, and higher taxes. Poul Thomsen, who led the IMF in the negotiations with Greece claimed, "[w]hat the government has committed to is a tough, front-loaded program that will correct things for the future, although it will take time. Indeed, it will be a multi-year effort. . . . The authorities have already begun fiscal consolidation equivalent to 5 percent of GDP and further legislative action is expected this week. There is also an emphasis on fairness, with measures to protect the most vulnerable. The authorities are asking the Greek people to share the burden fairly across all levels of society." The country erupted in protests against the bailout and the likely suffering of ordinary Greeks (see below for details). Moreover, even as the bailout was being negotiated there were doubts that it would solve Greece's problems. Indeed, following the bailout announcement, Greece's ten-year borrowing costs increased to 12.4 percent from 8.5 percent in the space of four days.[7] The markets and the people had no confidence in the bailout. They were proven correct; Thomsen's assurances would prove hollow.

The first bailout had no effect in controlling the debt crisis. The debt to GDP ratio reached 165 percent in 2011, and increased even further to 170 percent in 2012. In early 2012, the Greek economy had been in recession for over five years, with GDP declining by 6.8 percent in 2011. By late 2011 it was becoming clear that the first bailout, in addition to not helping the debt crisis, also had little effect in helping the economy as a whole. Following months of negotiations, a second bailout was agreed on in March 2012. The second rescue package was worth €130 billion, with the EU contributing the majority of the money, with the IMF contributing €28 billion. The first and second bailout packages were expected to pump approximately €173 billion into the Greek economy. Under the terms of the bailout, private sector holders of Greek bonds were "voluntarily" asked to accept a 53.5 percent nominal write-down on the value of the bonds—approximately a 70 percent reduction in net value. The European Commission notes that "[o]ut of a total of €205.6 billion in bonds eligible for the exchange offer, approximately €197 billion, or 95.7% have been exchanged."[8]

Of course, the second bailout came with strings attached: the number of austerity measures dramatically increased. Under the terms of the agreement, government spending had to be reduced by €3.3 billion: "1.1 billion euros would come from health spending, mainly by lowering pharmaceuticals prices; 400 million euros from public investment; 300 million euros from the defense budget; 300 million from pension cuts and 300 million from the central government. Some 325 million euros of cuts were put aside to be detailed later, with the remainder to come from a series of smaller measures to reduce ministry operating expenses." There also had to be mass privatization of state-owned assets: "Cumulative privatization receipts since June 2011 should be at least 4.5 billion euros by end-2012, 7.5 billion by end-2013, 12.2 billion by end-2014 and 15 billion by end-2015," with €50 billion in privatization being achieved in the medium term. In addition, there had to be a 22 percent reduction in the minimum wage, with a 32 percent reduction for those under 25, "automatic wage

increases based on seniority will be scrapped" and "social security contributions are to be reduced by 5 percent." Fifteen thousand government
workers would receive 60 percent of their pay and would be fired after
one year, with the public sector workforce declining by 150,000 by 2015
(only one person hired for every five people who retired).[9]

The price paid by Greece's citizens for the two bailouts and the
austerity policies was a high one. Indeed, it is a price that they are still
paying as of this writing. In regard to health care, public spending on
hospitals declined by 25 percent, and government spending on phar-
maceutical medicine decreased by 50 percent. The range of cuts to the
health budget is unprecedented across the Western world. David Stuckler,
writing in the medical journal *The Lancet*, states that "[t]he cost of austerity is being borne mainly by ordinary Greek citizens, who have been
affected by the largest cutbacks to the health sector seen across Europe
in modern times." As a result, over 800,000 people do not have access
to health care or state welfare. The situation is so bad that *Médecins du
Monde* (Doctors of the World) have begun providing health services to
the most vulnerable in some regions of the country. Disease prevention
schemes have been slashed, and this has led to diseases such as malaria,
not seen in the country for forty years, making a comeback. There has
also been a 21 percent rise in stillbirths, and infant mortality has increased
by 43 percent. Sociologist Alexander Kentikelenis claims that the Greek
government "failed to protect people at the time they needed support
the most. . . . What's happening to vulnerable groups in Greece is quite
shocking. . . . It's quite straightforward to measure what has happened,
it's much harder to quantify the long-term health implications for the
long-term unemployed and uninsured. . . . Leaving health problems to
get out of hand ends up costing a state much more in the long run."[10]

Affecting peoples' health is that, not surprisingly, the range of austerity measures has led to a dramatic rise in the unemployment rate. In
October 2009, when the true extent of Greece's debt problem came to
light, unemployment stood at 10.1 percent. In December 2010, the rate
was 14.8 percent; it was 21.6 percent in December 2011; and it reached
a peak of 28 percent in September 2013. Since then unemployment has
started to decline; in August 2014, the rate stood at 25.9 percent, but the
youth unemployment rate was still a staggering 49.3 percent (the record
was 58.9 percent in October 2013).[11] With more people out of work and
a dramatic reduction in public health care, there has been a large rise in
the number of people struggling to feed themselves. Out of a population
of eleven million, four million people are below the poverty line. People

have to make do with less; household "expenditures for food are reduced by 69.7 per cent, for bread by 70 per cent, for heating by 83.2 per cent, for clothing by 92.5 per cent, for transport by 79.4 per cent, for travel by 88.7 per cent, and for health and medication by 26.9 per cent." In 2001, at the main Athens soup kitchen, approximately one hundred people were seeking a free meal; ten years later, the number increased to thirty-five hundred. In 2005, the average age attending the soup kitchen was sixty; younger people have now been forced to seek help, and the average age has declined to forty-seven.[12]

The cost to the average Greek citizen has been immense. Arguably, the most painful aspect of the austerity measures is that Greek citizens have had no effect in reducing the country's debt. As mentioned above, by 2012 the debt to GDP ratio was 170 percent—significantly higher than when the crisis began. Despite a brief respite, the debt to GDP ratio is now at a record 175 percent. Rather than make things better, austerity policies have made Greece's economy worse, and the Greek people have paid a terrible price. As the European Economic and Social Committee Workers' Group argues,

> The impact is unevenly felt by workers, pensioners and by the law-abiding Greek taxpayers and their families. The uneven distribution of the economic and social cost of the anti-crisis measures is, among others, due to the inability of the government to address chronic structural flows of governance such as tax evasion, one of the many problems ensuing from a political system burdened by clientelism, rent-seeking and corruption. . . . Such flaws have proved lethal in the context of the anti-crisis policy and its deadlines. They have been instrumental in the inequitable allocation of the austerity burden: each time the government could not attain demanding fiscal targets it resorted to wage and pension cuts combined with heavy taxation instead of effectively combating tax evasion.[13]

Even the IMF was forced to admit that it made mistakes with the bailout and that the austerity measures went too far. On purely economic terms, austerity has been a failure. Arguably, the clearest measure is the contraction in GDP. Greek GDP grew by a paltry 0.8 percent in 2014. However, in just over the six years before then it declined by almost 40 percent. The size of the Greek economy was $341.6 billion in 2009. In 2013 it has shrunk to $241.72 billion. An internal IMF report on the first bailout states that "[f]orecasters significantly underestimated the increase in unemployment and the decline in domestic demand associated with fiscal consolidation." It goes on to claim that "[m]arket confidence was not restored, the banking system lost 30 percent of its deposits and the economy encountered a much-deeper-than-expected recession with exceptionally high unemployment." However, despite the self-criticism, this does not mean that the IMF would necessarily do things differently: "The results do not imply that fiscal consolidation is undesirable. . . . Virtually all advanced economies face the challenge of fiscal adjustment in response to elevated government debt levels and future pressures on public finances from demographic change. The short-term effects of fiscal policy on economic activity are only one of the many factors that need to be considered in determining the appropriate pace of fiscal consolidation for any single country." As the lead IMF negotiator for the Greece bailout, Poul Thomsen claims, "[i]f we were in the same situation . . . we would have done the same thing again."[14] Even though austerity in practice proved to be a disaster, the transnational elite and international organizations continued to believe that austerity was the cure.

Union Resistance to Austerity in Greece and Why It Failed

Not surprisingly, with the range of austerity measures and the problems they have caused, a wave of mass protests have risen up against them. As Richard Seymour argues:

> The social struggles taking off in reaction to austerity reached near-insurgency levels, and were perceived by many Greeks . . . as a "popular uprising." In the years between the beginning of Papandreou's government [2009] and the May 2012 election, there were 17 general strikes. The mass of small-business owners turned against austerity. The traditional social democratic governing party, PASOK, began to suffer an epochal decline. Eventually a radical left party [Syriza] compromising former Eurocommunists and various Maoists and Trotskyist groups came within a whisker of being the first party in the Greek parliament, on an anti-austerity programme.[15]

The use of a general strike as a tactic by the Greek labor movement is rarely seen by the labor movement in Northern Europe and is totally absent in the US. That such a tactic was used often in the fight against austerity on the surface demonstrates the unhappiness and outrage by organized labor of such measures. The Greek people have a history of engaging in protest action. Of the people who participated in protests against the 2010 austerity measures, more than 80 percent had previously engaged in a major protest in the previous ten years. That such a large number of people had previously engaged in either a strike and/or a major demonstration was an important factor in being able to mobilize people in the protests against austerity.[16] The trade union network (largely through the public sector) also played a significant role.

Thus, rather than accept that there was no alternative, it seemed that the labor movement was trying to protect the livelihood and living conditions of the Greek populace. As the labor movement around the world has done for centuries, the Greek trade union movement and the rank-and-file were standing up for ordinary workers and their families.

While the protests were against austerity, they were also in part against the ruling PASOK government who agreed to and implemented the austerity policies. PASOK is not a traditional right-wing party that embraces neoliberalism; it is a left-wing social democratic party. However, as we shall see below, not all unions and labor federations joined the protests due to austerity being embraced by their political allies. Nevertheless, it was not just the labor movement and the Left generally responding to austerity. As Seymour notes, "[a] section of the population feared and loathed the Left, and protesters, and strikers, and immigrants, as much as they detested austerity and the rule of European bankers. Since the semifascist Laos party had collaborated with the austerity government prior to the May elections, the neo-Nazi Golden Dawn was the major beneficiary on the far right, and in subsequent polls it has overtaken PASOK."[17]

Nonetheless, even with the mass protests against austerity by the Left and the Right, as well as the decaying fabric of Greek society, the reality is that the protests were largely ineffectual. Despite the votes in parliament being close, austerity policies were approved in the Greek Parliament to secure a bailout in 2010 and 2012, and more austerity policies passed through at other times, such as in February and March 2010 before the first bailout package was even negotiated.

The question, then, is why did the protests fail to sway government opinion? Why was the labor movement unable to stop austerity being imposed on the country? One reason the protests were not as effective as they could have been is that successive governments have enacted anti-union laws in an attempt to weaken the labor movement. University of the West of England academic Horen Voskeritsian notes that "a series of

laws radically changed core industrial relations institutions; collective bargaining, mediation and arbitration, the national minimum wage, and the
dismissals framework, leading to extreme decentralisation, the curtailing
of the trade unions' negotiating power, the elimination of any remnants of
social dialogue and the strengthening of employers' ability to unilaterally
control and manipulate the employment relationship." As I argued in the
previous chapter, part of the austerity agenda was to weaken organized
labor so as to further push neoliberal reforms. With organized labor weak,
it would be less likely to stage effective protests, and in turn it would be
easier for the government to further enact austerity policies. Moreover,
union density in Greece was not that great. In 2011, an estimated 28
percent of Greek workers belonged to a union. While this percentage
is certainly far greater than in the US, for example, it still means that
the overwhelming majority of workers are not union members. Of this
28 percent, only 18 percent of private sector workers belong to a union
(approximately 472,000), with 60 percent of public sector workers being
union members (approximately 311,000). Thus, the pay freezes and job
losses of public sector workers was of little concern to the majority of
union members because they were employed by the private sector. This
divided the labor movement, as it was easy to portray public sector workers as overpaid and inefficient. A divided labor movement that was already
weakened by antiunion legislation is highly unlikely to achieve major
change. Nonetheless, the labor movement's inability to prevent austerity measures being enacted and the resultant pain and suffering on the
population resonated badly with ordinary Greeks. In 2013, an opinion
poll found that 92.5 percent of respondents believed that the labor movement did nothing or very little to prevent austerity from occurring. One
reason is that Greece was used to, on average, two to three general strikes
per year, even in good economic times. As such, even though more than
fifty general strikes occurred since the beginning of austerity measures
through the end of 2014, the number of general strikes to protest against
austerity and people's suffering was viewed as insufficient by the majority
of Greeks. Whether the number of general strikes was sufficient or not,
the perception by the Greek people was that they were not. In the end,
perception is reality, and the "reality" for the public was that organized
labor did not do enough to stop austerity's descent onto the community.
Also hampering any response to austerity by organized labor is that it
did not have the organizational capacity and, more important, the general
support to engage in a mass number of general strikes. Indeed, a 2011
opinion poll found that only 7 percent of respondents had confidence in

all trade unionists; the overwhelming majority did not have confidence in the union bureaucracy. Such distrust in the union bureaucracy made it difficult to move "towards a mobilization which would require high levels of societal support."[18]

In other words, the community lacked faith that organized labor would put the interests of the public ahead of its own. The public believed that organized labor was self-interested and did not care about the wider community. As Voskeritsian forcefully argues, "[t]he disengagement with trade unionism, and the appeal that unions seem to have lost in large segments of Greek society, are not merely a result of weak industrial practices, but disillusionment with bureaucratic trade unionism. That is not to say that people are indifferent to social causes, as the various examples of solidarity networks in urban neighbourhoods, or the rising interest in voluntary work reveal. These civil society activities, however, usually occur independently of, or even in conflict with, the official trade union movement."[19] Organized labor was not considered part of the community; for the general public, organized labor's interests were not the same as their own. Thus, when the Greek public engaged in protests and the like, organized labor played little or no part.

Thus, even if the labor movement had the organizational capacity to conduct rolling general strikes, the distrust of the union bureaucracy would have potentially undermined such an action. General strikes and the like that involve hundreds of thousands of workers can bring pressure on the government to change or modify its course of actions. General strikes that do not result in a mass turnout are not only easily ignored by the government, but also make it more likely for the government to portray anti-austerity protesters as a minority. The relative weakness of the Greek labor movement made it easier for Greece politicians to push through austerity measures. A militant trade union movement that had no ties to political parties and/or that did not support the austerity agenda potentially would likely have been more effective. However, the major Greek labor federations believed, just like American unions during the so-called Golden Age of capitalism, that there was a social partnership between the state and unions. Greek trade unionist George Harissis claims that organized labor "cultivated the perception that the capitalist classes and their political parties are the 'social partners' with which the working classes can negotiate." With the rise of austerity, this view was badly mistaken. As organized labor believed there was a partnership with the government, the "reformist perceptions of social partnership, cross-class collaboration and social dialogue have become dominant within the Greek working classes and associated layers of society, weakening the previously dominant principles of class struggle, workers' demands and the class emancipation of exploited layers of society."[20] In other words, organized labor moved away from viewing itself as part of the struggle against capitalism and toward working with the government to arguably better society for all. Once the Greek government abandoned the social partnership, it was difficult for organized labor to once again view the fight against austerity as a class struggle. Partly due to this, a number of Greek unions believed that the economy could be salvaged simply by reducing debt. It is seemingly common sense that having a high debt level over a prolonged period is not sustainable. The analogy pro-austerity advocates often used was that a country's debt is similar to household finances. Neither could have high debt levels for any extended period. Whether this is true is open to considerable debate, but accepting the perception that debt is bad and believing there was a social partnership in place also had the effect of making organized labor assume that Greece's problems could be solved without a major change, when in fact there was a systematic challenge to the fabric of Greek society through austerity. Tied in with this, the trade unions aligned with PASOK and those aligned with the right-wing New Democracy—the two largest political parties in the country at the time—did not initially join the anti-austerity protests in 2010. These unions believed that reducing public spending would go a long way to solve Greece's problems, thus, while unfortunate, it was best for the country if public sector workers experienced massive job losses, reduction in pay, and worse working conditions. There was no need to protest against austerity; it was better for the country to accept its medicine.

Thus, from the outset organized labor was not united. Unions with ties to political parties were primarily concerned with their own self-interest and that of the parties they were aligned to. It was "fine" that public sector workers bore the brunt of austerity policies. As in New York City in the 1970s, as we have seen in the previous chapter, union self-interest condemned the anti-austerity movement and ushered in the era of concession bargaining. Unions putting their own self-interest above the wider community when it comes to austerity is a common theme in Greece, Spain, Ireland, the UK, and the US. In Greece, while a fully united labor movement may not have been unable to overturn austerity initially, a divided one had no chance. As the labor movement was not united, this made it easier for the government to enact legislation detrimental to organized labor, which in turn made it more difficult for organized labor to fight against austerity. Moreover, as a number of unions initially agreed to the Greek government's austerity agenda, this led to the Greek public having even less confidence in the union bureaucracy and believing that organized labor was not doing enough to overturn austerity policies, as discussed above. The Greek public's perception of organized labor became the reality; despite the large number of general strikes, the public believed the labor movement was not doing enough. Austerity became the new reality. All of these factors combined made it exceedingly unlikely that organized labor had any chance to overturn austerity.

Arguably, in part, because of this, the majority of Greek people for a number of years, despite large-scale protests and general strikes, accepted the view from politicians, the IMF, EU, and the mass media that there was no alternative to austerity. In 2012, before the second bailout agreement was voted on in parliament, a Greek general election took place. The public thus had an opportunity to vote for parties that vowed to end austerity policies and be no longer beholden to the bailout. Instead, they voted for a right-wing party that was pro-bailout. The conservative New Democracy party was elected to government with 29.6 percent (129 seats out of a 300-seat parliament), with the former ruling "left-wing" and pro-bailout party PASOK securing only 12.3 percent of the vote, giving them 33 seats in parliament. Thus, despite the anti-austerity and bailout protests, and the suffering of ordinary Greeks, in the end the majority of people voted for parties that promised more of the same. However, in reality there was very little democratic choice because the main political parties all embraced austerity. As Gill highlighted, under the new constitutionalism, government and opposition parties resemble each other in their economic policies. In one positive, the support for the Golden Dawn party in the election was not as great as expected. However, the neo-Nazi party still gained 6.9 percent of the vote which gave them 18 seats in parliament. Another positive for those opposed to austerity measures is that the left-wing Syriza party, who promised to tear up the loan agreements with foreign creditors, finished second with 27 percent of the vote, which gave them 72 seats. Syriza refused calls to form a coalition government with New Democracy and became the main opposition party. Considering that in its first year of contesting a general election, in 2004, Syriza received only 3.3 percent of the vote (6 seats) and in 2007 it received 5.04 percent, the huge gains show that there is room for a true left-wing party in Greece. This was further demonstrated in the 2014 Greece European Parliament elections, as Syriza finished first with 26.6 percent of the vote (6 seats), with New Democracy receiving 22.1 percent (5 seats). Ominously, Golden Dawn also improved their showing, receiving 9.4 percent (3 seats). Both Syriza and Golden Dawn also did well in local elections in 2014.[21]

Austerity policies in Greece damaged the economy, made the people suffer, and yet in the end the people still voted for parties that were pro-bailout (and hence pro-austerity). On the surface it seems an odd state of affairs, but the majority of Greeks felt there was no alternative. The media and pro-bailout parties made it seem that if the country pulled out of the loan agreements and/or abandoned austerity it would be catastrophic for the Greek economy, and people would suffer even more. Thus, despite the general strikes and the mass protests against austerity by the trade union movement and workers generally, in the end the Greek public believed that it is possible for things to be even worse if they abandoned austerity policies and the bailout. Quite simply, considering the awful state of the economy and the immense pain inflicted on ordinary citizens, this is a sad state of affairs. However, as I shall demonstrate in Chapter 5, in January 2015, the Greek people finally had enough of austerity and sought change. While change came, politicians did not (or could not) live up to their promises.

Austerity and Spain

Unlike Greece, Spain did not have a debt crisis. In 2007, Spain's debt to GDP ratio was only 26 percent. This was well below most other countries in the EU. Indeed, Germany's debt to GDP ratio in 2007 was 50 percent. Nonetheless, the problem with the Spanish economy arguably began in the 1980s. In 1979, the Spanish economy was the eighth largest in the world; it is now the seventeenth largest. Blyth summarizes what caused the decline: "Spain effectively deindustrialized, becoming a banking, services, and tourism hub. The problem is that the income streams such a growth model relies on come primarily from outside the country: when such people stop spending and lending, you are in serious trouble. It's even more of a problem when what domestic growth you do have is debt-financed and based on little more than the swapping of houses." Spain had one of the largest property bubbles in the world; between 1997 and 2007, house prices increased by 115 percent. The housing bubble was potentially more damaging than in most other countries because nearly 25 percent of Spanish GDP and employment was due to construction and related sectors. The combination of a large increase in tourism, which resulted in a 70 percent rise in tourist-related employment between 1997 and

2006, and the housing boom led to unemployment declining from over 24 percent in 1994 to 8.5 percent in 2006. As a result, when the housing bubble burst, as all bubbles eventually do, it had a major negative effect on the Spanish economy. The bursting of the housing bubble caused a banking crisis. The large Spanish banks were reasonably well protected from the housing bubble; the same was not true for the regional savings banks (*cajas de ahorros*). The regional savings banks were responsible for almost half of local banking-sector loans. The housing bubble was so large that private sector debt was increasing at a rate of 20 percent per year, and just before the crisis was more than 200 percent of GDP. Even with the large reduction in unemployment, debt was increasing in part because the real wage level was declining. While interest rates were low, even with the decline in real wages, the debt was "manageable." However, the 2008–2009 global economic crisis led to a credit crunch, which in turn led the European Central Bank to raise interest rates. As a result, the debt was no longer manageable. People were unable to pay back their loans, and an increase in bankruptcies occurred. Compounding the debt problem was that "Spanish mortgages are recourse loans, meaning that the bank can come after the debtor for the original loan—forever—and not for just the current value of the property, and mortgagers have every incentive to sit tight and not allow the market to clear, thus making the situation worse by inches. . . . In Spain, when you walk away from the house, the mortgage debt is still your problem."[22]

As a result of the bursting of the housing bubble and the credit crunch, in the third quarter of 2008 Spain's economy went into recession. In the first quarter of 2009, GDP declined by an astronomical 6.3 percent, with domestic demand decreasing by 7 percent. In response to the crisis, in 2009 the Spanish government implemented an economic stimulus package that was equivalent to 5 percent of the country's GDP, as well as a bank-bailout program. In addition to the bank-bailout program, the number of regional savings banks was slashed from forty-five to seventeen. The stimulus package and an increase in exports resulted in the economy moving out of recession in the first quarter of 2010. However, the crisis saw Spain's debt to GDP ratio increase to 60 percent by 2010, unemployment increase from 7.7 percent in 2007 to 25 percent in 2010, and by 2012 youth unemployment was a staggering 52 percent. The economic stimulus package also had the effect of increasing public debt to 11.3 percent of GDP. This worried the financial markets.[23]

The concern of the financial markets (while of course financial markets cannot directly dictate economic policy, they certainly can make their feelings known; they wanted austerity. The transnational financial networks pushed for austerity), the increase in debt, and the overall state of the economy led the Spanish government to believe that austerity was the only answer.

In May 2010, Spanish Prime Minister José Luis Rodríguez Zapatero of the ruling "Socialist" government announced a range of austerity policies in an attempt to end the economic crisis. As in Greece, it was a supposed left-wing party that first implemented austerity policies. Once again, under the new constitutionalism, very little separated political parties when it came to economic policies; the main political parties in Spain are pro-neoliberalism and pro-austerity. Indeed, there is a long history of supposed left-wing parties implementing neoliberal policies. Some such examples include the Democrats in the US under the presidency of Bill Clinton, the Bob Hawke/Paul Keating leadership of the Australian Labor Party in the 1980s and 1990s, and, as we shall see in the following chapter, the Tony Blair so-called New Labour in the UK in the 1990s and 2000s. Quite simply, throughout the twentieth and into the twenty-first century, we have seen a move of social democratic parties to the right. It has been common practice for so-called left-wing political parties to implement neoliberal policies.

Among the austerity policies the Spanish government implemented, the general VAT increased 2 percent to 18 percent, while the reduced rate increased to 8 percent from 7 percent; public sector wages were frozen, and overall public sector workers remuneration packages were reduced by 5 percent; pensions were frozen; and the retirement age was increased from sixty-five to sixty-seven. In addition, there was labor market "reform." As social researcher Luis Buendía notes, "[t]hese reforms include (a) relaxing rules to classify layoffs as due to economic causes which has the effect of lowering severance payments which are subsided by the state; (b) promoting new employment contracts which lower severance pay from 45 days for each year of services to 33 days; (c) reducing the power of unions to participate in decisions regarding workplace issues; (d) reducing the coverage of centralized bargaining; and (e) increasing the duration of fixed-term contracts which effectively perpetuate temporality."[24] As we saw with the Greek government, as part of the Spanish government's austerity agenda, the labor movement was targeted in an attempt to weaken the power of organized labor, which would allow further neoliberal and austerity measures to be more easily implemented. And, once again, it was a "left-wing" government that implemented austerity policies that had a major negative impact on workers, the poor, and the vulnerable (see below).

The austerity policies—and some would say not surprisingly—had no effect in helping the Spanish economy; indeed, they made things worse. However, in a sign that politicians believed that there was no alternative, in September 2011, the Spanish Parliament passed a constitutional amendment that forces all future governments in times of "normal" economic growth to have a balanced budget. In the general election in November 2011 (Zapatero brought forward the election from March 2012), Spanish voters elected the center-right People's Party to office, with Mariano Rajoy becoming the new prime minister. In the lead-up to the election, Rajoy promised that there would be tax cuts and that his government would protect health care and education. However, when it came to austerity, the new boss was the same as the old boss. Following the news that economic growth in the third quarter of 2011 had slumped to zero and another recession was on the horizon, rather than spend to stimulate growth, Mariano Rajoy announced a new array of austerity policies. In 2012, public spending cuts of 8.9 billion euros ($11.49 billion in US dollars) were implemented across all government departments, as well as tax increases, largely on wealthy Spaniards.[25]

Despite the range of austerity policies, the Spanish economy showed no signs of improvement. The economy slipped back into recession and unemployment continued to rise, as did the debt to GDP ratio. As there was seemingly no alternative, the Spanish government agreed to accept a bank bailout from the EU of up to €100 billion ($122.85 billion). As with Greece, the bailout came with austerity strings attached. As noted in the previous chapter, the major capitalist states wanted austerity to be implemented around the world. The VAT was increased: a "3 percentage point hike on products and services like clothing, cars, cigarettes and telephone services to 21 percent and a 2 percentage point increase on goods such as public transport fares, processed foods and bar and hotel services to 10 percent." In addition, public sector workers had their wages frozen for another year, were forced to work longer hours, and had to forfeit their December bonuses. There were some closures of state-owned companies, people would no longer be able to claim tax deductions for owning their own home, electricity bills were increased by 7 percent, and there was a further €660 million reduction in government spending. In a positive for retirees, their pensions were increased. However, in arguably the cruelest austerity measure of all, a reduction in unemployment benefits was implemented in an attempt to encourage those out of work to find jobs more quickly. Considering that unemployment was above 25 percent and there were very few jobs available, cutting unemployment benefits was further punishment to people already struggling to get by. Overall, the spending cuts and tax increases were worth €65 billion. The previous austerity measures were worth €75 billion (implemented by the former Socialist government) and €60 billion (previously implemented by Rajoy's government). Thus, overall the overall austerity measures were a staggering €200 billion. Rajoy claimed that "[t]his is the reality. There is no other, and we have to get out of this hole and we have to do it as soon as possible and there is no room for fantasies or off-the-cuff improvisations because there is no choice."[26]

In pure economic terms, the unemployment rate showed a steady decline from a record high of 26.94 percent in the first quarter of 2013 to 21.18 percent in the third quarter of 2015. While the decline is to be welcomed, it is still astronomically high. Likewise, after being in recession from 2011, the economy began to grow, albeit barely, in late 2013. Now whether these slight improvements were due to austerity or that it was impossible for the economy to do worse is uncertain. One must remember that it was austerity policies in the first place that led to large rises in unemployment and stifled economic growth. Moreover, the debt to GDP ratio, which was not a problem before the austerity measures, continued to increase. It reached a new record of 92.1 percent in 2013 and increased dramatically to 97.7 percent in 2014. The 2014 figure was actually viewed somewhat as a positive because it was expected to be above 100 percent.[27]

Union Resistance to Austerity in Spain and Why It Failed

Despite the minor improvements in the Spanish economy, as is the case in Greece, the people who paid the highest price for the austerity measures were the public. It was not surprising, then, that there were mass protests against the austerity policies beginning in 2010. However, just like in Greece, the anti-austerity movement was largely ineffective. Thus, one must ask again why organized labor was unable to overcome austerity.

A major reason the labor movement was ineffective in the struggle was that it became less militant once austerity policies were implemented. The percentage of Spanish workers belonging to a union has been relatively stable since the turn of the century, hovering between 15 and 18 percent. From 1996 to 2006, the number of strikes in Spain averaged between 618 and 807 per year. The number of strikes in 2009 was 1,001. With the implementation of austerity policies, the number of strikes declined to just under 1,000 in 2010 and in 2011. Thus, while the number of strikes did increase from the 1996–2006 average, once austerity was introduced unions were less militant, albeit only slightly. Moreover, the strikes were largely of a defensive nature; unions were in the main going out on strike only if austerity policies directly affected them, such as through labor market reform, or in an attempt to prevent job losses and wage cuts, rather than protesting against austerity as a whole (see below). Quite simply, unions were going out on strike to protect their own self-interests. Thus it was easy for the Spanish people to believe that organized labor was not doing enough to attempt to overturn austerity policies. The largest industrial action in 2010 was a general strike in September to protest against austerity and, moreover, the labor market reform. Whether the strike was a success depends on how one defines success. In a positive, millions of workers went out on strike; but still the strike had no impact in forcing the government to abandon austerity policies or the labor market reform. This leads on to a major reason why organized labor could not get the government to abandon austerity—namely, rather than fighting against austerity, a number of unions accepted such measures. In scenarios similar to what occurred in New York City in the 1970s and Greece in 2010, following the general strike, the two major Spanish union confederations— the *Comisiones Obreras* (Workers' Commissions) and the *Union General de Trabajadores* (General Unions of Workers)—agreed to the austerity policies being implemented. The austerity policies were implemented by the "Socialist" government with some minor modifications, such as the increase in retirement age being phased in over a number of years and the "number of years of social security contributions increased from 15 to 25 years." *Comisiones Obreras* and the *Union General de Trabajadores* agreed to the austerity policies even though the labor market reform had a major negative effect on unions. The labor federations believed there was no alternative and that it was best to accept the austerity measures with some slight favorable changes rather than to fight them. The labor federations were more interested in salvaging what they could for their members than in helping the entire community. *Comisiones Obreras* and the *Union General de Trabajadores* agreed to austerity, yet, as Angie Gago argues, the labor market reform had the effect of reducing unions "autonomy and changed the rules regulating their representation in the workplace. To this situation we also need to add the tendency towards the decentralisation of collective bargaining, and the current crisis in the negotiation of collective agreements. In fact . . . in the last five years the number of collective agreements signed in Spain has been reduced by almost 50 per cent, from 5,987 in 2008 to 3,378 in 2012." Related to this, both *Comisiones Obreras* and *Union General de Trabajadores* are advocates of the servicing model of unionism. As I argued in Chapter 1, under the servicing model, unions care only about their existing membership. They largely do not care about organizing the unorganized and what is happening in the wider community. The servicing model is a key component of business unionism, which led to the major decline of the US labor movement. Such an approach in Spain could, and did, succeed when the workforce consisted of full-time employees in "traditional" occupations. However, as both *Comisiones Obreras* and *Union General de Trabajadores* embrace the servicing model, they have struggled to organize workers in sectors that rely on temporary contracts, which, as noted above, is an ever-increasing amount of total Spanish employment. Gago goes on to argue that "labour organisations have traditionally relied on relatively stable supporters from industry and the public sector (insiders), and they are now facing significant difficulties relating to the new social groups affected by austerity measures, mainly young people, precarious workers and the unemployed (outsiders)."[28] Thus, for a large segment of the working population, as well as local communities, organized labor was not an important part of their day-to-day lives. In many ways, unions represented workers in the "old" economy and not those in the "new" Spanish economy.

At one time, around the world there were ties between unions and the local community. However, because of globalization this is becoming less common. As Michael Yates notes, in the US in 1935, "[w]orkers lived in close proximity to one another, and most of them worked close by. . . . Turn the clock ahead to 1995. There is a glass factory near Meadville, Pennsylvania, and some of the employees there want a union. The plant is located in an isolated area, and the company plans to hire people from a widespread area. When the shift ends, workers scatter in their vans and trucks to their rural and suburban homes. There is no sense of community."[29] As such, there used to be a natural affinity between unions and the community. Now unions have to actively attempt to form a bond with the community. However, Spanish unions often failed to do so, to their detriment.

All of these factors combined had the effect of limiting the labor movements' initial response to austerity. In other words, there was a similar situation in Spain as there was in Greece: large sections of organized labor agreed to the implementation of austerity policies in the mistaken belief that simply a reduction in debt would solve the problem, and they were not as militant as they had been in earlier years. Austerity was viewed as just another economic policy. *Comisiones Obreras* and *Union General de Trabajadores* cared more about themselves and their members' self-interests than they cared about the wider community. They did not realize, or did not care, that there was a push across the globe by intellectual elites and major capitalist countries for austerity to become the de facto economic policy. Through organized labor initially accepting the austerity agenda, any resistance movement was divided from the start. This basically condemned the anti-austerity movement; it had little or no chance to succeed. As a result, Spanish unions inadvertently paved the way for austerity to gain a much greater foothold in the country. That organized labor was self-interested caused austerity to take hold and result in suffering for large segments of the population (see below for details).

Indeed, with both *Comisiones Obreras* and *Union General de Trabajadores* agreeing to the 2010 austerity measures, the major austerity protests in 2011 largely came from the Indignados Movement—or, by its better known name, 15M (named after the date of its first major protest May 15, 2011). 15M was largely compromised of students, the unemployed, and underemployed young people. 15M, following in the footsteps of the Egyptian uprising, occupied public spaces and engaged in mass protests against austerity. Initially, 15M was hostile to the union movement, especially its collaboration with the government. Nonetheless, many rank-and-file workers were part of the protests, and 15M called for a general strike, but a strike not led by unions (see Chapter 5 for a larger discussion of 15M). The scale of 15M protests led to pressure being placed on the labor movement to once again mobilize in large numbers. Following the fall of the Socialist government and the rise to power of the People's Party, the labor movement once again returned to the general strike as a tactic. It was "easier" for the labor federations to stage mass protests against a right-wing government than a "socialist" one. Now while in principle it should make no difference, organized labor is less likely to stage mass protests against "left-wing" governments than those of the right. Of course, this also means, as I noted earlier, that so-called "left-wing" political parties have implemented a number of anti-labor polices across the globe with barely a sustained protest from organized labor in the fear that a right-wing political party will be elected to government in the future. There were further general strikes in March and November 2012, "the latter involving over 8 million workers, as the main unions were forced to respond to both the pressure from the streets and workplaces, and the sheer scale of the austerity being imposed by the government.

Again these actions had wide support from the social movements and in some cases saw more combative picket lines as groups of workers sought to organise from below. If these strikes are included in the figures, they show a significant rise in industrial action. But there were limits to the action in 2012: the seven months between general strikes, in which there was little or no direction given by union leaders, saw a wave of job cuts." Thus, while on the surface organized labor was more militant, there was no sustained pressure from them to force the government to abandon or modify austerity policies due to the many months between general strikes. One-off strikes may garner media attention, but if there is no sustained pressure it is easy for the government to ignore such protests. In addition, the 2012 general strikes were in a large part a protest against the European Central Bank, the EU, and the IMF rather than the austerity measures of the Spanish government. Under this reasoning, it was not the Spanish government's fault that they had to adopt austerity—it was "outsiders." It is certainly true that these outside bodies played a pivotal role in Spain adopting austerity. This is beyond dispute. However, Spanish unions were mistaken in believing that the government was forced to adopt austerity; successive governments adopted austerity in part because they wanted to do so. In the end, quite simply, despite repeated industrial action and general strikes, governments across the political spectrum in Spain supported and implemented austerity policies. However, even though there were general strikes and austerity was causing mass suffering to the general public across the country, large sections of the labor movement were still largely concerned about their own interests rather than that of the Spanish people as a whole. Gago argues that the "number of strikes does not show a shift towards a more militant position. First, the strikes have been called only when their constituencies were clearly attacked as in the case of labour market reforms. On the contrary, unions have not mobilised their constituencies against other cuts avoiding an open political confrontation in the national arena. Second, these strikes have had a clear defensive character. Mobilisation by the unions has been moderate, delaying the organisation of the strikes a few months after the enactment of the reforms." Moreover, a large number of strikes were in relation to job losses and/or companies failing to pay wages. In 2006 and 2007, approximately 50 percent of strikes were "offensive" in nature in which unions were demanding higher wages and better working conditions. In contrast, in 2011 only 20 percent of strikes were of a similar nature.[30]

In other words, once again, despite the shows of "militancy," Spanish unions were largely concerned about only their members' interests to the detriment of the wider community. They were largely indifferent to the suffering austerity caused if it was not related to themselves and their members. As we have seen, unions that care primarily about their and their members' interests have little chance in overturning or even modifying austerity policies to any great extent. The strikes were also far from being spontaneous in nature; occurring only well after the austerity reforms were enacted, the likelihood that industrial action would be successful was greatly diminished. A defensive and self-interested labor movement, as was the case in Greece, is a recipe for weakness. Thus it should not have come as a surprise that organized labor was totally ineffectual in the fight against austerity.

The Spanish labor movement, as well as Spanish social movements such as 15M, was seemingly powerless to stop the spread of austerity, and as a result ordinary Spanish people suffered. An article in *The Guardian* describes people's suffering: "How do you look after a now terminally ill 90-year-old aunt and her son with mental health problems, asks one, when both have lived off her €600-a-month pension? Another has given her spare room to a 57-year-old graphic designer friend who cannot find work and does not qualify for dole payments. How long will he stay? A doctor—and single mother—admits that she worked before Christmas with flu because she could not afford to take (unpaid) sick days." Household disposable income in real terms has declined by almost 10 percent since 2008, with savings rates declining as people are forced to use their savings to pay their bills. Likewise, a report in the *British Medical Journal* states that austerity policies in Spain have led to a rise in depression, suicides, and alcohol-related illnesses. There have been increasing numbers of people, especially the disabled, elderly, and the mentally ill, who have sought care within the public health system—a system unable to cope due to cuts in funding for public health care and social services. In addition, a lecturer in Global Health at the London School of Hygiene & Tropical Medicine claims that "[i]f no corrective measures are implemented, this could worsen with the risk of increases in HIV and tuberculosis—as we have seen in Greece where health care services have had severe cuts—as well as the risk of a rise in drug resistance and spread of disease."[31]

In January 2015, the *Center for Economic and Social Rights* released a report highlighting the impact of austerity on Spaniards. As a result of the austerity measures in 2014, almost thirteen million Spaniards are at risk of poverty and social exclusion. Since 2008, more than 800,000 children have become at risk of poverty and social exclusion; the total number in 2014 was 2.7 million. Twenty-five percent of Spanish children, 2.3 million, are at risk of malnutrition. Furthermore, the "[s]tate budget for social security benefits for children and families has been cut by 91% since 2008, while social protection allocations to immigrants, people with disabilities, the elderly and dependents, have all seen declines to historically low levels—with falls of 79%, 69%, 50%, and 26%, respectively, between 2008 and 2015." There has also been increasing inequality in the country. There has been a decline of 3.6 percent in average disposable income since 2007. However, the richest 10 percent of the population have experienced declines of only 1.4 percent. In contrast, the poorest 10 percent have experienced a 12 percent decline. The gap between the rich and the poor is the second largest in Europe (only Greece is worse); it has grown by 15 percent since 2007. Indeed, the six countries with the largest levels of inequality (Greece, Spain, Portugal, Italy, Ireland, and the UK) have all implemented austerity policies.[32]

In a positive development, in June 2014 the Spanish government announced a range of personal tax cuts. Under the proposed plan, there will be 12.5 percent reduction in income tax for 2015–2016. People earning less will see higher tax cuts. People earning less than €12,450 in 2016 will see their income tax fall from the 2014 rate of 24.75 percent to 19 percent in 2016, while those earning €300,000 or more will pay 45 percent tax in 2016 down from the 2014 rate of 52 percent. However, the government also plans to reduce the corporate tax rate by 5 percent to 25 percent in 2016. A cynic might claim that the reduction in the tax rates is due to the upcoming Spanish general election, and particularly to the rise of the left-wing Podemos party. Podemos, which has its roots in 15M, formed in 2014. It initially registered only 0.2 percent of support following its formation, but by December 2014 it has overtaken both the Socialists and the People's Party in the polls. Among the main policy platform of Podemos is eliminating austerity policies, ending corruption, and stopping mass privatization of government-owned assets, especially in relation to the health and education system.[33] Following years of pain and suffering and seemingly no alternative to austerity, the tax cuts and the rise of Podemos are positive developments. I will return to the rise of Podemos in Chapter 5.

Austerity and Ireland

Ireland is no stranger to austerity policies. In 1986, Ireland's debt to GDP ratio was 116 percent. Following their election victory, as Blyth argues, the right-wing government "cut transfers, the government wage bill, and taxes. Devaluation and negotiated wage moderation reduced unit labor costs by 12 to 15 percent. Growth rates and foreign investment both soared. Key to all this . . . was the large expenditure-based cut plus wage moderation and devaluation." Ireland was thus considered one of the success stories of austerity. However, debate continues on whether austerity led to the rise of the Irish economy. Stephen Kinsella argues that the Irish economy did not grow due to austerity, but largely because the austerity policies coincided with a boom in the international economy, the opening-up of the European single market, the Irish currency being devalued, an amnesty on income tax (approximately 2 percent of GDP), and industrial wages' increase by more than 14 percent between 1986 and 1989, which greatly increased government revenue and individual consumption.[34] Whether austerity truly led to the Irish boom is open to debate. What is beyond debate is that austerity was perceived to have led to an Irish economic boom. Thus, the next time the Ireland economy was in trouble, austerity was viewed as the savior. Austerity measures are what the country's politicians returned to.

By 2007 the Irish economy was in sound shape. The debt to GDP ratio declined from 116 percent eleven years earlier to 25 percent in 2007, and Ireland's net debt to GDP ratio was only 12 percent. The country was exporting goods and services to other booming economies, had an influx of multinational companies taking advantage of the country's low corporate tax rates, and its workforce became more highly skilled. Ireland's GDP per capita increased from €30,396 in 2001 to €40,702 in 2008. As a result, there was an increase in government revenue and public consumption. However, these factors also led to a housing bubble as people viewed property as a safe investment. The housing bubble was unofficially promoted by the European Central Bank as its interests rates were approximately zero percent. It was easy money. As a result, property prices exploded: "The average price of new construction in the country increased 91% from €169,191 in 2000 to a high of €322,634 in 2007, while second-hand home prices rose 98% from €190,550 to €377,850 over the same period. New home and second-hand construction in Dublin, the capital, increased 88% from €221,724 in 2000 to €416,225 in 2007, and second-hand home prices rose 107% from €247,039 in 2000 to a high of €512,461 in 2006." Buoyed by record low interest rates, people borrowed as much money as they could, with the banks happily giving out this seemingly "free" money.[35]

One consequence of the housing boom was that property prices increased at a faster rate than earnings. In 1995, an average property was four times a person's income; by 2006, a new home was ten times average income; and in Dublin a pre-owned home was seventeen times the average wage. The construction industry was crucial to the Irish economy. In 2006, it accounted for 24 percent of gross national product; in the second quarter of 2007, almost 19 percent of all employment was due to the housing industry (both directly and indirectly), and it accounted for 18 percent of tax revenue. However, as noted above, all property bubbles eventually burst. And for Ireland, considering how much its economy relied on construction, the bursting of its property bubble was catastrophic. Blyth writes that

> [t]o fund lending on such a massive scale, Irish banks increasingly turned to wholesale funding markets in the United States . . . essentially borrowing overnight to fund thirty-year mortgages. The three main Irish banks' combined asset footprint at the time of the crash was around 400 percent of GDP. One of those banks, Anglo-Irish, lent 67 billion euros to the nonfinancial sector (real estate) in 2007 alone. Anglo-Irish was particularly dependent on short-term funding. When the interbank market froze following Lehman's collapse, the ability of the Irish banks to service their loans collapsed along with Irish property prices, taking the entire banking sector down with it.

In response to the banking and financial crisis, the Irish government guaranteed the banking sector's debt. Thus, the debt, which equated to 400 percent of Irish GDP, was now the government's, and hence the public's, problem. Initially, the government gave three banks €5.5 billion in an attempt to stabilize them and eventually nationalized the Anglo Irish bank. Realizing that these moves alone would not prevent a banking collapse, the government formed the National Asset Management Agency (NAMA) in April 2009. Blyth further states that "NAMA bought the [bad banks'] assets at above book value with taxpayer money, sold shares of NAMA back to the banks, and they, in turn, used these shares as collateral to get liquidity from the ECB. In short, creative accounting and a helpful government enabled the banks to walk away scot-free from the carnage they had caused." The Irish government spent more than €70 billion in an attempt to prop up the banks. The bailout, not including the €70 billion, was worth 45 percent of GDP. Overall, the government debt to GDP ratio increased to more than 110 percent. The effect of the crisis saw Gross

National Product have the largest compound decline of any industrialized country for a three-year period beginning in 2007. Likewise, GDP declined by 3.5 percent in 2008, a massive 7.6 percent in 2009, and in 2010 by 1 percent. Unemployment increased from 4.6 percent in 2007 to 14.2 percent in June 2011, with 55 percent of those being unemployed for longer than 12 months. Savings rates increased from 1.6 percent in 2007 to 14.6 percent in 2010 as people braced themselves for bad times. As savings rates increased, consumption declined by 1.5 percent in 2008 and 7 percent in 2009.[36] As a result of the crisis, Ireland was forced to seek a bailout.

However, before receiving a bailout, Ireland had already begun to implement austerity policies in an attempt to control the crisis. The government, recalling how austerity solved the problems of the Irish economy in the 1980s and led to a boom, once again adopted a similar cure. In 2009, government spending was reduced by approximately 15 percent. The age in which public sector workers could receive a pension was increased to 66 from 65. The minimum wage was reduced by 15 percent, which brought significant hardship on those already on the margins of society. (The cut in minimum wage lasted for two years before the government reversed the reduction in 2011.) Welfare payments were also reduced. There was also the reinstatement of university fees, and increases in income tax for high earners. Considering the range of measures, one would assume that the labor movement would become more militant. Indeed, the number of industrial disputes initially increased dramatically from "356 [in 2008] to 278,000 in 2009, mainly through a series of one-day public sector strikes." However, the militancy was short-lived and soon to be forgotten. Rather than fight austerity policies, public sector unions agreed to industrial peace with the government. Organized labor abandoned militancy and the fight against austerity. Peter Rigney notes that "[i]n June 2010, the Public Services Committee of the Irish Congress of Trade Unions . . . backed what has become known as the 'Croke Park' agreement. The agreement . . . means a four-year pay freeze and commitments by the government not to implement compulsory redundancies and to maintain existing pension arrangements. In return, the trade unions agreed to a 'transformation' programme, expected to yield major productivity improvements and efficiencies—as well as a broad commitment to maintain industrial peace. The range of workers affected by the deal includes civil servants, health workers, teachers and employees in the security services." As a result, the number of industrial disputes declined markedly to 511 in 2010.[37]

The reduction in the number of strikes was a dramatic reversal from the previous year. By agreeing to the Croke Park Agreement, sections of the Irish labor movement accepted austerity. The situation in Ireland was very similar to those in New York City, Greece, and Spain. Faced with a situation in which the debt level was seeming spiraling out of control, organized labor accepted that there was no alternative with barely a fight. Organized labor in Ireland agreed to a raft of austerity measures, thinking this would solve the problem and things would eventually return to "normal." The unions agreed to austerity in the belief that if they did not do so, the government would have imposed harsher measures. However, just as in Greece and Spain, the initial austerity measures were the proverbial tip of the iceberg. Moreover, by accepting austerity and engaging in fewer strikes, organized labor was in principle agreeing to *all* the austerity measures being inflicted onto the wider community, not just those imposed on public sector workers. As such, by cutting an agreement with the government, the unions were de facto supporting austerity. They were putting their own self-interest above all others. Such an approach failed in Greece and Spain. It also failed in Ireland.

Despite the range of austerity policies in 2009 and early 2010, they had little impact in solving the crisis. Thus, in November 2010, the Irish government accepted a €85 billion bailout from the IMF and the EU. In some ways Ireland was forced to accept a bailout. The European Central Bank threatened the Irish government that it would no longer provide emergency funds if the government did not agree to an EU–IMF bailout package. The transnational financial network and the major capitalist states used the crisis in Ireland to further their austerity agenda. Nevertheless, earlier in the month, in anticipation of accepting a bailout, the Irish government announced a range of additional austerity policies in hopes of securing a rescue package. The Irish government also believed wholeheartedly in austerity. The austerity measures included €20 billion in spending cuts. There was an almost 15 percent reduction in the social welfare budget, an elimination of 24,750 public sector jobs, a €1.9 billion reduction in the health care budget, and a tax base so widened that some low-income workers and those receiving public sector pensions began paying tax for the first time. While all this caused significant pain to the general public, the government kept the corporate tax rate at a low 12.5 percent. Thus, there was misery for the general public, but not for the corporate sector. Moreover, as was the case in other crisis countries, the range of austerity policies was not enough. In December 2011, the government announced a further €3.8 billion in spending cuts and tax increases for "health care, social protections and child benefits."[38] Once again, the public suffered, not big business.

The austerity policies did not end there. In December 2012, the Irish government introduced further measures, including a new property tax (0.18 percent on homes worth up to €1 million and 0.25 percent on homes worth more than that), a €10 per month reduction in child benefits, a €61 million reduction in other household benefits, a €250 increase in university fees, and an increase in taxes on alcohol and tobacco. The tax increases and spending cuts amounted to €3.5 billion. It was still not enough. There was another austerity budget in 2013. The government claimed that this would be the "final austerity budget" the country would have to endure. There were a range of cuts to social welfare spending, such as a reduction in unemployment benefits to people under twenty-six, and the elimination of the bereavement grant to families of people who died. In regards to health care, prescriptions increased by €1 and reductions in health services occurred, including a tightening of rules for those over seventy years of age receiving medical assistance. And, in what was becoming a "tradition," taxes on alcohol and tobacco products increased. There were also increases in tax on bank deposits and state pensions. The 2014 budget did not contain any new austerity measures; indeed, there was some tax relief and other "voter-friendly" policies, although there was a further tax increase on cigarettes. But if the Irish people expected there would be no more austerity measures, they were in for a rude shock. Previously, water usage had been free. However, in accepting the EU–IMF bailout, the Irish government agreed to introduce a domestic water charge beginning on October 1, 2014.[39]

Thus, even though there were no "new" austerity policies, the effects of austerity still linger, even with the official ending of the bailout package in December 2013 and the government once again being able to borrow money from international markets. As in Greece and Spain, austerity had a largely negative impact on ordinary people, with the poor and vulnerable suffering the most, and the rich actually benefiting from the government's economic policies.

One of the first effects of austerity was that the number of people out of work climbed at a steady rate. The unemployment rate increased from 9.6 percent in January 2009 to 13.1 percent one year later. It eventually peaked at 15.1 percent in February 2012. Since then, the unemployment rate has shown a slow, steady decline; by September 2014, the number of people looking for work stood at 11.1 percent, which is still well above the January 2009 figure. However, the unemployment rate dramatically declined in 2015, and by October the rate was "only" 8.9 percent. However, while the decline is to be welcomed, the figures are somewhat misleading. For many people, it was better to leave the country rather than wait for an economic turnaround and/or protest against austerity. In 2007, 46,300 people emigrated from Ireland. The number increased to 80,600 in 2011, 87,100 in 2012, and 89,000 in 2013 before declining to 81,900 in the twelve months to April 2014. The rate of emigration is so great that if the numbers are factored into the unemployment rate, it would add approximately another 8 percent to the official figures. Moreover, if one also includes those people who are currently in part-time positions but want a full-time job and those who are discouraged from seeking a full-time position, that would raise the unemployment rate by another 4 percent. Homelessness has increased almost 20 percent since 2010, with about six people per day becoming homeless in Dublin. Julien Mercille notes that "[i]t's hard for homeless people to start renting because in Dublin, there are 2,500 people chasing 1,500 accommodation units and rents have increased by 18% since 2011 while the rent allowance payable by the Department of Social Protection has fallen by almost 30% since 2011. In theory, there is also social housing, but there is a waiting list of nearly 90,000. The government said it would build some new homes over the next two years, but that would only reduce the waiting list by 2%."[40]

In addition, a survey of 11,000 people with young children found that an astonishing 67 percent "could not afford basic necessities, and were behind on utility bills, rent and the mortgage." The number of young people who have endured serious deprivation has doubled to 20 percent since 2007, and 51 percent of them cannot adequately access health care because of the cost. Indeed, health care funding has been slashed by 20 percent, with a decline in staff of 11–12 percent. A 2012 survey determined that 40 percent of people (1.8 million) had €100 or less every month after bill payments, while 602,000 people had no disposable income remaining. As is often the case, it is women who suffer greater economic hardships than men during bad economic times. The Economic and Social Research Institute determined that between 2009 and 2013 women had higher declines in disposable income in every income group as compared to men. On average, women experienced a 14 percent decline in disposable income, while men experienced a 9 percent decline. However, not everyone is struggling; the rich are doing well. Indeed, "inequality in Ireland is four times the OECD average." In 2010, the richest segment of the population experienced an 8 percent rise in disposable income, while the poorest segment had a 26 percent decline in disposable income. Government policies have greatly contributed to the rising inequality. In addition to austerity measures, the 2013 budget resulted in those earning €20,000 paying an extra 1.2 percent in tax, those earning €100,000 paying an extra 0.2 percent in tax, and those earning €200,000 paying only an extra 0.1 percent in tax. It was those struggling to get by who were hit hardest by the tax increases.[41]

Nonetheless, despite many people suffering, one reason that Ireland is being portrayed as an austerity success story is the recent growth of its economy. Following a decline in 2009 and 2010, Ireland had small GDP growth in the years following the crash. However, as noted above, many multinationals have their headquarters in Ireland and declare their earnings in the country to take advantage of the low corporate tax rate; thus, "Irish GDP is inflated by global firms booking huge revenues through Ireland for tax purposes. When one looks at Irish GNP, which takes out such revenues, growth declined by 2.5 percent in 2011." Revenue of multinationals headquartered in Ireland is counted toward service exports. Martin Malone of the brokerage firm *Mint Partners* argues that "[t]he entire increase from 2007–2012 in Ireland's service exports is almost complete fluff . . . they are overstated by Euro 30 billion, which as a measure versus GNP comes to almost 25 percent of the total." Thus, the Irish recovery is not as great as the raw figures would have one believe. Indeed, the austerity measures have had no positive impact on the debt levels; by 2012, debt levels had increased to 117.4 percent of GDP, and it increased even further in 2013 to a record 123.7 percent, before falling to 109.7 percent in 2014.[42] Even though eliminating debt is the top priority for austerity advocates, the debt to GDP ratio is still well above the level before austerity policies were implemented. Thus, for such advocates Ireland is considered a success story, but debt is still well above 100 percent of GDP even though the country has been subjected to vast austerity policies.

Simon Tilford, the chief economist at the Centre for European Reform in London argues that "Ireland is the closest thing to a success story that European leaders have. . . . But it doesn't really stand up to scrutiny because there's been a huge fall in the domestic economy and living standards." The impact of austerity on Ireland was so great that one of the architects of the IMF/EU bailout package—Professor Ashoka Mody— argues that there was too much austerity in the country. Mody claims that "[w]e are seeing a belated recognition of the fact that the constraint imposed only by austerity was untenable. . . . Clearly the experience, if experience was needed, has demonstrated that reliance on austerity is counterproductive." He went on to claim that "[g]iven that Europe is dragging itself down the austerity process, some of the growth projections are not likely to be met. In that case these debt burdens will remain higher for longer than we currently think. Something has to give."[43]

Resistance to Austerity?

As noted, considering the range of austerity measures and the suffering they have caused, one would assume there would be massive public protests against them, with the labor movement at the forefront. This did not happen in Ireland. In addition to accepting the Croke Park Agreement, public sector union members, in some cases against the wishes of union leaders, agreed to its successor the Haddington Road Agreement. This was a case where the union bureaucracy wanted to fight against austerity, or more to the point, attempt to modify the new range of austerity measures the government was attempting to impose on workers. Union leaders were not interested in attempting to force the government to abandon austerity altogether. However, public sector workers had seemingly no fight left in them and accepted the Agreement. The Haddington Road Agreement provisions include an increase in weekly working hours, cuts to pay and pensions, and a more "flexible" work force. The Agreement will reduce government spending on the public sector by one billion euros starting in 2015. Union members thought that resistance was futile. Stephen Bach and Alexander Stroleny claim that "[a]fter trade union rejection of an earlier set of proposals in spring 2013, the government introduced legislation to cut public sector wages unilaterally. Unions could exempt themselves from the legislation if they individually endorsed modified proposals, termed the Haddington Road Agreement. . . . The agreement included some modest government concessions (e.g. on increases in working hours) and was eventually ratified under duress by virtually all public sector unions in membership ballots." Both the Croke Park Agreement and the Haddington Road Agreement created division between the public and private sector as they gave the impression that the public sector needed immediate reform; its workers were privileged. As such, organized labor in Ireland was divided. As there was no unity between public and private sector workers, it was relatively easy for the government to portray public sector workers as overpaid and inefficient. As we have seen, a divided labor movement is bound to fail. One potential reason that the membership agreed to Haddington Road was, as Bach and Stroleny note, that if the public sector unions did not accept the proposed reforms, the government would have unilaterally imposed the austerity measures onto the public sector and they may have been even harsher. Thus, the public sector workers believed that the austerity measures could have been even worse and, thus, rather than fight and potentially fail and suffer even more pain, it was "best" to accept the government offer that included very minor concessions.[44] In other words, they were already defeated and believed it in their best interests to capitulate.

Another reason the majority of union members were not willing to engage in continued mass militancy against austerity is that, like unions in the US, organized labor in Ireland became complacent during times of prosperity when a social contract was in place. As Ronald Erne argues, "[d]uring the Celtic Tiger years, most Irish unions uncritically supported a competitive corporatist development model, which did not leave room for autonomous union action. . . . Given the unprecedented growth rates that Ireland experienced from 1987 to 2007, union leaders seemed to have good reasons to celebrate the Irish social partnership model. . . . But when the Celtic Tiger bubble burst, a very passive union movement generated by years of social partnership and economic growth had lost the capacity to act independently."[45]

Thus, as with unions in the US, Greece, Spain, and countless other countries, Irish trade unions and their members were ill-prepared by the abandonment of the social partnership by the government. Irish unions somewhat fool-heartedly believed that good times would never end and that the government would be a lifelong partner. This made it very difficult for unions and their members to go from a relatively passive benign partner to one that is militant in a short period of time and, more important, to be able to sustain such militancy.

Thus, even though there were at times large-scale protests against austerity, for the most part the labor movement and the Irish population generally believed that there was no alternative to austerity—it was best just to accept it. Neil Irwin argues that the "Irish seemed to deal with the coming era of austerity—and even their loss of economic sovereignty—with greater acceptance than the Greeks had. In the Mediterranean nation that spring, protestors had staged a nationwide strike, tried to storm parliament, and firebombed a bank, leaving three dead. By contrast, there was no significant violence in the streets of Ireland."[46] There was seemingly little fight in the Irish when it came to the austerity onslaught.

However, as highlighted above, there have been sporadic protests. Moreover, half of the private households refused to pay the newly introduced household tax in 2012; in Dublin, there have been public protests in which more than 100,000 people marched against austerity, as well as, in 2014, large protests throughout the country against the water tax, with some arguing that the Irish people can no longer take austerity. There have been numerous reasons given why the Irish people have seemed to accept austerity, including religion, history, and that people would rather emigrate than fight. Another reason is that the Irish electorate is largely right wing "with 80–90% of votes going to centre-right parties deriving from the independence movement (a pattern shared with other postcolonial countries)." Nonetheless, with the continued austerity policies there has been a shift to the left: "In recent elections, a substantial chunk of votes have moved leftwards out of this camp, which is now capable of securing perhaps 55–60% in actual elections. Much of this leftward movement is contradictory, supporting the Labour Party, which is enthusiastically implementing austerity as a coalition partner (with the center-right Fine Gael) or Sinn Féin, which is doing the same north of the border." A source for hope for those against austerity occurred in the 2014 local and European elections. The elections saw both the Labour Party and Fine Gael suffer major losses, with independents and Sinn Féin—which contradictorily is anti-austerity in the Republic of Ireland and pro-austerity in Northern Ireland—seeing large rises.[47] While this is a positive development, out of the four main political parties, only Sinn Féin does not advocate austerity in the Republic of Ireland. Once again, there is a reduction in citizens' democratic choice, as government and opposition parties resemble each other in their economic policies. As Sinn Féin supports such measures in Northern Ireland, one must question how truly committed the party is to eliminating austerity. It is fair to say that the Irish people are still firmly under the grip of austerity.

Austerity, Economic Hardship, and the Labor Movement

Austerity in Greece, Spain, and Ireland cannot be considered a success. Even Ireland, which is the closest to what one might call successful, has suffered greatly due to austerity policies. Considering the widespread suffering by the general public in these countries, one would assume that the labor movement would have been at the forefront of the attempts to overturn or, at the very least, help protect people from austerity. Indeed, in Greece, Spain, and Ireland, the labor movement did organize mass protests, went out on strike, and generally campaigned against austerity and the political parties that implemented such policies. However, at the same time, unions in Spain and Ireland collaborated with the government for the implementation of a range of austerity policies. Even in Greece, with a number of general strikes and seemingly militant actions, sections of organized labor were seemingly more concerned with their political partnerships than with understanding the true nature of austerity that was being forced on the population. As with the municipal unions in New York City in the 1970s, certain Greece, Spanish, and Irish unions were putting the interests of their members and their partnership with a political party above the interests of the wider community. Moreover, while on the surface organized labor's repose was militant, in many ways it was defensive in character; namely, in each country unions had already accepted that concessions were a given and austerity was a necessity. As such, the general strikes and the protests were trying to minimize the pain for their members. They staged mass protests only to try to limit the damage. Organized labor that is self-interested, lacks unity (the divide between public sector unions and private sector unions in each country was often quite pronounced), and is defensive has little chance of succeeding in its struggles. Indeed, the labor movements in Greece, Spain, and Ireland had little or no effect in preventing the spread of austerity. Of course, it was not just unions that "accepted" austerity. Despite the suffering, the general public consistently voted for political parties that advocated bailouts and austerity measures. Even though there were general strikes, mass protests, and campaigning against austerity for a long time, the general public accepted the conventional wisdom that no alternative to austerity existed. There was also a situation in Ireland in which union members agreed to a raft of austerity measures, against the wishes of the union leadership, because the fight was seemingly out of them and they could not envisage an alternative.

However, in recent years, in each of these countries, parties that are anti-austerity have begun to make political gains: the left-wing Syriza and right-wing Golden Dawn in Greece, Podemos in Spain, and independents and to a lesser extent Sinn Féin in Ireland. (I will return to the rise of anti-austerity parties in Chapter 5.) There is a growing acceptance that the austerity measures in these countries went too far and that the suffering has not been worth it. Even the IMF has admitted that in certain instances the austerity policies have caused too much suffering. However, this does not mean that the policy elites have abandoned the idea of austerity. Indeed, in the UK and the US austerity has largely been embraced by center- and right-wing political parties and policy elites. Even so-called left-wing parties sprout the benefits of austerity, but they do so in a less boisterous manner. We turn to these two countries in the following chapters.

Chapter 3

Austerity and the Labor Movement in the United Kingdom

As we saw in the previous chapter, organized labor in Greece, Spain, and Ireland was unable to overcome or even mitigate the harshest austerity policies. Moreover, a number of unions and labor federations put their own self-interest above the wider community by agreeing to a range of austerity measures. In the United Kingdom, union membership stands at 6.5 million, with public sector membership at 3.8 million (55.4 percent of the public sector workforce) and private sector membership at 2.6 million (14.4 percent of the private sector workforce). While a long way from its peak power, organized labor still can wield considerable muscle. This combined with the public's early opposition to austerity rendered it not unrealistic to assume that such economic policies could have been overturned. However, as this chapter shall demonstrate, a number of unions followed the path of organized labor in Greece, Spain, and Ireland and put their own interests above all others. This led to austerity becoming the dominant economic policy, which was a detriment to the majority of the UK public.

Austerity in the UK

The UK's economy in 2009, while not as dire as the Greece, Spain, and Irish economies, was certainly not robust. The country was mired in the longest recession on record; GDP declined by 7.2 percent between the first quarter of 2008 and the second quarter of 2009. The unemployment rate increased to 7.6 percent from 5.6 percent in 2008, while the debt to

GDP ratio increased from 44.5 percent in 2007 to 52.3 percent in 2008, and then to 67.1 percent in 2009.[1] Quite simply, the UK, like nearly every other country in the world, was suffering in a large part due to the global economic crisis.

In response to the economic downturn, both politicians and the intellectual "elite" began to push the austerity agenda. In November 2008, the opposition Conservative Party began making noises that the Labour Party's strategy of engaging in an economic stimulus in the Keynesian-ism tradition to improve the British economy was the wrong course of action. The Tories argued that government spending should be curtailed. In 2009, then opposition Conservative Party leader David Cameron went so far as to claim that if elected his government would implement an "age of austerity." He stated that "[o]ver the next few years, we will have to take some incredibly tough decisions on taxation, spending and bor-rowing—things that really affect people's lives. . . . There is only one way out of this mess and this is through massive change. . . . I'm frustrated it's not happening. I'm impatient to get on with it." Cameron was also signaling that he wanted to cut public sector salaries: "Where this has gone to nurses, doctors, teachers, police and other frontline stars, that is money well spent. . . . But it is certainly not true of the wage bill for the swarm of unaccountable quangos that has infested our country under Labour." Cameron's rhetoric was shared by George Osborne, who was to become the new chancellor following the Tories' election victory. In the lead-up to an emergency budget that promised large spending cuts (see below for details), Osborne claimed, "You can see in Greece an example of a country that didn't face up to its problems, and that is the fate that I want to avoid." He made it clear that Britain would rather cut its way out of trouble than seek a bailout: "I'm absolutely clear, I don't want the question even asked, 'Can Britain pay its way in the world?' I'm going to prove . . . that we can." Likewise, in the lead-up to the general election, Osborne, following the yet to be discredited research from Reinhart and Rogoff, claimed that if government debt reached 90 percent of GDP it would hinder economic growth. He stated, "[t]he latest research suggests that once debt reaches more than about 90% of GDP the risks of a large negative impact on long term growth become highly significant. If off-balance sheet liabilities such as public sector pensions are included we are already well beyond that. And even on official internationally comparable measures of debt, we are forecast to break through 90% of GDP in just two years time. . . ."[2]

Helping the Conservative Party's austerity agenda, apart from the downturn in the economy, was what Gill calls the "organic intellectuals," who were also on the austerity bandwagon and made their desires known in the UK press. As Blyth claims, the *Financial Times* "became a kind of bulletin board for elite economic opinion." There were numerous opinion pieces arguing that the only way countries struggling economically could recover was to adopt austerity. For example, Jeffery Sachs argued that the Keynesianism era was over: "The hastily assembled stimulus packages were a throwback to naive Keynesianism. The relevant fact was that the US, UK, Ireland, Spain, Greece, and others had over-borrowed for a decade, so a decline in consumption after 2007 was not an anomaly to be fought but an adjustment to be accepted." He concluded by stating that "[w]e need, in sum, to reset our macroeconomic timetables. There are no short-term miracles, only the threat of more bubbles if we pursue economic illusions. To rebuild our economies, the watchword must be investment rather than stimulus." Likewise, the president of the European Central Bank Jean-Claude Trichet wrote that it was wrong for countries to use stimulus packages to try to overcome the economic crisis:

> With hindsight, we see how unfortunate was the oversimplified message of fiscal stimulus given to all industrial economies under the motto: "stimulate," "activate," "spend!" A large number fortunately had room for manoeuvre; others had little room; and some had no room at all and should have already started to consolidate. Specific strategies should always be tailored to individual economies. But there is little doubt that the need to implement a credible medium-term fiscal consolidation strategy is valid for all countries now.[3]

Not surprisingly, the austerity agenda was also advocated by the Governor of the Bank of England, Sir Mervyn King. In February 2010, in the lead-up to the general election, King argued that reducing budget deficits could have a stimulus effect on the economy, but added the disclaimer that it depended on circumstances. Nonetheless, he went on to claim, "what is very important, and why I totally agree with Jean-Claude Trichet, is that at all times governments need to have a clear and credible plan for reducing a structural deficit." In addition, in the first quarter of 2010, King personally met with Cameron and Osborne at his offices. It was alleged that King was advising the soon-to-be prime minister and chancellor on economic policy. As for King's motivations in hosting so many meetings with Cameron and Osborne, Kate Barker, who was a member of the Monetary Policy Committee, claims, "[t]he cynical view would be that this was Mervyn's effort to get the Bank into a good working relationship with the next regime. The uncynical view is that he was worried markets could lose confidence, which is certainly plausible, so you can argue Mervyn was right to say, 'This can't go on.' But the way he expressed his views on fiscal policy meant they could be interpreted in a political way." Former IMF Chief Economist Simon Johnson also went on the record in February 2010 stating that there were similarities between the UK and crisis countries such as Greece, Portugal, and Spain. He stated, "[n]ow Greece is an extreme example—there I think you can see that it's going to get very messy very quickly—but unfortunately the budget situation in these other countries [Portugal, Spain] is also weak. . . . And I have to add the UK to this list. Unless you can persuade the markets that you're really going to bring the budget under control within the foreseeable future and you're going to have some credible actions—and you're going to have to do some persuading—you're going to have big trouble."[4] The right-wing policy elite, the organic intellectuals, were preparing the groundwork for austerity.

However, it was not just right-wing newspapers and individuals arguing for austerity. In *The Guardian*, left-wing, so-called Keynesian Larry Elliot argued that austerity was inevitable and that there was no alternative: "These are the facts of fiscal life. The City knows them. The chancellor knows them. George Osborne knows them. Public spending will be cut and taxes will rise. All that is at issue is when, for how long and by how much. Certainly, the scale of the retrenchment will dwarf that of the 1990s, when policy was tightened aggressively after sterling's exit from the European exchange rate mechanism."[5] Quite simply, organic intellectuals, the media, and politicians were engaged in a none-to-subtle ideological campaign to convince the public that if the UK was to avoid an even more severe economic downturn and not end up like Greece, for instance, austerity was essential. Austerity was the cure.

The austerity, and more generally neoliberalism, agenda of right-wing politicians and sections of the media had the effect of influencing public opinion. The idea of "big" government being wasteful and less spending on social welfare being needed had been gaining traction in the UK for a number of years. The British Social Attitudes Survey in 2009 found that the public opinion was moving to the right and was almost as right wing as in 1979 when Margaret Thatcher came to power. The survey showed that people were increasingly against a large government; as we have seen, a reduction in the size of government spending is a key pillar of austerity. Likewise, an Ipsos-Morris study found that a majority of people supported spending on social welfare irrespective if it raised taxes in the late 1980s. However, in the late 2000s less than 30 percent of people supported spending on social welfare, with up to 40 percent opposed to government spending on social welfare if it raised taxes. Richard Seymour argues that this change occurred at a time when

> more people [were] likely to see themselves as being on a medium rather than low income. The change was particularly marked among young people. In general, the positive view of the welfare state, as "one of Britain's proudest achievements" that predominates among older people is far less evident among the young. They are less likely to support the government bearing responsibility for the care of the elderly, and are among the most likely (apart from the pre–Second World War generation) to say that less generous benefits would force people "to stand on their own two feet." If anything, the credit crunch and recession seemed to accelerate the reversal and drive people further to the right.

Seymour goes on to note that the Tories, in addition to preaching that there was no alternative to austerity, were smart enough to include a few populist measures in their first austerity budget, "such as a small windfall tax on banks, designed to give the impression that the government was cracking down on the parasites and helping the poor, despite the overall impact of the budget. This sweetened the deal for many people who were resigned to the bitter pill of cutbacks."[6]

Once people accept that there is no alternative, such little measures can win their hearts and minds. Under this mindset, a person accepts the notion that the government is not an ideologically driven beast that wants to implement austerity because it fits the government's worldview; rather, the government is implementing austerity because it has to and is doing as much as possible to prevent the ordinary voter from suffering.

In addition, the government used a divide-and-conquer strategy when it came to welfare, attempting to portray welfare recipients as taking money away from the employed. In October 2010, Cameron claimed that

> I do think it's time for a new conversation about what fairness really means. . . . Yes, fairness means giving money to help the poorest in our society. But you cannot measure fairness

just by how much money we spend on welfare. . . . Fairness
means supporting people out of poverty, not trapping them in
dependency. . . . But here's something else about fairness. Fairness isn't just about who gets help from the state. . . . Taking
more money from the man who goes out to work long hours
each single day so the family next door can go on living a life
on benefits without working—is that fair? Fairness means giving people what they deserve—and what people deserve can
depend on how they behave.[7]

In short, in Cameron's world it seems that only men go out to work, and
that welfare recipients are figuratively stealing from the working "man."
All of these factors had the effect of further making neoliberalism and
austerity more palatable to the general public.

Nonetheless, following the 2010 election, there was a brief period
when it seemed that the Tories may not be able to form government.
The Conservative Party was able to win only 307 seats in parliament (an
increase of 97), short of the 326 required to gain an outright victory. The
Labour Party, boosted somewhat by its Keynesianism stimulus package
in its last year in office, won 258 seats (a decrease of 91), a much better
than expected showing. The Liberal Democrats who ran on a platform
that austerity was needed, but promised to oppose any increase in the
VAT rate and university tuition fee increases, won 57 seats. The Liberal
Democrats were the kingmakers. The prospect of austerity measures not
being implemented frightened sections of the media. It also seemed to
frighten the civil service, as the most senior civil servant, Cabinet Secretary Sir Gus O'Donnell, whose position entails being the "head of the
permanent apparatus which governs the country," told the Tories, Labour,
and the Liberal Democrats that if a coalition government was not formed
it was possible that the UK could end up defaulting like Greece had and
there could be a breakdown of society. O'Donnell then proceeded to draft
" 'guidance' for the negotiating parties, newly codifying certain practices
in the state, in order to make a coalition more likely than a minority
government. This ensured that a government could be formed on the
basis of an ad hoc agreement between two parties that had never been
put to the electorate." Such guidance favored a Tory–Liberal Democrat
government. In face of criticism of such an approach, a Cabinet Office
spokesperson argued that "Everyone had confidence in the system . . . the
markets didn't panic. . . . They had a clear sense of what was meant to
happen. It was very useful to have a document which provided clarity."

O'Donnell defended himself by claiming that a Labour–Liberal Democrats minority government "would not have had the strength in parliament to be able to pass the tough measures that would be needed to get us through this problem." In other words, austerity was "meant" to happen and a Labour–Liberal Democrat minority government would not have implemented austerity. The era of austerity was about to descend on the UK despite only 36.1 percent of the electorate voting for the Conservative Party. Despite the promises of the Liberal Democrats to oppose drastic cuts in the lead-up to the election, once they were in power the party accepted full-blown austerity. Indeed, once he became Business Secretary in the coalition government, Liberal Democrat Vince Cable claimed that the parties' opposition to any VAT rise in the lead-up to the election was simply posturing: "We were trying to score a point against the Conservatives, if you like. Okay, well that was in the election. We have now moved past the election."[8] Austerity hit the UK hard beginning with the first emergency budget in June 2010. Similar to other examples of austerity around the world, it was the poor and vulnerable who suffered the most pain.

A Range of Austerity Policies

In announcing the emergency budget, Osborne argued that without austerity measures there would be "higher interest rates, more business failures, sharper rises in unemployment, and potentially even a catastrophic loss of confidence and the end of the recovery. We cannot let that happen. This Budget is needed to deal with our country's debts. This Budget is needed to give confidence to our economy. This is the unavoidable Budget." The measures announced in the budget included a two-year wage freeze on all public sector workers earning more than £21,000, tax cuts tied to the consumer price index rather than the retail price index, a three-year freeze on child benefits, limits on housing benefits, and a VAT increased by 2.5 percent to 20 percent. The reduction in public spending was the largest since World War II. In addition to the cuts in spending and higher taxes, as noted above, Osborne made sure to include a few populist measures in an attempt to win the public's support. While the budget was tough on the average person, the same was not true for business. Announced in the budget was that the corporate tax rate would eventually be lowered from 28 percent to 24 percent. Osborne had already announced that he would be lowering the tax rate to 25 percent, so business got an extra bonus. Tax on small business would be reduced to 20 percent, and any new companies not in the east/southeast would not have to pay employer national insurance contributions, up to £5,000, for their first ten employees. Overall, the tax and spending cuts would amount to £40 billion ($59 billion US), or 2.2 percent of GDP by the end of the 2014–2015 financial year, while the welfare cuts would amount to £11 billion over the same period. With lower business taxes and spending, the government was following the neoliberal agenda by limiting the government's involvement in the market. Considering that in the lead-up to the election the Conservative Party only mentioned some token welfare cuts, the budget sprung a major and unwelcome surprise for the most vulnerable members of society. Nonetheless, Osborne argued that the budget "pays for the past. And it plans for the future. It supports a strong, enterprise-led recovery. It rewards work. And it protects the vulnerable in our society. Yes it is tough—but it is also fair." He went on to state that "[t]oday we have paid the debts of a failed past and laid the foundations for a more prosperous future. The richest paying the most and the vulnerable protected: that is our approach."[9]

The budget was many things, but it was alleged that it was unfair and that the vulnerable were not protected. General Secretary of the Trades Union Congress (TUC) Brendan Barber claimed that despite the Tories arguing that everyone is in it together it, "[t]he one thing we can now say is that we are very definitely not all in this together. . . . Those on middle and low incomes have done worse than expected, and the rich have been let off much of what they feared. We will all suffer from an economy that is now likely to be sluggish at best and with a double-dip recession at worst." While one would expect the TUC to claim the budget targets the poor and not the rich, what was not expected was that the *Financial Times* economics editor Chris Giles argued the same thing. He noted that in contrast to the Treasury's claim that the budget contains progressive measures, the independent think-tank the Institute for Fiscal Studies argued that the budget will hit the poor and vulnerable the hardest, especially in regards to the cuts in public services. The *Financial Times* determined that the announced 15 percent cut in public services would result in an 8 percent reduction in income for the poorest 20 percent of the population, while those in the top 20 percent would have less than a 3 percent reduction in income. It went on to outline that in 2008–2009, due to public spending, the poorest benefited to the tune of £6,315 and the richest benefited by £3,870. As such, it is almost impossible to slash public services without hurting the poor and vulnerable the most.[10] Thus, Osborne's claim that the budget was fair and would protect the most vulnerable was very hollow indeed. That the economics editor of the *Financial Times* argued that the budget would hit the poor and vulnerable hardest, considering that the paper was in favor of austerity, clearly demonstrates how transparently regressive the budget truly was.

As we will see below, the June 2010 emergency budget did not solve the UK's problems. There were other austerity policies in subsequent years. However, in a theme, business benefited as the government announced in March 2011 that the corporate tax rate would be reduced to 23 percent by 2014. In November 2011, on the realization that the policies were not working as quickly as expected, the government announced that the austerity measures would continue until at least 2017, that there would still be a reduction of 600,000 public sector jobs, with public sector workers wage rises being fixed at 1 percent for a further two years. As inflation was above 1 percent, public sector workers wages were actually declining in real terms. In the March 2012 budget, among the measures announced was that tax-free allowances for people over sixty-five were frozen (benefiting the treasury to the tune of £33.5 billion). However, there would be tax cuts for business amounting to £730 million because the corporate tax rate would drop to 23 percent by April 1, 2013, and by 21 percent by 2014. The rich also benefited in that the top individual tax rate was reduced by 5 percent, to 45 percent. Thus, 300,000 wealthy individuals, as well as corporations, benefited from the budget, while 5 million pensioners were potentially worse off. There were not as many austerity policies in the March 2013 budget, but it was announced that the current austerity policies would now continue until 2018, and corporations benefited even more as the corporate tax rate would now drop to 20 percent in April 2015—the joint lowest level among G20 countries. A bedroom tax was introduced in April 2013 that included the provision that welfare recipients who have an extra unoccupied room in their dwelling would have their payments reduced. This was not the end of new austerity policies for the year. In June 2013, the government announced further austerity policies that would begin in 2015. These included a 10 percent reduction for local governments and the justice budget, as well as a reduction in welfare payments; also, people seeking unemployment benefits would have to wait seven days from beginning an active job search before receiving payment.[11]

Cameron and Osborne were convinced that the austerity policies implemented in the emergency budget and subsequent budgets would lead to a revival in the UK's economy. Indeed, in September 2013, following the fastest growth since the 1990s, in a speech to business leaders Osborne proclaimed that the austerity policies were a success and that those people against austerity were proven wrong. In the speech, Osborne stated that "[t]he economic collapse was even worse than we thought. Repairing it will take even longer than we hoped. But we held our nerve when many told us to abandon our plan. . . . And as a result, thanks to the efforts and sacrifices of the British people, Britain is turning a corner." Continuing, he claimed that "[t]he pace of fiscal consolidation has not changed, government spending cuts have continued as planned, and yet growth has accelerated and many of the leading economic indicators show activity rising faster than at any time since the 1990s." However, Osborne made it clear that the age of austerity in the UK was not coming to an end—far from it. He went on to state that "[t]he plan is working, but the recovery is still in its early stages, plenty of risks remain and more years of hard decisions lie ahead. . . . This is a hard, difficult road we have been following. But it is the only way to deliver a sustained, lasting improvement in the living standards of the British people." Osborne found support from Alan Greenspan, the former chairman of the US Federal Reserve, who stated, "[w]hat Britain has done with its austerity program has worked much better than I thought it would. . . . I have had discussions with George Osborne and others and as far as I can judge, it is coming out pretty much the way they had expected."[12]

Coming out pretty much the way they had expected is an interesting way to describe the UK in the years following the emergency austerity budget in 2010. I will return to the human cost of the era of austerity below. For now, let's look at the impact of austerity on the economy and on the public.

The Impact of Austerity on the Economy

One of the key ideological principles of austerity is that budget deficits are bad. Indeed, in the speech celebrating austerity's success story in the UK, Osborne stated that "[n]ever again should anyone doing my job be so foolish, so deluded, as to believe that they have abolished the age-old cycle of boom and bust. So I can tell you today that when we've dealt with Labour's deficit, we will have a surplus in good times as insurance against difficult times ahead. Provided the recovery is sustained, our goal is to achieve that surplus in the next Parliament. That will bear down on our debts and prepare us for the next rainy day." There was just one small problem with Osborne's claim: debt was not under control. In 2009, the UK's debt to GDP ratio stood at 67.1 percent; it increased to 78.4 percent in 2010, to 81.8 percent in 2011, to 85.8 percent in 2012, to 87.3 percent in 2013, and to a record high of 89.4 percent in 2014.[13] Rather than getting debt under control, because of or despite austerity, the debt to GDP ratio has constantly increased and, at the time of this writing, is at the highest it has ever been.

Writing in *The New Yorker*, John Cassidy notes that in 2009 and 2010 Osborne was arguing that austerity was essential or else the UK would end up like Greece. He notes Osborne claimed that the "public-sector debt as a proportion of G.D.P. would peak in 2013–14, at 70.3 per cent, and then start falling. That promise is another one that has gone by the wayside. The Office for Budget Responsibility is now predicting that the debt burden will keep climbing until 2015–16, when it will peak at eighty per cent of G.D.P.—almost ten percentage points above Osborne's original figure." Considering that the Office for Budget Responsibility does not have the best track record in predicting how the economy will do, one must be wary of any prediction they make, especially as the ratio is currently almost 90 percent. In addition, in the June 2010 budget Osborne stated that the structural budget deficit was 4.8 percent of GDP. However, after three years of austerity he predicted that the structural budget deficit—which is the underlying budget deficit—would decline to 1.9 percent. This was to prove very optimistic. John Lanchester notes that "by the end of those three years [by 2013], after £59 billion of tax rises and spending cuts, the figure is set to be 4.3 per cent. Even that number was achieved only thanks to a kitchen sink's worth of special inputs, including a £3.5 billion windfall from auctioning off the 4G telecom spectrum, and some exuberant, almost rococo creative accounting to do with the transfer of Royal Mail pension liabilities, state ownership of the Bradford and Bingley building society, and interest credit from the Bank of England's quantitative easing scheme." Moreover, rather than declining further, in 2014 the structural budget deficit ballooned to 5.7 percent of GDP. By way of comparison, for the entire Eurozone it is 1.5 percent, in Italy it is 0.8 percent, while Germany has a surplus of 0.5 percent. The government now claims that structural budget will be balanced by 2017–2018.[14] Thus, in regards to controlling the UK's debt, which was not all that large of a problem before implementation of the government's austerity strategy, austerity has failed.

There was better news in regards to unemployment. In June 2010, the unemployment rate stood at 7.8 percent, before peaking at 8.4 percent in September 2011. The rate remained relatively steady, hovering around the upper sevens before a steady decline beginning in mid-2013: by November 2013, the unemployment rate stood at 7.1 percent; by June to September 2014, it was down to 6 percent; and it declined to 5.4 percent in late 2015. This was the lowest level since April 2008, with the number of people looking for work below two million. However, while the unemployment rate was declining, average weekly earnings were generally below the inflation rate. Since the global economic crisis began in 2008, in almost every quarter inflation outstripped the rise in workers' pay; on average, real wages have fallen by approximately 2 percent per year, with wages falling by approximately 13 percent for people aged twenty-five to twenty-nine, and by more than 15 percent for eighteen- to twenty-four-year-olds. In other words, for a six-year cycle, workers' pay was declining in real terms, with real wages at one of its lowest ebbs in a decade. Thus, while unemployment levels have been declining, there has not been a corresponding increase in average weekly earnings. In other words, a lower unemployment rate is certainly beneficial, but for employed people the amount of goods and services they can buy with their income is lower than it was before the global economic crisis began. Moreover, "because unemployment has not risen by as much as in previous recessions, when and if it falls, there is less scope than in the past for it to boost wage growth through the usual wage curve mechanisms." Indeed, the June 2010 Budget estimated that growth in real wages would be 2.4 percent by 2014, a figure reiterated in March 2012. However, in 2014, the Office for Budget Responsibility predicted a real wage growth of 0.3 percent, but wages actually increased by 0.8 percent. While any increase is to be welcomed, this is a very minor increase following years of hardship.[15]

In regards to GDP, following a 5.2 percent decline in 2009 due in large part to the global economic crisis, GDP grew by 1.7 percent in 2010, 1.1 percent in 2011, 0.3 percent in 2012, and 1.7 percent in 2013. Thus, while the economy was growing, it was hardly buoyant. However, in the first quarter of 2014, GDP grew by more than 3 percent, in the second quarter by 0.9 percent, and a further 0.7 percent in the third quarter of 2014. Overall, GDP rose 2.4 percent for the year. The large rise in GDP in the first quarter led austerity advocates to claim that this showed that such a strategy was the best course of action. Indeed, Mark Gilbert, writing in *Businessweek*, argued that the "U.K. government under Prime Minister David Cameron and Chancellor of the Exchequer George Osborne has championed austerity, rather than Keynesian pump-priming, as the solution to the economic downturn. Now Britain's own bruising experiment with austerity is starting to pay off."[16] Now whether one should be arguing that policies that took over three years to "pay off" are a good thing is certainly open to debate. Plus, is it really the case that austerity is now working?

It was a positive that the UK economy grew in 2014, but as Larry Summers, former economic adviser for President Obama, notes, while the US GDP is above its pre-crisis level, the same is not true in the UK. The UK's GDP levels are below the pre-crisis peak and "even further short of levels predicted when austerity policies were implemented." The Office for Budget Responsibility predicted that GDP would increase by 1.3 percent in 2010, 2.6 percent in 2011, and 2.8 percent in 2012 and 2013. Partly as a result of GDP not increasing as much as expected, as I outlined above, the country's debt to GDP ratio has increased dramatically. Also, while GDP has been increasing, so has the UK's population. In this regard, population growth has outstripped the increase to GDP. Thus, GDP per capita is approximately 1 percent lower in real terms since the beginning of the crisis. Summers also argues that the "acceleration in growth has less to do with austerity spurring growth than with a slowdown in the pace at which policy became more austere. The pace of fiscal contraction has slowed over the past two years. Slowing fiscal contraction means the decrement to growth caused by fiscal policy becomes more attenuated. Other things equal, this would be expected to produce more favorable growth performance." In addition, the Cameron government has implemented decidedly non-austerity policies designed to encourage lending, the most important being the Help to Buy program. The program "gives low, teaser-rate mortgages to some borrowers and guarantees the mortgages of others so that they can put only 5 percent down. There are also special programs to reward banks for lending to small business and to get the central bank involved in export finance." Now while it is a good thing that the government is encouraging lending, such lending programs that guarantee mortgages put the government at risk if there is another economic crisis. Moreover, such programs have led house prices to increase dramatically, especially in London. This favors existing homeowners over renters and runs the risk of causing another housing bubble. Overall, then, what has been the cost of austerity to the average person in the UK? An Economics professor at Oxford University, Simon Wren-Lewis, claims that "Gross National Income was £1,557,503 million in 2012, and there were 26.4 million households, so that gives gross income of £59,000 per household. So the 6% figure [total cost of austerity policies on GDP] implies that austerity has cost the average UK household a total of about

£3,500 over these three years. Although all governments like to give the impression that they can have a big impact on people's prosperity, few actually do. These numbers suggest that the current UK government has managed to do so, but unfortunately by making us all poorer." Wren-Lewis also argues that the recovery is not illusory—it is real to a certain extent. Nonetheless, "neither does it atone for the sins of the past. Above all else, it must not lead to complacency. We have still a long way to go to repair all the damage caused by the recession. Even when that has been done, the problems that led to the financial crisis have not been fixed. With inflation targets still at 2%, and perverse fiscal responses, we remain dangerously vulnerable to any future large negative demand shock."[17]

However, while it is undoubtedly true that the government has adopted austerity policies, in some ways they have been austerity-lite in that the measures have not been targeted at schools and hospitals, and pensioners have not been as hard hit as other segments of the population because—as John Lanchester, writing in the *London Review of Books* notes—pensioners do go out and vote. Lanchester argues:

> But whereas the cuts are real, austerity . . . [is] less easy to locate. We're undergoing sharp reductions in overall levels of government spending, yes? Well, actually, no we aren't. There are reductions compared to the previous rates of spending growth, sure, and there are sectorally specific cuts also, but the figures for total government spending, as given by the OBR [Office of Budget Responsibility], go as follows: 2012–13, £674.3 billion; 2013–14, £719.9 billion; 2014–15, £731.0 billion; 2015–16, £744.7 billion; 2016–17, £755.1 billion; 2017–18, £765.5 billion. There's a simple point to make about these numbers: they go up. The population is predicted to go up too, so they don't represent a dramatic spending increase, but they do represent an increase and therefore, as some right-wing commentators . . . are pointing out, this is not austerity.

Lanchester argues that even though the government is implementing austerity-lite and not full-blown austerity, the government claims it is doing the latter in part to placate the bond markets in an attempt to keep down the costs of borrowing. It is also doing it because, as noted above, the public has shifted to the right in relation to government spending, especially when it comes to welfare. The UK public believes that government spending should be curtailed; indeed, less than 30 percent of the population believes that the government should spend more on welfare. In the previous recession under a Tory government, which occurred in the 1990s, 58 percent of the populous wanted more government spending on welfare. Overall, Lanchester claims that "the British economy makes an extraordinarily complicated picture. We have an economy . . . [that] is rapidly growing jobs; we have brutal cuts in government spending, while government spending continues to rise; we have a country where things feel as if they've been bad for a long while, and yet on the figures, most of the hard times are still ahead."[18] It is the impact on ordinary people to which we now turn. The situation does not make for pleasant reading.

The Impact of Austerity on the Public

Under the previous government's economic stimulus, in an attempt for the UK economy to recover from the global economic crisis, the income level for the poorest 20 percent of the population increased by 3.4 percent. This was the highest level of growth for any segment of the population. In contrast, the richest 40 percent's income grew by only 0.2 percent, which was the lowest level of growth. The poor benefiting the most through government policies did not occur under austerity policies. Instead, the poor and vulnerable suffered—and still are suffering, greatly. Between 2010 and 2014, the poorest 20 percent of the population had the second largest decrease in their net income. Furthermore, it is estimated for the period 2010–2015 the poorest 10 percent will have the greatest decline of net income—a 38 percent reduction. In contrast, the richest 10 percent will have the least decline in their net incomes, falling by only 5 percent. However, the mega-wealthy have not suffered due to austerity. The income for the richest one thousand people in the UK increased in real terms by £138 billion between 2009 and 2013. Quite simply, as the old adage goes: the rich are getting richer, while the poor are getting poorer.[19]

In a report looking at the cost of austerity in the UK, *Oxfam* notes that the "top one per cent of earners pocketed 10p of every pound of income earned in the UK in 2010–11, up from 7p in 1994–5. Meanwhile, the poorest 50 per cent of the population took home between them only 18p in every pound, down from 19p." It is the richest 1 percent that benefited due to neoliberalism, with neoliberalism causing increased inequality. Due to austerity policies, the Institute for Fiscal Studies has determined that by 2020, if the current austerity policies are not abandoned, an additional 800,000 children in Britain will be living in poverty—nearly 25 percent of Britain's child population. In addition, 1.5 million working adults will sink into poverty—17.5 percent of the working population. In 2012, more than 900,000 people sunk into absolute poverty. *Oxfam* further states that

> [u]nemployed people will experience a loss of income close to 7 per cent. The decision to change how social security payments increase will have a particularly damaging effect; linking payments to a lower inflation index, the Consumer Price Index (currently 2.9 per cent), instead of the Retail Price Index (3.3 per cent) means incomes will not rise to match increases in the cost of living. These changes will affect the poorest hardest, as basic costs for food, energy and housing have outpaced inflation over the last few years. This impact is compounded the poverty premium and recent measures to limit increases of some social security payments—including Jobseeker's Allowance, Housing Benefit and Child Benefit—to just 1 per cent annually for the next three years, which greatly affects those in in-work poverty.

Furthermore, at the height of cuts to public spending by the Thatcher government in 1983, 14 percent of households could not afford at least three basic living necessities: "These include living in adequately heated homes, eating healthily, and owning basic clothing items such as properly fitting shoes." Following the implementation of austerity measures, this figure increased in 2012 to 33 percent. Among the *Poverty and Exclusion Project* findings were that approximately four million adults and one million children do not own "at least one basic item of clothing, such as a warm winter coat, while 3 million adults of working age (including over a fifth of those looking for work) cannot afford appropriate clothes for a job interview." Other findings included the following: "One-third of all adults can't afford to pay unexpected costs of £500 (such as if a cooker breaks down), 31% can't afford to save at least £20 a month, and 1 million children can't afford to join sports training or drama clubs." The problems extended to housing as approximately "11 million people cannot afford adequate housing conditions and nearly one in ten households are unable to afford to fully heat their home."[20]

In addition to limiting the increases in social security payments, the government also made it easier to suspend welfare payments if people do not religiously follow the rules. Between June 2012 and June 2013,

860,000 welfare recipients were sanctioned, an increase from 500,000 during the previous year. The figure further rose the following year—to a record 900,000. Of those 900,000, one third had been claiming benefits for less than 13 weeks, which seems to suggest that many were potentially unaware of all the rules they had to follow. Furthermore, in the first three months of 2014, 15,955 people on the Employment Support Allowance—"the benefit for people with health conditions that cannot work"—were subjected to sanctions. Of these, 9,851 had a mental illness—62.44 percent of the total number of sanctions. In February 2009, only 27.78 percent of people sanctioned had a mental illness, and in April 2010, the percentage was 40.72. Whether the increase was due to more people being diagnosed with a mental illness and/or tougher measures is uncertain, but a consistent rise occurred between 2009 and 2014. The Department for Work and Pensions notes that the primary reason for imposing sanctions is people being late for meetings. However, as the Methodist Church's policy adviser, Paul Morrison, argues, "[s]anctioning someone with a mental health problem for being late for a meeting is like sanctioning someone with a broken leg for limping. The fact that this system punishes people for the symptoms of their illness is a clear and worrying sign that it is fundamentally flawed."[21]

Indeed, while the UK public is increasingly viewing people on welfare as "dole bludgers," "welfare queens," and the like, often those sanctioned are a result of bureaucracy gone mad. Writing in *The Guardian*, Owen Jones notes that "[s]ocial security for the poor is shredded, stripped away, made ever more conditional." He provides examples of welfare recipients sanctioned for superfluous reasons:

> Glyn, a former gas fitter from Manchester, was sanctioned three weeks before Christmas 2013, and received no money. He had missed a signing-on day because he was completing a job search at Seetec, one of the government's corporate welfare-to-work clients. Then there's Sandra, a disabled Glaswegian who lives with her daughter. She was sent a form asking to declare whether she lived with someone; assuming it meant a partner, she said no, and was called in to a "compliance interview." Because her daughter was not in full-time education, Sandra was stripped of her entitlement to her £50 per week severe-disability allowance.

There are many more examples like this, people being forced to suffer because a get-tough approach on welfare recipients is electorally popular.

The crackdown on benefits also led to a rising number of people seeking help at food banks. Food banks are places where people in need are able to obtain food so that, quite simply, they do not go hungry for any extended period. Trussell Trust, a leading food bank, noted that between April 1 and June 1, 2012, it gave out three-day emergency supplies of food to 152,000 people—more than three times as many as it did in the corresponding period in 2011. The crackdown on welfare led to more people seeking help from food banks. Welfare sanctions and/or delay in people being able to claim benefits resulted in almost 50 percent of all referrals to food banks, and an 80 percent increase in people seeking help due to benefit sanctions. Of course, it is not just welfare recipients seeking help from food banks—just over 22 percent of people seeking help were the working poor. The Chief Executive of Trussell Trust David McAuley said that "[i]ncomes for the poorest have not been increasing in line with inflation and many, whether in low paid work or on welfare, are not yet seeing the benefits of economic recovery. . . . Instead, they are living on a financial knife edge where one small change in circumstances or a 'life shock' can force them into a crisis where they cannot afford to eat." Although they condemn the rise of the welfare state, this does not mean that conservative politicians mind benefitting from it. For example, Conservative Party politician Richard Benyon, whose family is worth approximately £110 million, owns a number of properties and receives £120,000 in housing benefits from his tenants. Likewise, Tory politician Richard Drax received $13,830 in housing benefits in 2013.[22]

Moreover, on the same day that there were announcements on the record number of people having benefit sanctions and the number of people being referred to food banks, Conservative peer Baroness Jenkin claimed that a major problem was that "[p]oor people don't know how to cook. I had a large bowl of porridge today, which cost 4p. A bowl of sugary cereals will cost you 25p." Instead of eating cake, the poor should eat porridge. Not to mention, it was also revealed that the House of Lords spends £65,000 yearly on champagne. When it was suggested that the catering service for the House of Commons and the House of Lords be merged to save money, the idea was rejected on the grounds that the quality of champagne would suffer.[23]

Quite simply, due to austerity policies, more people are sinking into poverty and greater inequality, with the poorest and most vulnerable suffering the most and the rich "suffering" the least (while also being more likely to quickly regain any lost wealth if the economy shows continued signs of improvement). Meanwhile, most of the mega-rich benefit economically from austerity policies.

In addition, as is often the case, women suffer the most during tough economic times. Susan Pashkoff notes:

> With incomes falling in the advanced capitalist world as part of the general economic condition since the late 1970s, women face greater threats than men. Women receive lower incomes and lower pensions (due to historically lower wages), and face the increasing reluctance of the state to support women in the workplace through the provision of childcare and after-school programs or by shouldering caregiver responsibilities for the elderly and infirm. As the general pattern of work tends more towards increasing underemployment and part-time labor, women will begin to face competition from men for part-time jobs that women traditionally held while at the same time benefits decline.[24]

In the aftermath of the 2008 global economic crisis, it was initially men who suffered more duress due to the high number of jobs lost in the construction, manufacturing, and finance sectors. However, following the layoffs and the beginning of austerity, the largest burden fell to women. It is estimated that £5.8 billion of the £8.1 billion tax increases and reduction of benefits will affect women. This is because "on average, one-fifth of women's income is made up of welfare payments and tax credits compared to one-tenth for men. Put another way, benefits make up twice as much of women's income as men's." Women were also hit hard due to the reduction in the public sector workforce, with estimated job losses of 730,000 by 2016–2017; women are over-represented in the public sector as they compromise approximately 65 percent of the workforce. Female unemployment increased from 678,000 in 2008 to 1.08 million in 2013—the latter being the highest level since 1988. As Pashkoff claims, "[t]he impact of women's responsibility for social reproduction is evident looking at economic inactivity in January–March 2013. Out of a total of 9 million people who are economically inactive, 2.3 million people cite household and caring responsibilities as the reason for their economic inactivity; of these, 220,000 are men and 2.1 million are women. Of the 2.3 million of those that say that they want a job, 630,000 report that they are looking after home and family, with this breaking down to

76,000 men compared to 556,000 women." In other words, women want to work, but are unable to do so, often because they have to look after children and/or other family members. Pashkoff goes on to argue that the reduction in housing benefits (see above for details) also disproportionally affects women: "Fifty percent of those receiving housing benefits are single women (often single parents) and there are one million more women than men claiming housing benefits. Additionally, the bedroom tax (an over-occupancy charge for extra bedrooms) for those in social housing is hitting people with disabilities and single mothers disproportionally, as they are primarily the people who live in social housing." Moreover, single mothers suffer the greatest due to austerity; by 2015, they would have lost approximately 8.5 percent of their after-tax income. In contrast, single fathers would have lost 7.5 percent, couples who have children would have lost 6.5 percent, and couples without children would have seen a 2.5 percent reduction of their income.[25]

Thus, austerity policies resulted in financial pain and suffering for ordinary Britons. Furthermore, the poor and the vulnerable, as well as women, have been hit disproportionally hard because of austerity in the UK. Considering that austerity causes people to suffer, one would expect that, as in years past, the labor movement would be at the forefront of austerity policy protests and/or strikes. It is this issue to which we now turn. As we shall see, organized labor in the UK behaved no differently from New York unions in the 1970s and unions in Greece, Spain, and Ireland when faced with austerity—it put its own interests above the wider community. As a result, austerity continues to dominate the UK economic landscape.

The UK Labor Movement and Austerity

Following the June 2010 emergency budget, there was predictable outrage by the trade union movement. As noted above, the TUC claimed that the budget unfairly targeted the poor and middle class compared to the rich. Likewise, UNITE Joint General Secretary Derek Simpson noted, "[w]here is the promised fairness in cutting the wages of needy households yet fighting shy of closing the tax loopholes which allow the wealthy to dodge their duty to this country? And increasing VAT is reckless—it will stop people spending, harm UK business and choke off the recovery." There was similar outrage across the union spectrum. Yet while condemning the budget there was a decided lack of talk about protests and/or strike

action. Most union leaders were seemingly content with voicing their outrage rather than taking immediate action. An exception was the general
secretary of the Rail Maritime and Transport (RMT) union, Bob Crow.
Crow argued that

> David Cameron has launched a full-frontal assault on the trade
> union movement on a scale which is unprecedented since
> Margaret Thatcher's government set out to smash the National
> Union of Mineworkers. . . . When someone's winding up to
> give you a kicking you have a clear choice—you can either take
> them on right from the off or you can roll over and hope that
> they go away. RMT is calling on the trade union movement
> to start the fight-back right here, right now before Cameron
> and Clegg have had a chance to pull their boots on. This is
> not the time for talking, it's the time for action. We need an
> emergency meeting of the Trade Union Congress to co-ordinate
> the political and industrial action that we will need to take as
> a united movement to drive back the ConDem [Conservative/
> Liberal Democrats] attack on our members.[26]

For those wanting unions to take militant action, Crow's pronouncements
were very much the exception rather than the rule.

Indeed, the fight-back did not start straight away or even in 2010.
Somewhat shockingly, and on the surface very surprising, this was a time
of passivity for most unions. In the preceding twelve months until March
2011, the number of days lost to industrial action was the lowest since
records began in 1931. Considering the range of austerity measures that
negatively affected almost all sections of the community, and with the
poor, vulnerable, and working class (especially public sector workers)
suffering the most pain, one would have assumed that the union movement would be out in force almost immediately. There was a lot of talk
by union leaders about how bad austerity was, but very little by way
of militancy, or indeed any action at all. That the UK union movement
did not mobilize its membership against austerity put it on the defensive
almost immediately. As we have seen, a defensive labor movement has
resulted in austerity being unable to be overturned in Greece, Spain, and
Ireland. That organized labor in the UK did not mobilize immediately,
or indeed at any time in 2010, put it at a distinct disadvantage because
a number of austerity measures were already implemented and accepted
to a certain extent as necessary by the public. With the government and

the majority of the media continually arguing that austerity was necessary if the UK was not to end up like countries such as Greece, this had the effect of convincing some of the UK public to take their "medicine." This was especially true as, noted above, the public were increasingly hostile to the idea of a "big government." Austerity and neoliberalism more generally support the notion that a reduced role for the government is beneficial to all concerned. Nonetheless, 2011 was to be the year of strikes and mass protests in the UK, with organized labor seemingly willing to become the militant movement it once was. The first major TUC protest occurred in March, 2011. The protest witnessed somewhere between 250,000 and 400,000 people marching through London demanding an end to austerity. The protest was one of the largest in UK history and the biggest since the February 2003 anti-Iraq War demonstration. Such a large turnout even surprised the union movement. The general secretary of UNISON, Dave Prentis, claimed the strike was "absolutely enormous and showed the anger of ordinary working people at the Government's cuts." The general secretary of UNITE, Len McCluskey, told the protesters "you represent a spirit of resistance in every workplace and community that says we are not going to have our way of life killed so that the rich and greedy can live as they please." The most impressive part of the anti-austerity protest was the large cross-section of people demonstrating. Organized labor had the support of wide sections of the community in the fight against austerity. Community support for anti-austerity protests was essential if there was any hope for such economic measures to be modified or abandoned. Writing for the *BBC*, Paul Mason noted that "[t]he demographics were interesting. Unison—a union which has a reputation in the trade union movement for passivity—had mobilised very large numbers of council workers, health workers and others: many from Scotland and Wales; many from the north of England. Unite likewise, and the PCS seemed capable of mobilizing very large numbers. What this means, to be absolutely clear, is people who have never been on a demo in their lives and in no way count themselves to be political. I also saw many small self-selected groups not mobilised by unions: family groups, school groups, speech therapy groups."[27]

It was indeed an impressive show of force. But by the time the strike occurred, austerity measures were well established. It is much more difficult to get policies overturned than to stop them from being implemented initially. This is especially true because the government was firmly committed to austerity. Organized labor began the austerity fight from a position of weakness because it took too long for it to mobilize its members.[28]

Nevertheless, considering the large turnout, it was not a surprise that some unions decided to go on the offensive. While it can certainly be argued that they should have struck much earlier and often, there was beginning to be sustained pressure on the government. The National Union of Teachers, the Association of Teachers and Lecturers, the University of College Union, and the Public and Commercial Services Union went on a one-day strike on June 30, 2011, with somewhere between 100,000 (government estimate) and 200,000 (labor movement estimate) protesting against the proposed changes to public sector pensions and austerity more generally. The strike caused disruption at 11,114 of the 21,500 state schools "along with airports, benefits offices, driving tests and galleries and museums." Due to the turnout and the disruption it caused the strike was a moderate success. Not surprisingly, the government condemned the strike. What was surprising, however, and not helping the strikers was that the then Labour Party leader Ed Miliband refused to endorse the strike. He claimed that "[t]he most important thing for the unions is to get the public to understand what their argument is. I don't think the argument has yet been got across on public sector pensions as to some of the injustices contained on what the government is doing. Personally I don't think actually strike action is going to help win that argument and I think it inconveniences the public. I think strikes must always be the very last resort." He also wrote on Twitter that "[t]hese strikes are wrong at a time when negotiations are going on. People have been let down by both sides—the Govt has acted recklessly." Likewise, former Labour Prime Minister Tony Blair was against the strike: "I just think the best thing is for them [public sector unions] to engage with the process of change."[29] A process of change in other words means for unions to accept austerity to a certain extent.

Such statements undermined the action by the public sector unions. When the former Labour Prime Minister and its then current leader believe that the unions should not have gone out on strike, this influences the general public against unions and public sector workers. This is especially true when Blair is claiming that public sector unions need to accept austerity. Unions, especially public sector unions, undertaking industrial action generally have a difficult time winning community support. When its supposed allies in the Labour Party are against industrial action, it makes unions' efforts to win community support almost impossible (I will return to the union movement's relationship with the Labour Party later in the chapter). Despite Labour's leaders' pronouncement against strike action, unions and the rank-and-file flexed their considerable muscle later that year.

On November 30, 2011, over thirty unions and up to two million people across the UK went out on strike to protest, once again, the cuts in public sector pensions and austerity more generally. The striking workers were against government plans to reduce employer contributions to pensions, while increasing personal contributions and increasing the retirement age to sixty-seven in 2026 instead of 2034. The strikes led to the "closure of most state schools; cancellation of refuse collections; rail service and tunnel closures; the postponement of thousands of non-emergency hospital operations; and . . . delays at airports and ferry terminals." The size of the protest is seen in the figures: over 62 percent of state schools remained closed for the entire day, 14 percent were partially closed, and more than 900,000 health, civil service, and local government workers also went out on strike. The union movement was ecstatic at such a large turnout. Following the mass turnout, even David Cameron was forced to concede that it was indeed a "big strike," after previously telling his colleagues that the strike would be a failure. However, he claimed that "[s]triking isn't going to achieve anything, particularly when negotiations are ongoing. I think it's irresponsible. There are negotiations ongoing. I'm sure they can be brought to a conclusion but in the end we have to make sure that public sector pensions are good for public sector workers, but affordable for everyone else who is going to work and contributing to them." Nonetheless, that Cameron was forced to admit that it was a "big strike" showed that he was concerned about the increased militancy of organized labor and whether continued strikes could begin to destabilize the austerity agenda. Whether organized labor could overturn the full range of austerity measures or even stop the most recently announced austerity policies is debatable. However, what the union movement could do was demonstrate that a large mass of people across all walks of life viewed the measures as electorally unpopular and try to destabilize the government through continued mass action. This could have potentially prevented the government from continuing with austerity measures or to modify the harshest aspects. While Cameron and Osborne might have believed wholeheartedly in austerity, Tory politicians in marginal seats would begin to agitate if they thought austerity policies would lead to their losing their seats in parliament. Cameron and Osborne needed a clear majority of the party to support austerity and to be able to continue with such policies in the future. Through the militancy of continued mass protests, there was optimism from the Left that the union movement and workers were regaining power and would use that power to fight other austerity measures. Writing in *The Guardian*, Seumas Milne argued, "It's not just the scale of the strike, though, but its breadth, from headteachers to school cleaners in every part of the country, that has set it apart. Most of those taking action were women, and the majority had never been on strike before. This has been the 'big society' in action, but not as Cameron meant it." Once again, large sections of the community were with organized labor in the fight against austerity. That a majority of the strikers had never been on strike before, and yet were out protesting, demonstrates that the anti-austerity protests were gaining a foothold across the community. In a hopeful tone, Milne concluded the article by claiming, "One strike isn't, of course, going to force the government to turn tail. After Osborne's pay and jobs battering, the likelihood must be of more industrial action, with no guarantee of success. But today was a powerful demonstration of democratic workplace strength—which offers a chance to begin to turn the tide of a generation."[30]

The crucial point in the article is that, as Milne correctly identifies, one strike is not going to change government policies, or even slightly modify them. It is exceedingly unlikely that a one-day strike would make the government overly concerned. For change to occur, what was needed was continued mass action. Of course, whether sustained pressure would have resulted in the government abandoning or modifying austerity is impossible to ascertain, but a series of one-off strikes months apart was doomed to fail.

Indeed, Milne's optimism was misplaced. Instead of pushing for the government to abandon or modify other austerity policies, the unions largely concentrated on negotiating a compromise on the public sector pension changes. The unions put their own self-interest above all others; in December 2011, "[b]ased upon only marginal changes to the government's original plans, Unison, Unite and the GMB have agreed a provisional framework for a settlement on the local government pension scheme while Unison has accepted the final offer on the health service pension scheme as the basis for a negotiated agreement."[31]

That three large unions accepted a settlement so quickly undermined the entire labor movement's power and basically condemned the entire anti-austerity protest movement. Moreover, it demonstrated to large sections of the community who had never before undertaken protest action that unions are self-interested and only care about themselves and their members. As I have highlighted previously, when unions concentrate only on their own narrow self-interest rather than the entire fight against austerity, the only "winners" are the government and a section of the workforce who could have had harsher austerity measures imposed on them. What happened in New York City in the 1970s and in Greece, Spain, and Ireland in the latest austerity drive repeated itself in the UK. One can certainly question why the unions quickly capitulated and largely accepted the austerity measures. Self-interest is certainly one answer; another answer is that the unions were going into the strike on the defensive and were trying to salvage anything they could, even if it meant undermining the entire anti-austerity movement and those negatively affected by austerity policies.

The sentiment of the unions who cut deals with the government and accepted austerity was best summed up by the health secretary of UNISON Christine McAnea. She argued, "[w]e have been able to protect some categories of members . . . but as far as we are concerned this was always a damage limitation exercise." In other words, she and her union believed that the labor movement was never going to be able to overturn all or even the majority of austerity measures. Thus, the union getting a slightly improved pension offer from the government was the best that could be hoped for, even if the offer "benefited" its members to the detriment of all other sections of the community. In this case, the unions believed that by accepting lower wages and worse working conditions for their members, the so-called "damage limitation," this benefited the membership, as otherwise the government might have imposed even harsher measures on the workers. To repeat once more, conditions of narrow self-interest in which unions care only about their members to the detriment of everyone else have led to a decline in the union movement in the US and the UK, as well as harming entire communities. In addition, when a number of unions agreed so quickly to the government's "final offer," this undermined the efforts of teachers and civil service workers to gain a better deal. By focusing on what they could salvage, a number of unions not only undermined the anti-austerity protests, they also "sold out" their fellow unions. In January 2012, the Association of Teachers and Lecturers (ATL) who represent 160,000 workers also agreed to the final offer, while the Association of School and College Leaders agreed to it in principle after a survey showed more than 75 percent of its members would agree to the offer. ATL president Alice Robinson said that "[a]lthough the government's final offer does not give us everything we wanted, it is the best deal we could get in the current economic climate, and members do not want a significantly worse deal imposed on them if they rejected this one."[32] Once again, union leaders were not talking about the government's offer in positive terms; it was a bad deal for union members, but it was not as bad as it could have been.

This was the same situation as when the Irish trade union members accepted the Haddington Road Agreement (see Chapter 2). Union members believed there was no alternative. It was in their best interests to accept the government's offer, in fear that if they did not the government would force a worse deal on them. While one can criticize the members for not being militant and standing up to fight against the government, faced with a similar situation many workers would accept the government's offer, especially in tough economic conditions including a seemingly all-out assault on the public sector workforce. Organized labor was already divided, and as a result of the lack of unity there was little fight left in the teachers' unions' membership when it came to opposing the austerity measures. It was better for them to capitulate than to struggle when their "allies" had already abandoned them. Union solidarity is essential, and it had been abandoned by a number of unions. Moreover, such actions made it exceedingly clear to first-time protesters and the public as a whole that organized labor cared only about its own members and that unions were willing to undermine each other's efforts. Solidarity did not exist even among unions, let alone within the wider community. Quite simply, unions did not expect to fight successfully against all or even the majority of austerity measures; they were just engaging in damage control in an attempt to secure the "best" deal from the government. In such a situation, it would have been counterproductive for the remaining unions to not accept the government's offer. Organized labor was seemingly never interested in overcoming austerity; thus, it was in no-one's interest for the unions who had yet to accept the government's deal to remain militant and attempt to fight.

Due to the number of unions agreeing to the government's final offer, the next public sector strike in May 2012 was not as large, involving fewer than 400,000 workers. While still a relatively large and impressive showing, its strength was nowhere near as powerful as five months earlier. Quite simply, any chance the union movement could overturn austerity policies—although, as we have seen, this seemingly was never the goal of all sections of the union movement—were long gone; strike action was a defensive action to begin with, and once sections of organized labor began putting their and their members' interests above everybody else's, the battle was lost before it had even got started. Union members, their supporters, and the wider community had begun to realize this. In addition, because five months passed between the large-scale protests, austerity measures became further entrenched, and the government and large sections of the media had the opportunity to further solidify the idea that there was no alternative to austerity. By October 2012, a TUC-sponsored protest involved only about 200,000 workers. While in sheer numbers the protest sounds impressive, it was only about 10 percent the size of the November 2011 protest, and it occurred five months afterward. Quite simply, how could nonunion members trust organized labor to care about them considering its previous action? The short answer is that they could not. Organized labor had made it very clear what it was most concerned about—its own members, and seemingly nobody else. Moreover, how could one union trust another union considering that a number of unions secured deals with the government to the detriment of other unions? In many ways the October 2012 protest was simply an act of defiance that the government could, and did, ignore. The waning power of the labor movement, or at the very least, their unwillingness to be militant is demonstrated in strike statistics. In 2011, strike action led to 1.4 million days being lost; by 2012, this dropped to only 248,800—one of the lowest numbers on record. Any militancy remaining in the labor movement vanished once unions began rushing to accept the government's "final offer." In a positive, the number of days lost due to strikes increased to 443,600 in 2013, but the number of overall stoppages actually declined from 131 to 112, and the total number was almost one million less than in 2011. In addition, while the number of days lost to strike action increased, strikes were primarily focused on pay disputes—95 percent of the total.[33]

Workers deserve a fair wage and good working conditions, but the increased "militancy" in 2013 demonstrates that unions were focused on narrow bread-and-butter issues rather than on anything affecting the wider community, such as austerity. While UK laws may prevent unions from staging sympathy strikes and the like, for the general public, when unions strike only over pay, the perception is fed that the labor movement cares little about the wider community. Considering a number of unions undermined the anti-austerity movement by focusing on members' self-interest in 2011–2012, unions striking over bread-and-butter issues made that perception so much stronger. The UK labor movement would do well to remember its own past when it achieved strong growth and was part of the community in the 1960s and 1970s, when it became involved in a raft of protests against the Vietnam War, nuclear disarmament, and other issues. During this period, the labor movement did care only about wages and working conditions—it cared about everything that affected the wider community. Such an approach—social movement unionism—benefited not only the labor movement but the community at large. I will further analyze this strategy in Chapter 5.

There were further actions against austerity in 2013 and 2014, including a strong protest of fifty thousand by unions in September 2013 on the opening day of the Conservative Party conference in Manchester. The demonstrators were protesting cuts to the health service. While getting that number of people out to protest is impressive, there was, once again, little by way of follow-up. Thus it was easy for the Conservatives to act as if the protest never occurred. As stated above, one-off protests might garner media attention, but they are exceedingly unlikely to change government policy. Another mass protest occurred involving hundreds of thousands of workers against austerity by public sector unions in July 2014. The unions were protesting the pay freeze and declining living standards of ordinary workers caused by government policies. The TUC's general secretary, Frances O'Grady noted at the time that "[n]early half a million local government workers earn less than the living wage. But even as the economy starts to grow, ministers have told them that the pay cap will last until at least 2018. . . . This is why today's strikers deserve public support. They are saying that ordinary workers should not be locked out of the recovery, and that we should all get a fair share as the economy grows again."[34]

While not as impressive as the 2011 protests, the July 2014 protest was still an imposing show of force. However, one must ask what the TUC expected to accomplish. Did they really expect that the government would abandon or modify austerity that was well entrenched on the basis of another one-off protest? More to the point, it was not realistic for organized labor to expect large-scale support from the general public considering that at the height of the anti-austerity movement a number of unions decided that self-interest trumped the interests of the community at large. Did O'Grady really expect public support for public sector unions? Unlike the 1960s and 1970s, when the union movement fought for the entire community, this time sections of it were unwilling to do so, and even went so far as to undermine other unions' efforts in overturning or modifying austerity. By July 2014, any potential the labor movement had in forcing the government to abandon austerity or modify such policies was nonexistent. It was way too little, and way too late. In many ways, the protest was an exercise in futility. Union self-interest guaranteed this. Furthermore, as I have argued, one-off demonstrations that are not followed up on, and which are protesting long-established policies, are highly defensive in nature and quite unlikely to succeed. Organized labor never truly set out to fight austerity measures. Thus we should not be surprised that such policies became entrenched in the UK.

Austerity and Political Parties

A provocative question concerning the union movement's protests against austerity was this: even if unions were determined to go all-in in their fight, how could austerity be overcome? As organized labor abandoned militant action as a strategy, seemingly the only action remaining was trying to help elect a "friendly" political party to office. The Conservative Party has embraced its version of austerity and is highly unlikely to reverse course to any large extent unless it becomes electorally unpopular. Thus, one would assume that the union movement was attempting to get the Labour Party elected to office in the 2015 general election. There was a major problem with this strategy, however (and not just that Labour was soundly defeated; see below): the Labour leader at the time, Ed Miliband, repeatedly went on record stating that a Labour government would not reverse the spending cuts. In June 2013, Miliband said, "[i]f we win the election, we will come to power in tougher economic circumstances than we have seen in generations and that will have to shape the way that we govern. . . . Our starting point for 2015/16 will be that we cannot reverse any cut in day to day, current spending unless it is fully funded from cuts elsewhere or extra revenue—not from more borrowing. . . . So when George Osborne stands up . . . and announces his cuts in day to day spending, we won't be able to promise now to reverse them because we can only do so when we can be absolutely crystal clear about where the money is coming from." He not only reiterated this position in February 2014, but astonishingly promised more spending cuts: "Clearly the next Labour government will face massive fiscal challenges. Including having to cut spending. . . . That is why it is all the more necessary to get every pound of value out of services. . . . And show we can do more with less. Including by doing things in a new way."[35] In other words, both of the main UK political parties supported austerity to a varying degree. Thus, organized labor's electorally strategy was bound to fail no matter the outcome of the general election. Even had the Labour Party been elected to office, there would have remained a level of austerity in the country.

This is another example of Gill's new constitutionalism. Both of the central political parties in the UK were advocates of austerity, thus limiting democratic choice when it came to economic policies.

It could be argued, however, that organized labor would have had a greater chance to convince the Labour Party to abandon or modify austerity than they had with the Conservatives. This is on the surface true only if one ignores recent history. Quite simply, in many ways it is surprising that the UK labor movement still believes that the Labour Party is not beholden to other interests well above those of working people. Indeed, it is relatively common knowledge that following a string of election defeats, along with the belief within Labour Party circles that the defeats were due to the Party's alliance with unions, that so-called "New" Labour has a much greater ideological embrace of neoliberalism, beginning when Tony Blair was elected party leader. Such a strategy paid off electorally as Labour swept to power in 1997. Before this, as political economist Steve Coulter notes, "unions had three main channels of influence over the Labour Party. The first was via their control of party institutions. Labour's governance and policymaking institutions (Conference, the National Executive Committee and National Policy Forums) were dominated by unions to various degrees through their voting strength, augmented by their ability to act as a bloc." The second channel of influence was through the unions giving Labour money in exchange for "unofficial" influence of Party policy. The third was " 'insiderist' lobbying by sections of the union movement close to the Party leadership who exploited overlapping goals and shared values to participate in policymaking. However, under Blair, the unions control over Labour Party institutions was largely dismantled; there were very few, if any, examples of unions being able to gain influence over Party policy, despite Labour relying heavily on unions for financing, and the TUC had to battle "Blair's determination to do as little as possible for the unions." Thus, union influence over Labour Party policy was long gone, even though they were largely responsible for electing Miliband as Party leader.[36]

Consequently, even if the union movement was successful in helping the Labour Party get elected, workers and the general public would still have been subjected to a level of austerity policies. In other words, the UK public continue to suffer through austerity implemented by the ruling Conservative Party and its coalition partner, the Liberal Democrats. Meanwhile, the main opposition, the Labour Party, also largely supports austerity policies, with its leader arguing that more spending cuts are needed. The UK public has been basically forced to choose between political parties that in one form or another supports austerity. This indeed represents a new constitutionalism. Organized labor's strategy to overcome austerity, if such a strategy even existed, was bound to failure even before it began. If there existed a left-wing political party that was against austerity, as was the case in Greece with Syriza and in Spain with Podemos, there is a strong likelihood that they would benefit from the main parties supporting austerity. Instead, a right-wing political party that hints at some economic populist policies is the one that has benefited.

The United Kingdom Independence Party (UKIP) was formed in 2003, but it came to prominence in 2009 when the Party came in second in the European Parliament elections with 16.5 percent of the vote. The Party was not as successful in the 2010 UK general election, in which it achieved only 3.1 percent of the vote and could not get a politician elected to parliament. However, as austerity continued to cause suffering, the UKIP's anti-immigration, anti-European Union platform has become more popular. It is easier to blame "others" for one's economic woes, even though, as I noted above, the decline in real wages cannot be blamed on immigration. In the 2014 local elections, UKIP won 163 seats, an increase from 35. It also got two people elected as MPs in by-elections; and in the 2014 European Parliament election, UKIP received 27.49 percent of the vote, the highest vote-getter of any British party. This was the first time that Labour or the Tories did not receive the most votes in an election held across the UK. In an attempt to capitalize on its increasing popularity and the austerity backlash in the community, UKIP, which was to the Right of the conservatives in regards to economic policy, has moved to the Left in this regard, even though it is still in favor of free trade. UKIP now argues that companies should have a social obligation to its employees; supports the National Health Service being free (although UKIP's then-leader Nigel Farage's suggestion in the lead-up to the May 2015 general election that the NHS may be privatized in the future led to internal conflict within the party); is opposed to the bedroom tax; no longer supports a flat-tax rate but prefers a progressive system in which top-earners should pay at least 40 percent tax (which is below the current top rate); and, in a by-election, its candidate campaigned on a "protect your benefits" platform. Such a strategy is popular with UKIP's supporters because they want a larger state and more public spending. Moreover, "78 per cent [of its supporters] support the nationalisation of the energy companies and 73 per cent back the renationalisation of the railways. Rather than a 'code of conduct' for employers, 57 per cent simply want zero-hour contracts [employment contracts with no guarantee on the number of hours an employee works in a week] to be banned. Rather than a flat tax, the same number support the reintroduction of the 50p rate." While UKIP has moved slightly to the Left in regards to economic policies, it is still virulent anti-immigration and anti-Europe.[37] In other words, it is a far-Right party that moved somewhat to the Left economically in an attempt to garner more support.

The composition of UKIP voters is quite interesting in the sense that its supporters are largely those who used to vote Conservative, with a mixture of working-class support. University of Oxford academics Geoffrey Evans and Jon Mellon, in a study of UKIP voters from 2005–2014, determined that the Party is

> attracting, primarily, disaffected former Labour voters from the Conservatives and elsewhere, but the working class basis of UKIP has been markedly over-stated. Working class voters are a little more likely to support UKIP than other classes, but there is stronger support among the self-employed and business owners, who were Mrs. Thatcher's hard-core supporters, not Labour's. Even within the working class, the strongest UKIPers are the lower supervisory category, who are not the disadvantaged semi- and unskilled workers that have been thought to provide the core of UKIP support.

Evans and Mellon go on to argue that UKIP voters are similar as voters to "radical right" parties across Europe: "an alliance between the working class and the self-employed (and employers)—rather than a party of the 'left behind.' Even more significant, in electoral terms, the differences in sizes between the social classes means that numerically the bulk of UKIP's support comes, counter-intuitively, from the larger professional [and] managerial middle classes." Thus, as UKIP voters were not traditional Labour supporters, they believed that in the 2015 General Election UKIP posed a bigger threat to the Conservatives than did Labour.[38]

The election result seemed to paint a different picture. The Conservatives won an outright majority by securing 331 seats (a gain of 24), Labour won only 232 seats (a loss of 26), the Liberal Democrats won only 8 seats (a loss of 49—largely due to the Party's embrace of austerity), while UKIP managed to win only 1 seat. While on the surface it seemed UKIP was a bigger threat to Labour, a study by University of London academic Eric Kaufmann found that "there is a silent minority of English nationalists whom UKIP draws upon. The Tories managed to scare enough of them away from non-voting and UKIP to win while convincing a small but important group of voters from other parties."[39]

One could thus reasonably conclude that Labour supporting austerity policies had little effect on the outcome of the election. Union members and the working class as a whole were still solidly behind Labour. Nevertheless—in a worrisome sign for future prospects of the Labour Party, if it does not take a different approach—in the twenty seats with the lowest voter turnout, Labour was successful in each of them. In Labour's heartland, people were not bothered to turn out and vote, signifying widespread disillusion with the Party. UKIP came in second in nine of these seats, and their vote was 4 percentage points higher in these seats than their UK average. In other words, there is a greater likelihood that an increasing number of people in traditional Labour seats might turn to UKIP, or a similar party, in the future. Moreover, while UKIP managed to secure only one seat, almost 3.9 million people voted for them (12.6 percent of the electorate—an increase of 9.5 percent). No other party came close to matching UKIP's rise. Indeed, UKIP secured almost 41.5 percent of Labour's total, yet due to the UK voting system won only 1 seat compared to Labour's 232. At this stage it is uncertain whether such results will disenfranchise UKIP's supporters or galvanize them in future elections. What they do signify is that a large segment of the population seeks an alternative to the austerity agenda backed by both the Conservatives and the Labour Party.[40]

Through the union movement's ties to a strategy of overturning austerity via electoral politics, and if the Labour Party continues to support austerity, and with there being no credible anti-austerity left-wing party, the far-right UKIP, by turning somewhat to the left economically, has the potential of gaining even more support among a large segment of the population in future elections. UKIP's anti-immigration and anti-Europe stance is popular with segments of conservative voters and sections of the working class, while its shift to the left economically is popular with those disillusioned with Labour's acceptance of neoliberalism and austerity. Such a combination could well lead to UKIP gaining further support.

A Sad State of Affairs

The UK economy was suffering because of the global economic crisis. However, with the implementation of austerity policies, not only has the economy not sprung back to life, wide-scale suffering has prevailed, with women, the poor, and vulnerable enduring the most pain. While the labor movement has attempted to combat austerity through a series of strikes and demonstrations, they have generally focused on a narrow scope of wages, pensions, and working conditions. As happened in Greece, Spain, and Ireland, the labor movement has been unable to combat the spread of austerity and protect ordinary workers and their families from the damage that austerity causes. Union self-interest condemned the anti-austerity protests. In addition, the UK labor movement's main hope of overturning austerity is the election of the Labour Party to government. Unfortunately, the party was generally supportive of austerity and signaled that a future Labour government would have implemented even more cuts. Such a strategy was an unmitigated failure, as the Conservatives won re-election in a landslide. They managed to convince enough voters that there was indeed no alternative to austerity. This should not have been a surprise considering that the two main parties, as well as the majority of the UK media, supported austerity to varying degrees. If people are constantly told there is no alternative, over time they will tend to believe such a message. Yet, at the same time, the fact that there is no left-wing, anti-austerity party, as exists in Greece and Spain, has led to the far-right UKIP gaining considerable support. Thus, not only has the labor movement been unable to overturn austerity, austerity in the UK might result in a party that is anti-immigration, anti-Europe, and supportive of free trade, with some economic populist policies continuing to gain more electoral support. For the labor movement and its supporters, this is truly a sad state of affairs.

In an ironic postscript to the labor movement's half-hearted struggle against austerity, following Labour's disastrous 2015 General Election, UNITE General Secretary Len McCluskey claimed that one of the main reasons the party lost the election is that it embraced austerity. Writing in *The Guardian*, he stated that "Labour didn't lose votes by proposing to tax the wealthiest a bit more, or intervene in the housing and energy markets. It did lose support because of its muddled message on austerity." He goes on to claim that "[i]gnoring the views of many economists, it accepted a need to balance the budget and eliminate the deficit which left them playing on Tory ground. Once this was conceded, Labour was on a hiding to nothing—no one will ever believe that they would be more reliable cutters than the Tories. So Labour was left trying to protect the victims of the Tory cuts agenda while accepting its underlying premises, also depriving itself of a coherent narrative linking together popular individual policies."[41] Considering that a number of unions accepted the austerity agenda by agreeing to deals with the government that undermined the anti-austerity movement and condemned the poor and vulnerable to increased suffering, McCluskey should be criticizing unions, such as UNITE, for being self-interested. Indeed, it was under McCluskey's leadership that UNITE cut a deal with the government and condemned the anti-austerity protest at the height of its power. While Labour might have embraced austerity to a certain extent, it was the self-interest of a number of unions that ensured that austerity would remain the economic policy of choice on 10 Downing Street.

Chapter 4

Austerity and the Labor Movement in the United States

Unlike the situation in some European countries, there was no "catastrophic" (of course this depends on how one defines catastrophic) economic collapse in the United States that led the US government to turn toward austerity, as happened in Greece, Spain, and Ireland. However, the US economy was indeed suffering as a result of the global economic crisis. The US's austerity turn, federally, did not develop because the incoming government ideologically advocated austerity as an economic policy, as happened in the UK (though a turn to austerity did occur at the state level in Wisconsin due to the ideology of the incoming government). Rather, austerity at the federal level in the US happened arguably by stealth.

This chapter provides an overview of how austerity policies have become almost pervasive at the federal, state, and local levels across the US. We will look at how austerity has hurt the US people, as well as at the resistance to austerity by the labor movement. Unlike in Europe, where there have been mass protests against austerity, the fight against austerity in the US has been relatively nonexistent nationwide. Instead, resistance has been focused more at the state and local level. We will look at two of the most high-profile struggles against austerity: the rise of the Wisconsin Workers Movement and the Chicago Teachers Union's strike. As in Europe, the US labor movement has been for the most part powerless to prevent austerity, but the Chicago Teachers Union (CTU) was partly successful in its fight. The CTU struggle provides a lesson that the rest of the US labor movement, and indeed, labor movements across the globe, should learn from.

Austerity in America

The austerity policies being implemented in a number of countries across the globe were largely uncommon at the national level in the US until the late 2000s. As Blyth correctly argues, "[b]efore 2008 no one, save for a few fringe conservatives in the United States and elsewhere, were concerned with 'excessive' national debts or deficits. Deficit hawks in the United States, for example, pretty much disappeared in embarrassment as, under the banner of fiscal conservativism, the Bush administration pushed both debts and deficits to new heights while inflation remained steady." Austerity was, however, used at the local level—the New York City budget crisis in the 1970s being a prime example (see Chapter 1). However, as happened in Europe, the global economic crisis resulted in austerity becoming fashionable once again in the US. As happened in other countries, a housing boom was a precursor of problems to come. From the turn of the new century, housing prices were on the rise across the US. By summer 2005, the prices of homes in Florida, Arizona, Nevada, and California were approximately 150 percent higher than they were in 1999. As Krugman notes, "[o]ther cities saw smaller increases, but there had clearly been a national home price boom that bore all the signs of a classic bubble: belief that prices never go down, a rush by buyers to get in before prices went still higher, and lots of speculative activity; there was even a reality-TV show named *Flip This House*. Yet the bubble was already starting to leak air; prices were still rising in most places, but houses were taking much longer to sell." Nationally, house prices peaked in spring 2006. Although prices began to decline, and the bubble was rapidly leaking air, there was not an immediate crash.[1]

However, beginning in mid-2007, banks began to get caught up in the housing crisis; they were incurring significant losses on mortgage-backed securities. This was followed by a credit crunch later that year as banks would not lend to each other; the credit crunch combined with a decline in construction and consumer spending pushed the US into a recession. By September 2008, the US economy was struggling with unemployment rising, but it was not a dire situation. However, the September 15 collapse of the global financial firm Lehman Brothers had a dramatic effect: "Lenders who had previously been willing to roll over their loans to the likes of Lehman no longer trusted the other side to make good on its promise to buy back the securities it temporarily sold, so they began requiring extra security in the form of 'haircuts'—basically putting up extra assets as collateral." Unfortunately, investment banks did not have extra assets. They thus began selling their assets to cover their "cash needs," which in turn drove prices lower, caused more panic, and drove the price of "interest rates on all but the safest assets" sky high. Blyth notes that "[b]y the third quarter of 2008, the height of the crisis, the top six US banks, Goldman Sachs, JP Morgan, Bank of America, Morgan Stanley, Citigroup, and Wells Fargo, had a collective asset-to-GDP ratio of 61.61 percent. They ran leverage ratios (assets/ equity) as high as 27 to 1 (Morgan Stanley) and as low as 10 to 1 (Bank of America). Compare this to Lehman Brothers' footprint. Lehman was running 31 to 1 leverage on an asset base of $503.54 billion, which is equivalent to about 3.5 percent of US GDP." As happened elsewhere across the world, the big banks were too big to allow to fail. This led to the Federal Reserve providing loans to banks and financial institutions to ensure they did not run out of money. In addition, the Bush administration created a $700 billion bank bailout fund.[2]

The net effect of the economic crisis led to household net worth declining by $13 trillion in 2008. It was impossible for the Federal Reserve to cut interest rates in an attempt to stimulate the economy because short-term interest rates were already at zero percent. The incoming Obama administration thus turned partially to Keynesianism and enacted a $787 billion economic stimulus package entitled the *American Recovery and Reinvestment Act*. However, the Act was inadequate to overcome the sense of doom in the economy. Krugman states that the Act "surely mitigated the recession, but it fell far short of what would have been needed to restore full employment, or even to create a sense of progress. Worse yet, the failure of the stimulus to deliver clear success had the effect, in the minds of voters, of discrediting the whole concept of using government spending to create jobs. So the Obama administration didn't get a chance for a do-over." The bank bailout, along with the economic stimulus policy, had the effect of increasing public debt. The government debt to GDP ratio increased from 64.8 percent in 2007 to 76 percent in 2008, 87.1 percent in 2009, and 95.2 percent in 2010.[3]

The increasing public debt as well as the perceived failure of the economic stimulus led to an ever-growing number of so-called elites arguing that austerity was the cure. Indeed, in January 2009, over two hundred economists signed an advertisement sponsored by the libertarian CATO Institute against the stimulus. The advertisement stated:

> Notwithstanding reports that all economists are now Keynesians and that we all support a big increase in the burden of government, we the undersigned do not believe that more government spending is a way to improve economic performance. More government spending by Hoover and Roosevelt did not pull the United States economy out of the Great Depression in the 1930s. More government spending did not solve Japan's "lost decade" in the 1990s. As such, it is a triumph of hope over experience to believe that more government spending will help the U.S. today. To improve the economy, policymakers should focus on reforms that remove impediments to work, saving, investment and production. Lower tax rates and a reduction in the burden of government are the best ways of using fiscal policy to boost growth.[4]

In other words, Keynesianism, or any other left-wing economic policy, was not the answer; instead, the Austrian economists claimed, austerity was the cure.

While the Obama administration did not immediately move toward austerity, in 2010 President Obama formed the National Commission on Fiscal Responsibility and Reform, also known as Bowles-Simpson (the names of the co-chairs were Alan Simpson and Erskine Bowles). The Commission was "charged with identifying policies to improve the fiscal situation in the medium term and to achieve fiscal sustainability over the long run. Specifically, the Commission shall propose recommendations designed to balance the budget, excluding interest payments on the debt, by 2015. This result is projected to stabilize the debt-to-GDP ratio at an acceptable level once the economy recovers." Quite simply, the Commission's overriding goal was to determine how to balance the budget and reduce debt. The preamble to the Commission's report stated: "Together, we have reached these unavoidable conclusions: The problem is real. The solution will be painful. There is no easy way out. Everything must be on the table." It goes on to powerfully claim: "After all the talk about debt and deficits, it is long past time for America's leaders to put up or shut up. The era of debt denial is over, and there can be no turning back."[5]

If such dire warnings were not enough, in March 2011, in a speech to Congress, Erskine Bowles went even further. Bowles, a Democrat, forewarned,

> [t]his problem is going to happen, like the former chairman of the Fed said or Moody's said, this is a problem we're going to have to face up to. It may be two years, you know, maybe a little less, maybe a little more, but if our bankers over there in Asia begin to believe that we're not going to be solid on our debt, that we're not going to be able to meet our obligations, just stop and think for a minute what happens if they just stop buying our debt. What happens to interest rates and what happens to the U.S. economy? The markets will absolutely devastate us if we don't step up to this problem. The problem is real, the solutions are painful and we have to act.

Bowles's assertion was clear: a debt crisis would occur if no action was taken. Likewise, Alan Simpson noted to Congress that a debt crisis would happen in less than two years. Thus, the US needed to take immediate action to prevent a debt crisis. It was not that they wanted fiscal responsibility, austerity, or whatever name one chooses. Action was necessary because "we love our children, our grandchildren, and our country too much not to act while we still have the chance to secure a better future for all our fellow citizens."[6] Austerity was seemingly the only hope.

Backing the austerity brigade was the yet-to-be discredited work of Reinhart and Rogoff. Numerous Republican politicians mentioned Reinhart and Rogoff's findings that a debt to GDP ratio exceeding 90 percent greatly hinders economic growth. For example, Paul Ryan, Chairman of the House Budget Committee, claimed that "[e]conomists who have studied sovereign debt tell us that letting total debt rise above 90 percent of GDP creates a drag on economic growth and intensifies the risk of a debt-fueled economic crisis." Dave Camp, chairman of the powerful House Ways and Means Committee, noted, "[i]ndependent economists have found that debt loads greater than 90 percent of GDP could result in the loss of up to a million jobs." Likewise, Jeff Sessions, the ranking member on the Senate Budget Committee stated that "[f]our major academic studies have shown that gross debt in excess of 90 percent of GDP results in weaker economic growth."[7] Moreover, even after Reinhart and Rogoff's work was discredited, a number of Republicans continued to refer to the work when arguing that austerity was necessary. These politicians were either unaware that the work had been discredited—difficult to believe, considering how much the news was publicized—or they simply did not care.

However, if excessive debt was truly a problem, one would assume that interest rates on long-term bonds would increase, as occurred in crisis-hit countries such as Greece and Spain. This did not happen in the US. In late 2010, the interest rates on long-term bonds hovered between 3.25 and 4 percent. By late 2011, even though debt was increasing, the interest rate declined to just over 2 percent. Since then the rate has fluctuated, but the last time it was above 4 percent was in May 2011.[8] Thus, while excessive debt may have been a problem in the eyes of politicians, the financial markets were not overly concerned. Nonetheless, as is often the case, perception becomes the reality. Thus, for both Democrat and Republican politicians, the debt problem had to be overcome. Austerity descended on the US.

In December 2010, President Obama authorized a two-year pay freeze for federal employees. At the time, Obama claimed, "[t]he hard truth is that getting this deficit under control is going to require some broad sacrifice, and that sacrifice must be shared by employees of the federal government." The pay freeze would not end in two years. In late 2012, Obama issued an executive order overturning the freeze on March 27, 2013, granting federal employees a very modest 0.5 percent wage increase. However, in March 2013, Congress agreed to extend the wage freeze until the end of 2013. There was "joy" for federal employees in 2014, and again in 2015, as they were granted wage increases of 1 percent per year, an increase well below inflation. Indeed, the average pay increases for federal employees under the Obama administration are the lowest for any administration since at least 1970.[9] As we shall see, Democrat politicians are often not the panacea that organized labor views them to be.

While federal employees endured wage freezes, other sections of the public service were also about to endure major budget cuts. The *Budget Control Act* came into existence on August 2, 2011. Under the Act, discretionary spending (spending the president requests that must be approved by Congress—approximately one-third of the Federal Budget) was set to be reduced from 9 percent of GDP for the 2011 financial year to 6.2 percent by the 2021 financial year. The 2021 figure, if achieved, would be the second lowest on record since 1962. The overall goal was to reduce the budget deficit by $2.1 trillion over that period. In addition, $760 billion was saved through budget cuts in 2010 and 2011. However, as is often the case, the market was not satisfied. On August, 5, 2011, Standard & Poor's reduced the US's credit rating from AAA (this occurred partly due to the debt ceiling). While many were predicting that this was catastrophic, the overall result was negligible.[10] Nonetheless, Standard & Poor's action was a clear signal that, at the very least, certain sections of the market wanted further cuts; they wanted greater levels of austerity.

At the federal level, austerity continued. In 2012, $850 million in spending cuts and tax increases came into being via the Budget Control Act. In March 2013, automatic budget cuts (known as sequestration) were enacted to the tune of $1.1 trillion. With the additional cuts and tax increases, the budget would be reduced by $3.9 trillion in ten years.[11]

Austerity has become entrenched in the US. In a remarkably candid document entitled "Ten Facts You May Not Know About the Federal Budget," the head of the Senate Budget Committee, Democrat Patty Murray, outlined the level of austerity (without obviously using that term) at the federal level as of October 2014. It is not clear whether she views the almost unprecedented decline in federal spending as a negative, but Murray is certainly not arguing that austerity is bad. Here are Murray's ten facts:

1. Federal spending usually increases every year, even just to account for inflation. However, between 2009 and 2014 federal spending remained virtually unchanged. The last time this happened was "during the post–World War II phase down from 1946 to 1951."

2. Federal spending as a portion of GDP in 2014 was 20.4 percent. It was 24.4 percent in 2009. It is the largest five-year decline since 1946 to 1951.

3. The lowest level of Federal spending under the Regan administration was 20.5 percent. As noted in point 2, in 2014 it was 20.4 percent.

4. "Chairman Ryan [Republican] proposed in his [Financial Year] FY2012 budget resolution that federal spending for FY2012 to FY2014 would total $10.67 trillion. Actual spending was $10.50 trillion, $175 billion less over that time frame. For FY2014, Chairman Ryan called for $3.583 trillion in spending, but actual spending was $3.504 trillion."

5. The deficit was 2.8 percent of GDP in 2014; the forty year average is 3.1 percent.

6. "In January 2012, the 2014 deficit was projected to be $658 billion, using reasonable assumptions of current policy, including sequestration. In fact, the deficit in 2014 was only $483 billion, even though the Murray-Ryan deal [December 2013 Budget Act] replaced two-thirds of the nondefense discretionary cuts and roughly one-half of the total discretionary cuts for 2014."

7. "In the five years from 2009 to 2014, the federal deficit as a percentage of GDP dropped from 9.8 percent to 2.8 percent, a swing of 7 percentage points. In the seven years from 1993 to 2000, a 3.8 percent deficit turned into a surplus of 2.3 percent, a swing of 6.1 percentage points. The 1990s are generally viewed as a period of substantial improvement in the federal budget."

8. The National Commission on Fiscal Responsibility and Reform argued that federal spending as a portion of GDP should be 21.4 percent by 2014. As noted in point 2, in 2014 it was actually 20.4 percent. In addition, Bowles-Simpson argued that in 2014 revenue as a percentage of GDP should be 18.8 percent; it ended up being only 17.6 percent.

9. "The Bowles-Simpson commission called for a revenue target equivalent to 20.7 percent of GDP by 2022 and recommended a path to achieve that. Based on the revenue-to-GDP levels called for by Bowles-Simpson, it would take over $4.5 trillion in new revenue to meet the Commission's targets."

10. In June 2010 it was estimated that by 2050 the federally held public debt would be 339 percent. In July 2014 it was estimated to be only 126 percent by 2050.[12]

Quite simply, the current level of austerity being inflicted onto the economy and the American people is almost unsurpassed in US history. Compared to austerity in Europe, there were no pronouncements that the US was entering into an "age of austerity," no claims that austerity was the only solution—austerity just happened. It was in many ways austerity by stealth. This is also another example of new constitutionalism, as both the Democrats and Republicans support austerity as an economic policy. Such a level of austerity would clearly have a large impact on the American economy. It is to that subject we turn now.

Austerity's and Neoliberalism's Impact on the American Economy

As noted above, the debt to GDP ratio increased from 64.8 percent in 2007 to 76 percent in 2008, 87.1 percent in 2009, and 95.2 percent in 2010. One would assume that, at least based on so-called economic orthodoxy, austerity measures would lead to a reduction in the debt to GDP ratio. As occurred in Greece, Spain, Ireland, and the UK, what has been happening is that the percentage is increasing. The government debt to GDP ratio increased to 99.94 percent in 2011, 100.1 percent in 2012, 101.53 percent in 2013, and 102.98 percent in 2014. One reason that the debt to GDP ratio has been increasing despite the cuts in government spending is because the GDP growth rate has been quite slow. US GDP grew by 2.5 percent in 2010, 1.6 percent in 2011, 2.3 percent in 2012, 2.2 percent in 2013, and 2.4 percent in 2014. While it is a positive that the economy is growing, considering the American economy declined by 0.3 percent in 2008 and 2.8 percent in 2009, the economy has only grown by 5.5 percent over the last six years—an average of 0.917 percent per year. In other words, GDP growth has largely been stagnant.[13]

The decline in discretionary spending is a large reason that GDP growth has been minimal. As Krugman wrote in March 2014, if the level of discretionary spending remained the same as it was under the second term of George W. Bush's presidency, it "would be about a third—or more than 2 percent of GDP—higher. Since there is good reason to believe that the multiplier is 1.5 or more, this would mean real GDP 3-plus percent higher, closing much if not most of the output gap, and probably an unemployment rate below 5.5 percent. In short, we would have had a vastly healthier economy but for the de facto victory of disastrous austerity policies."[14]

Regarding the unemployment rate, in August 2011 it stood at 9 percent. Since that time unemployment has trended downward; it was 8.1 percent in August 2012, 7.2 percent in August 2013, 6.1 percent in August 2014, and was 5.8 percent in November 2014. On the surface this is cause for optimism. However, austerity policies have had an impact on the rate. In March 2014, the unemployment rate was 6.7 percent, but as Krugman argues, it should have been below 5.5 percent. One reason there has been a reduction in the unemployment rate is that there has been a constant decline in the number of people looking for full-time jobs. In September 2014, when the unemployment rate fell below 6 percent for the first time since July 2008, the number of people looking for work declined by 97,000. Indeed, the number of working-age people in the workforce fell to 62.7 percent—the lowest level since February 1978.[15]

Combined with the number of people leaving the workforce, as in the UK, US wages have largely stagnated for a number of years. In September 2014, the average hourly wage for nonmanagement private-sector workers was $20.67—an increase of 2.3 percent compared to September 2013. While it is a positive that the wage is increasing, the rise is well below 2006 and 2007, when the average wage increased by 4 percent per year. It is important to note that today's purchasing power is approximately the same as in 1979. Real wages were at their highest in January 1973; the hourly rate then of $4.03 is equivalent to a current wage of $22.41. In regards to wages, the old adage that the rich get richer while the poor get poorer still holds true today. People in the lowest 10th percentile have witnessed wage declines of 3.7 percent in real terms since 2000. In contrast, people in the 90th percentile have seen wage increases of 9.7 percent.[16]

As wages have stagnated, it is not a surprise that median household income is well below its peak. In 1999, the median household income adjusted for inflation for all American homes was $56,895. Following the dot-com crash, income declined before increasing in the mid-2000s to reach $56,436 in 2007. Since then there has been a decline. In 2012, median household income was $51,578, while in 2013 it increased very marginally to $51,939—8 percent below the 2007 figure, 9 percent below the 1999 peak, and 1 percent lower than in 1989. In other words, there was a large decline before the impact of the global economic crisis, and for the last twenty-five years average household income has largely stagnated. Still, however, the rich are getting richer. In 2013, a household needed to earn $196,000 to be in the top 5 percent—a 2.5 percent increase from 2012. The top 5 percent of all households now earn 22 percent of all income. Austerity and neoliberalism more generally have been good for the rich.[17]

As wages have stagnated and household income declined, it is not a surprise that the median net worth of households has also either declined or largely stagnated. In 2010, the median net worth of households in 2013 dollars was $82,300. In 2013 it was $81,400. Thus, little change in three years. However, in 2007 the median net worth of households was $135,700. There has been a staggering decline in real terms over six years. For White Caucasian households, the figure was $192,500 in 2007, $138,600 in 2010, and $141,900 in 2013. For African American households, the figure was $19,200 in 2007, $16,600 in 2010, and $11,000 in 2013. For Hispanics, the median net worth of households was $23,600 in 2007, $16,000 in 2010, and $13,700 in 2013. The number of White households owning their own home declined from 75.3% in 2010 to 73.9% in 2013, a 2 percent decrease. In contrast, the "homeownership rate among minority house-holds decreased from 50.6% in 2010 to 47.4% in 2013, a slippage of 6.5%." Thus, while all households suffered greatly due to the global economic crisis, White households have recovered some of their losses since 2010, while African American and Hispanic households have suffered even further hardship. Writing for the *Pew Research Center*, Rakesh Kochhar and Richard Fry note that "[t]he current gap between blacks and whites has reached its highest point since 1989, when whites had 17 times the wealth of black households. The current white-to-Hispanic wealth ratio has reached a level not seen since 2001." They go on to conclude that "[p]eak values for the wealth ratios were recorded in the 1989 survey—17 for the white-to-black ratio and 14 for the white-to-Hispanic ratio. But those values of the ratios may be anomalies driven by fluctuations in the wealth of the poorest—those with net worth less than $500. Otherwise, the racial and ethnic wealth gaps in 2013 are at or about their highest levels observed in the 30 years for which we have data."[18]

Overall, while GDP has been growing and there has been a decline in unemployment, Whites have only slightly "benefited" over the last three years, while the situation for African Americans and Hispanics has become worse. Austerity measures have thus not only resulted in a decline in the debt to GDP ratio, they have not helped most Americans recover wealth lost due to the global economic crisis.

Of course not everyone has suffered. There is rising inequality in America. A key measure of inequality is the ratio of wealth to house-hold income. In a 2104 report, the international financial services group Credit Suisse states that "[f]or more than a century, the wealth income ratio has typically fallen in a narrow interval between 4 and 5. However, the ratio briefly rose above 6 in 1999 during the dot.com bubble and broke that barrier again during 2005–2007. It dropped sharply into the 'normal band' following the financial crisis, but the decline has since been reversed, and the ratio is now at a recent record high level of 6.5, matched previously only during the Great Depression. This is a worrying signal given that abnormally high wealth income ratios have always signaled recession in the past." It is interesting to note that the current record levels of inequality were matched only during the Great Depression—another instance when austerity policies were implemented in the US. Economists Emmanuel Saez and Gabriel Zucman determined that the share of total household wealth by the top 0.1 percent increased from 7 percent in the late 1970s to 22 percent in 2012. The current level is near its peak that occurred during the 1920s. During the decades of Keynesianism in America following the Great Depression, the level of household wealth owned by the top 0.1 percent declined, but following the implementation of neoliberalism in the late 1970s and the abandoning of the social contract, the mega-rich got even richer. Furthermore, the "share of wealth of the bottom 90 percent of families did gradually increase from 15 percent in the 1920s to a peak of 36 percent in the mid-1980, it then dramatically declined. By 2012, the bottom 90 percent collectively owns only 23 percent of total U.S. wealth, about as much as in 1940." Saez and Zucman go on to argue that "[s]ince the housing and financial crises of the late 2000s there has been no recovery in the wealth of the middle class and the poor. The average wealth of the bottom 90 percent of families is equal to $80,000 in 2012—the same level as in 1986. In contrast, the average wealth for the top 1 percent more than tripled between 1980 and 2012. In 2012, the wealth of the top 1 percent increased almost back to its peak level of 2007. The Great Recession looks only like a small bump along an upward trajectory."[19] In short, Keynesianism helped the average American, while the advent of neoliberalism has led to the rich becoming richer. Likewise, austerity has helped the rich recover their wealth after the global financial crisis, while failing to do the same for the middle class and the poor.

The extent of inequality has reached such a level that it bothers even Janet Yellen, Chair of the Board of Governors of the Federal Reserve. Yellen has admitted that "[t]he extent of and continuing increase in inequality in the United States greatly concern me." She went on to claim that "income and wealth inequality are near their highest levels in the past hundred years, much higher than the average during that time span and probably higher than for much of American history before then."[20]

Now, although austerity measures are not totally to blame for the rising levels of inequality, as we have seen in the preceding chapters, austerity has always hurt the poor and most vulnerable wherever and whenever it has been implemented. In the US, African American and Hispanic households have seen their economic wealth decline since 2010, while White households have had only slight increases. Moreover, just as has happened in Greece, Spain, Ireland, and the UK, austerity has adversely affected people's health and well-being.

In a July 2014 report, the Coalition for Health Funding noted that the overall public health service federal funding declined by nearly 11 percent between 2010 and 2014, with some services being cut by 25 percent. As a result, "more than 50,000 state and local public health professionals have been laid off since 2008—those who monitor and respond to outbreaks, immunize children and the elderly, and inspect restaurants. In addition, public health departments in 33 states and the District of Columbia report that they reduced their budgets between 2011 and 2013." Professor David Stuckler of Oxford University notes that there have been "cuts to the women and children's health program, which provides food to pregnant women, and has been shown to prevent infant mortality—this is one of the programs facing significant cuts. Another is the Centers for Disease Control, which was a great protector during meningitis outbreaks, and outbreaks of West Nile Virus, which has been seen in California, and most recently in Dallas, Texas." Among the range of cuts, funding for tuberculosis has declined from approximately $125 million in 2010 to approximately $108 million in 2014. While one in five infant deaths is caused by a birth defect, and the "causes of about 70 percent of all birth defects remain unknown," funding for the "the Centers for Disease Control and Prevention's . . . birth defects research and prevention activities" has declined by 18 percent between 2010 and 2014. Funding constraints have also resulted in Severe Combined Immune Deficiency (SCID)—more commonly known as "bubble boy disease"—being added to newborn screening in only twenty states. In 2013, 3,800 babies were born daily in states that do not screen for SCID. There are many other examples of cuts in federal health spending due to austerity, generally unrecognized by most people unless they or someone they know is directly affected.[21]

In addition to the range of cuts in federal public health care spending, which is impacting millions, the number of people in the federal food stamp program has increased by 50 percent between 2009 and 2013. As of this writing, about 46.5 million people—including 12 million children and 7 million seniors—in the US need help affording food. More than 14 percent of the population is on some kind of food stamp program. Between 1970 and 2000, only 7.9 percent of the population was on food stamps. In 2012, "17.6 million households had limited or uncertain access to adequate food supplies." In a 2014 survey conducted by John Zogby, who has been researching hunger in America since 1987, found that 9 percent of the respondents "have gone without food for 24 hours at a time because of a lack of money or food in the past month." Other findings were that 13 percent of "18–29 year olds and 12% of 30–49 year olds experience hunger" and that "[t]he West has the highest occurrence of people going hungry (13%), no doubt in part caused by the highest concentration of Hispanics, 20% who say they fall into this category." Moreover, because the survey was conducted online, the number of people experiencing hunger is probably substantially higher since poor households are less likely to have Internet access via computers and smart phones.[22] Dorothy Rosenbaum, senior fellow for the Center on Budget and Policy Priorities, sums up the situation well: "There are people who receive benefits who nonetheless are hungry because the benefit levels tend to run out towards the end of the month. . . . There are people who qualify for low benefits—for example, senior citizens, people with disabilities—who may get SSI [Supplemental Security Income] or Social Security. Those programs bring them close to the poverty line but their SNAP [Supplemental Nutrition Assistance Program] benefits are relatively low, and they face a hard time getting access to food."[23]

What has austerity meant to America? In the richest country on Earth, a substantial number of people go hungry and cannot afford to eat. Quite simply, while the impact of the global economic crisis has led to a number of people seeking help so they can eat, austerity and neoliberalism have caused even further suffering across the US. Austerity has been a failure for the overwhelming majority of Americans, yet it remains the de facto economic policy of choice—a sad state of affairs.

Union Resistance?

Considering the range of austerity cuts implemented by the government that affect the poor and vulnerable the hardest, one might assume that the labor movement would be out in full force attempting to overturn austerity, or at the very least trying to mitigate its harshest effects. One might expect that organized labor would stage mass protests across the country to draw attention to the damaging effects austerity has had on large segments of the population and on the US economy as a whole. In other eras, this would have indeed been the case. Whatever their shortcomings, labor federations in Greece, Spain, Ireland, and the UK staged numerous nationwide protests against austerity. AFL-CIO President Richard Trumka has rebuked austerity many times, claiming austerity measures primarily target working people and should be extended to corporations and the rich. For example, in March 2011 Trumka wrote that "[i]f we were really talking about things we can't afford, at the top of that list would be tax breaks for corporations that ship jobs overseas, tax breaks for hedge fund managers, more tax breaks for corporations that hide their profits outside the country and continuing tax cuts for the top 2 percent. Just closing one destructive loophole—tax cuts for corporations that ship jobs overseas—would be enough to replace almost half of the jobs-destroying sequester." In the same article, Trumka blames Republicans and not the Democrats for austerity: "In the face of high unemployment and slow growth, out-of-touch Republicans are throwing tantrums and threatening to harm our economy through a series of manufactured crises. What are the demands of these hostage-takers? They want Democrats to agree to cut Social Security and Medicaid and Medicare benefits, cutting the safety net out from under middle-class families who have borne the brunt of decades of slow growth and diminished opportunities."[24]

However, while the AFL-CIO has raged against austerity, when it comes to protesting on a national level, the response has been decidedly mute—almost nonexistent when compared to the mass protests occurring in other countries. The AFL-CIO and Change to Win, the other US national labor federation, have basically been all talk with little to no action. Considering the decided lack of militancy, it seems on the surface that the labor federations believe that very little can be done to overcome austerity outside of the political arena. Under such an approach, austerity will be overturned only if Democrats get elected to office.

There have been *some* protests, albeit on a very small scale. In January 2013, the AFL-CIO and its allies sponsored a National Day of Action for fiscal fairness. Unlike in Europe, where similar actions led to hundreds of thousands of people taking to the streets, the US saw only hundreds of people (at best) participating in local demonstrations. One example of action undertaken occurred as follows: "In Seattle members of Washington Community Action Network, wearing athletic uniforms, threw dodge balls inscribed with the word 'TAX' at each other during lunch hour in front of the downtown office of Wells Fargo, one of the 'dirty thirty' giant corporations that pay no federal income tax. Together with a group of 80 union members they marched to the Federal Building, held a rally and sent delegations to meet with aides in the offices of Senators Patty Murray and Maria Cantwell."[25]

Not to disparage such an event, but small-scale protests like this are not likely to change politicians' positions. Unfortunately, politicians would not pay the slightest attention to such a protest. Indeed, as noted above, Senator Murray was seemingly proclaiming the unprecedented level of austerity in America almost two years after the Seattle action. The protest action had zero effect on her. Since the US labor movement's response to austerity has been largely nonexistent, it should come as no surprise that austerity has taken its stronghold. There have been no mass strikes, protests, or demonstrations against austerity. While the AFL-CIO and Change to Win have constantly noted the damage that austerity is doing, neither organization has sought to protest nationally. Considering the lack of success organized labor has had in Greece, Spain, Ireland, and the UK in overturning austerity—although each country has seen mass demonstrations—one must question whether organized labor in the US feels austerity cannot be overcome through large-scale demonstrations. Another possibility is that organized labor at the national level does not view austerity as negatively as one would think it would. For if the AFL-CIO and Change to Win do in fact believe that austerity is damaging, how do they think austerity will be overcome? Certainly not through mass protests as occurred in these other countries. Seemingly, the only answer is that they believe that if Democrats can take control of the presidency, Congress, and the Senate, the Party will then enact Keynesianism legislation rather than neoliberalism—legislation that is more pro-labor than pro-capital. This is a similar strategy to that undertaken by organized labor in the UK, albeit with much more protest action. Following this line of thinking, change cannot come through the power of the people forcing politicians to modify their positions, but only through the ballot box. The AFL-CIO and Change to Win apparently believe that the Democrats will abandon the austerity-by-stealth policies currently being forced on the US public. Thus, the role of organized labor is merely to help their preferred politicians be elected. However, as I shall argue below, it is a mistaken strategy for organized labor to pin their hopes on the Democratic Party to enact legislation that benefits working people. Despite promising the world, the Democrats have given organized labor and working people very little since the late 1970s and the abandonment of the social contract.

While the response to austerity in the US has been virtually nonexistent at the national level, the same is not true at the state and local level. The two most high-profile battles against austerity by the labor movement have been in Wisconsin and Chicago. It is to these struggles that I now turn.

Wisconsin Workers' Movement

In November 2010, Republican Scott Walker was elected Governor of Wisconsin after defeating Milwaukee Mayor Tom Barrett. Walker's election campaign was greatly aided by financing from billionaires Charles and David Koch. The Koch brothers were increasingly well known through their ties to the Tea Party. The Koch Industries PAC gave Walker's gubernatorial campaign $43,000, its second highest contribution (housing and realtor groups gave $43,215). In addition, the Koch Industries PAC also donated one million dollars to the Republican Governors Association. The Association then donated $65,000 via independent expenditures to Walker's campaign and also spent $3.4 million on television advertisements and political mailings critical of Barrett. As well as Walker being elected, Republicans controlled both houses.[26]

Wisconsin's long-term deficit resembled that of many other US states—it was quite large. However, it was lower than what faced former Wisconsin Governor Jim Doyle when he was elected, and the current budget was projected to be in a slight surplus. While Walker had presented himself as a moderate, his first few months in office showed he was anything but. Indeed, in his first week in office Walker announced $137 million in tax breaks to companies. Two weeks later, on February 11, Walker announced that a Budget Repair Bill was needed due to a short-term budget deficit of $140 million (caused in large part by the $137 million in tax breaks just announced) and a long-term deficit of $3.6 billion. The Repair Bill basically eliminated the right of government workers to collectively bargain effectively. Under the Bill there is a "[p]rohibition of any unions or collective bargaining for most state workers. Those that continue to have any union representation at all will be limited to bargaining for wages only which will have a mandatory limit which will be set annually by the State Legislature." At best, wages can rise only in line with inflation. In real terms, public sector workers would be "treading water." As a result of unions being limited to collective bargaining only in regards to wages, they could not bargain "over insurance (so employees can be given high deductible junk insurance with no say in the matter), benefits, pensions, holidays or personal days, vacation, working conditions, adequate staffing, class size, worker safety issues, mandatory overtime, shift selection, requests for days off," and so on. Furthermore, unions would be forced to recertify every year; basically unions would have to engage in a National Labor Relations Board election every year, and be successful, if they were to represent Wisconsin public sector workers.[27] In other words, union power would be greatly diminished, even if they could remain to be the certified bargaining agents for public sector workers—not a small feat in itself. As we have seen, similar situations have occurred around the world; as part of their austerity agenda, politicians target organized labor in an attempt to weaken its power. A labor movement stripped of its power benefits the rise of austerity and neoliberalism.

As *Washington Post* journalist Erza Klein argues, "[t]he best way to understand Walker's proposal is as a multi-part attack on the state's labor unions. In part one, their ability to bargain benefits for their members is reduced. In part two, their ability to collect dues, and thus spend money organizing members or lobbying the legislature, is undercut. And in part three, workers have to vote the union back into existence every single year. Put it all together and it looks like this: Wisconsin's unions can't deliver value to their members, they're deprived of the resources to change the rules so they can start delivering value to their members again, and because of that, their members eventually give in to employer pressure and shut the union down in one of the annual certification elections." Simply put, the power of the public sector unions would be dramatically curtailed. In addition, weakening the power of the unions enhanced the chances that Republicans and other right-wing parties and candidates would be elected to positions of power throughout Wisconsin. This would further increase the chances that antiunion legislation would be enacted; it was a vicious circle, and one the labor movement seemingly could not escape from. However, it is important to note that not all public sector unions were targeted. Police and firefighter unions were not included in Walker's draconian measures despite their members generally having the highest wages and best benefit packages. While one can debate the reasons that these unions were excluded, when compared to other union members, public safety union members have a long history of voting for Republicans over Democrats, public safety unions are much more likely to endorse Republican candidates, and public safety unions generally supported Walker in the election.[28]

In addition to the assault on public sector unions, one month later Walker also signed into law a range of spending cuts over two years to the tune of $4.2 billion—equivalent to 6.7 percent of Wisconsin's budget. The range of cuts: spending to state schools decreased by $834 million (7.9 percent, or $550 per student), the Medicaid budget was reduced by $500 million, and local governments' budget was decreased by $96 million (almost 11 percent). In announcing the cuts, Walker claimed that "[w]e need a leaner and cleaner state government. . . . As we decrease spending, we also increase flexibility so local government and state government have the tools to deal with reduced revenue." Walker wanted austerity. This is another example of a government targeting organized labor in an attempt to weaken it so that austerity policies could be more easily implemented. Walker was supported by his Republican colleagues. For example, Senate President Mike Ellis stated, "It's the first budget we've had in 12 years that's going to actually be a balanced budget without any funny money." In contrast, Democrats derided the spending cuts, especially in regards to education. Representative Tamara Grigsby called the education cuts an "absolute annihilation. . . . He does this under the guise of fixing the budget, but what he's really doing is waging war on Wisconsin. . . . [It is a] blow that I don't think we [Wisconsin] can stand up to."[29]

Considering the assault on public sector unions, as well as the range of spending cuts announced the following month, it was not a surprise that unions staged mass protests against the measures. On February 15 over 10,000 teachers, other public sector workers, and their supporters staged a mass demonstration at Capitol square. Unlike most other protests, their numbers continued to grow over the following days. On February 19, approximately 70,000 people were protesting at Capitol square, and 100,000 on Saturday, February 26. Another mass protest of 100,000 took place on Saturday, March 12. The protests were a considerable show of force and acts of a militant movement.

The protests had more of a political focus (in attempting to overturn policies detrimental to organized labor) than an economic one (the protests were not solely about bread-and-butter issues such as wages and working conditions). It is not necessarily the case that economic struggles do not have a political dimension. Likewise, political struggles can have an economic dimension. However, for the Wisconsin Workers' Movement, the focus was on the political dimension. The focus was political to such an extent that some union leaders were willing to support the austerity spending cuts in the state budget—as well as to accept concessions, such as workers paying an increased amount toward their own pensions and health insurance—if Walker would agree not to implement the draconian anti–public sector collective-bargaining measures. Thus, there were sections of organized labor that cared more about their own interests than those of the wider community that would be hit hard by austerity policies. They were putting their self-interest above all else. In addition, in an attempt to not seem militant, in late February union leaders withdrew their support of protestors occupying the Capitol building. The union bureaucracy believed that such militancy would undermine their cause and that nothing would be achieved by a continued occupation.[30]

The unions' continued focus on a political strategy to overturn the antiunion laws led them to seek a recall election. They came to the conclusion that the only way the legislation would be eliminated would be through electing Democrat politicians—not through militant action such as large-scale protest. By January 2012, more than 900,000 people had signed a petition demanding a new election. As only 540,208 signatures were needed to trigger a new election, Wisconsin voters went back to the polls in June 2012. Unions were confident that Walker would be defeated. In June and July 2011, six Republican and three Democrat state senators had endured recall elections. The results saw all three Democrats retain their seats, while two Republicans lost theirs. In the lead-up to the election, the Republicans spent over $45.5 million and the Democrats $17.9 million in an attempt to get their candidate (Walker for the Republicans, Barrett for the Democrats) elected. The combined spending of over $63 million was a new record for Wisconsin elections; the previous record was "only" $37.4 million, set in 2010.[31]

Despite their optimism, the election result was an unmitigated disaster for the labor movement and its supporters. Walker was not only reelected—the first governor to be victorious in a recall election—but the Republicans held on to their majority in the Senate. Following the election result, labor journalist Doug Henwood claimed that

> [t]here were several things wrong with the electoral strategy. . . . Barrett was an extremely weak candidate who'd already once lost to Walker (though by a slightly narrower margin than this time). Potentially stronger candidates like Russ Feingold refused to run, probably out of fear of these results. And the bar was very high for a recall. Only 19 states have recall provisions, and Walker was just the third governor to face one. Well over half of Wisconsin voters think that recalls should be reserved only for misconduct—and less than a third approve of recalls for any reason other than misconduct.[32]

In addition, as much as the labor movement and its supporters may not want to admit it, unions are generally not that popular with the American public. In a Gallup poll, only 25 percent of Americans want unions to have more influence (close to the lowest level on record), while 42 percent want unions to have less influence. The low opinion of unions by the general public is largely a result of an overwhelming majority of people (68 percent) believing that unions are more concerned with their own members than the community at large. In short, people believe unions are self-interested. It is no surprise that the public views unions this way, given that a number of unions agreed to Walker implementing austerity policies so long as he would not implement antiunion laws. Unions were telling the wider community that they care more about themselves than they do the public. The unions were clearly self-interested, and it cost them dearly. Such a negative perception of unions was seen in the recall election. As Henwood notes, "while only about 30% of union members voted for Walker, nearly half of those living in union households but not themselves union members voted for him. . . . In other words, apparently union members aren't even able to convince their spouses that the things are worth all that much." For the labor movement, it is bad enough that 30 percent of union members voted for Walker, but 48 percent of people living with a union member also voted for Walker. The labor movement was unable to convince a sizeable minority of its own members and nearly 50 percent of people living with a union member not to vote for Walker. Thus, it was no surprise that a large majority (61 percent) of nonunion households voted for Walker and his antiunion policies. In addition to surviving the recall election in June 2012, in November 2014 Walker was once again victorious in the nationwide governor elections with a relatively unchanged margin of victory of 5.7 points (compared to 6 points in 2010 and 6.8 points in 2012).[33] While one could complain that the amount of money spent to get Walker and other republicans elected dwarfed that spent by the Democrats, the simple reality is that Wisconsin voters wanted the antiunion, austerity advocate Walker as their governor.

Since unions were unable to overturn the draconian antiunion laws, it comes as no surprise that union density and worker's wages in Wisconsin have declined. Union membership has declined from 13.3 percent in 2011 to 11.7 percent in 2014. Public sector unions have experienced large losses. Writing in *The Washington Post,* Robert Samuels notes that "[t]he state branch of the National Education Association, once 100,000 strong, has seen its membership drop by a third. The American Federation of Teachers, which organized in the college system, saw a 50 percent decline. The 70,000-person membership in the state employees union has fallen by 70 percent." Indeed, public sector union membership declined from approximately 50.3 percent in 2011 to 30.9 percent in 2014. The electoral strategy by Wisconsin unions was an unmitigated failure. Henwood argues that unions should have engaged in a much more rank-and-file campaign with an emphasis on how the attack on unions affects everyone in the community. Henwood states: "Suppose instead that the unions had supported a popular campaign—media, door knocking, phone calling—to agitate, educate, and organize on the importance of the labor movement to the maintenance of living standards? If they'd made an argument, broadly and repeatedly, that Walker's agenda was an attack on the wages and benefits of the majority of the population? That it was designed to remove organized opposition to the power of right-wing money in politics? That would have been more fruitful than this major defeat."[34] Whether such a strategy would have been successful is impossible to ascertain, but it is beyond dispute that, despite the brief hours of promise when people took to the streets and embraced militancy, the labor movement in Wisconsin was soundly defeated. As a result, there were antiunion laws *and* austerity. Union leaders moved away from militant action in which they were supported by the majority of the community to a political strategy that was a disaster. Agreeing to the implementation of austerity policies demonstrated to the public that the labor movement cared more about itself than about the wider community. As we saw in Greece, Spain, Ireland, and the UK, self-interested organized labor has little chance in overturning austerity. The labor movement hurts both itself and the wider community through their self-interest.

Indeed, lost in the focus on the assault on public sector unions is that Walker implemented major spending cuts that had an adverse effect on Wisconsin. In the twelve months to February 2012, while Walker promised to create 250,000 new jobs, Wisconsin actually lost 16,900 jobs. This is despite the $137 million in tax breaks given out to business when Walker first came to office. It was these same tax breaks that led to the short-term budget deficit and was used as an excuse to implement the antiunion laws. The Bureau of Labor statistics from March 2011 to March 2012 show that Wisconsin experienced the highest amount of job loss in the country—a loss of 17,800 public sector jobs and 6,100 private sector jobs. Indeed, the loss of only private sector jobs was also the highest in the country. In contrast, more than 24,000 jobs were created in 2010. In March 2013, the Bureau of Labor statistics ranked Wisconsin 44th in the country in creating private sector jobs. Slightly better news for the state was it was ranked 35th in job creation in September 2013. However, the job growth of 1.2 percent was well behind the national average of 2.1 percent. Likewise, "[t]he latest federal figures, comparing March 2013 to March 2014, show Wisconsin's job growth rate at 1 percent, below the national average of 1.7 percent, and its wage growth rate at 2.9 percent, behind the national average of 3.8 percent." Indeed, from 2011, Wisconsin ranks 40th in job growth, nationally, and 42nd in wage growth. There has been largely stagnant job growth, with private sector workers suffering as well as those in the public sector, and wages for public sector workers are declining in real terms. Writing in *The New York Times,* Steven Greenhouse notes that Walker's impact "has already emboldened other Republican-controlled states to enact measures that weaken unions and cut benefits. Tennessee and Idaho passed laws that cut back bargaining rights for public schoolteachers, while Ohio curbed collective bargaining for all state employees—though that law was repealed in a 2011 referendum. Even longtime union strongholds like Michigan and Indiana have enacted right-to-work laws that undercut private-sector unions by banning any requirements that workers pay union dues or fees."[35]

Thus, the labor movement's failure to overturn the antiunion laws and austerity policies has had an adverse impact not only in Wisconsin but across the country. The self-interest and political strategy of organized labor in Wisconsin hurt public sector workers and unions, large sections of the community in Wisconsin, and unions across the country, which in turn has had an adverse effect on people nationwide. In addition, the strategy of electing Democrats to office in the hope of pro-labor legislation is sadly flawed. It is wrong to assume that simply by electing Democrat politicians we can avoid antiunion laws. Kim Moody and Charles Post note that "[i]n 2011, Democrats in Massachusetts supported legislation to strip public healthcare workers of bargaining rights, Connecticut Democrats attempted to reclassify college faculty as managers to make them ineligible for union representations, New Jersey Democrats joined Republicans in attempting to exclude healthcare from collective bargaining and Illinois Democrats succeeded in restricting teacher union rights." Indeed, Wisconsin Democrats do not have the best record when it comes to labor and social issues. It was somewhat ironic, then, that the Wisconsin labor movement viewed electing Democrat politicians to office as their best chance to overcome the antiunion laws. Even though militant action seemed to be working in swaying public opinion, union leaders decided the best strategy was political. As it turned out, these politicians may or may not have enacted pro-labor legislation.[36]

Of course it is not just Wisconsin Democrats who promise organized labor the world, but end up delivering very little. The same process has been occurring across the country at all levels of government for a number of years. It was the abandonment of the social contract by both Republicans and Democrats in the late 1970s that led to politicians on both sides being generally lukewarm to organized labor's desires. For example, Jimmy Carter refused to support legislation that would have allowed unions to engage in boycotts, the Clinton administration was wholeheartedly behind neoliberalism and free-trade agreements such as NAFTA, and while there was hope that the Obama administration would support pro-labor legislation such as the Employee Free Choice Act, this did not come to fruition.[37]

The Democrats are happy to accept union funding and manpower come election time, but they are not willing to support legislation that would actually benefit working people. Instead, they appear to support the level of austerity being inflicted on the country and to advocate neo-liberalism. Once again, this is an example of new constitutionalism. The situation is similar as in the UK. As we saw in the previous chapter, the Labour Party is happy to accept union financing, but is nowhere near as willing to support prounion policies and in fact embraces austerity to an extent.

In the end, the labor movement in Wisconsin was unable to over-come the antiunion laws and austerity policies implemented by Governor Walker. In Chicago, however, the labor movement—specifically, the Chicago Teachers Union—enjoyed more success. The union did not rely on a strategy of trying to elect labor-friendly politicians, but instead mounted a militant grassroots campaign that involved the community in the fight against austerity.

Chicago Teachers Union

In February 2010, the Chicago Public School System faced an overall deficit close to $1 billion. The head of the school system, Ron Huberman, claimed that there would have to be pension reform and unions would have to engage in concession bargaining and accept job losses. Earlier in the year, the "district trimmed millions in programs, laid off 536 employees and mandated six furlough days for nonunion staff." In announcing the deficit, Huberman said there would be a further five hundred job losses for nonunion staff and three weeks of furlough days. These measures, which would save the city $25 million, were not neces-sary to balance the yearly budget, but were done to demonstrate "fiscal responsibility"—they were austerity measures. Late that year, the school system wanted the Chicago Teachers Union (CTU) to accept $100 mil-lion in wage and benefit concessions. When the CTU refused, the school district unilaterally fired 1,300 teachers and 500 paraprofessionals and school-related personnel.[38]

The city's demand for wage concessions occurred at the same time that new leadership took hold of the CTU. Beginning in the 1960s, CTU leadership was dominated by the United Progressive Caucus (UPC). Until 1987, the UPC-led CTU was fairly progressive and engaged in eight strikes. However, following a 1987 strike, the CTU began to be more compliant with the city, even while teachers' rights were being eroded. In 1995, legislation was enacted that "unilaterally targeted Chicago teachers by severely restricting what the CTU could legally negotiate with regard to wages and benefits, and eliminating system-wide seniority. This meant that all matters relating to class size, pedagogy, and other areas that clearly affect the working conditions of Chicago teachers (students and parents) could only be negotiated if both sides agreed to do so."[39]

Given the complacent nature of the UPC-led CTU, it was no surprise that reform groups arose to challenge UPC's dominance of the union. In 2001, the Pro Active Caucus of Teachers (PACT) managed to elect Debbie Lynch as president of the CTU. While there was an improvement in the way the CTU was run, PACT was forced to focus on factional wars within the union. This led in part to CTU agreeing to a substandard collective-bargaining agreement in 2004. The agreement was initially voted down by the rank-and-file, before being approved with only minor improvements. The factional warfare and the substandard contract led to the UPC once again gaining control of the CTU in 2004. Also in 2004, a program called "Renaissance 2010" began in Chicago to close one hundred underperforming neighborhood schools (a third of all Chicago public schools) and in their place to open privately run charter schools. The charter schools are decidedly nonunion, with teachers' salaries and benefits below what unionized teachers in public schools earn. Moreover, state funding was diverted from the public school system to private charter schools. Tom Alter argues that "[t]he Civic Committee of the Commercial Club of Chicago, an organization of Chicago's top corporate heads, played an instrumental role in convincing Daley and Arne Duncan, chief executive officer (CEO) of CPS at the time, to adopt the plan. Tom Vander Ark, executive director for education at the Bill and Melinda Gates Foundation, called the plan 'the most important thing that's happened in high school reform in this generation.'" The CTU could do nothing to prevent this from occurring. Moreover, the then president-elect of the CTU, Marilyn Stewart, stated that she would "reserve judgment" on the plan even though it was clear that public-run schools with unionized jobs would disappear and be replaced by privately run charter schools with nonunion jobs. Whether Stewart decided to reserve judgment because the

Democrats formulated the plan is uncertain, but when in June 2009 the US Secretary of Education Arne Duncan announced that the "Chicago Plan" would become national policy, Stewart applauded.[40] As such, the CTU was seemingly powerless, as well as being complacent, in the decline of the Chicago Public School System.

The next challenge to the old guard occurred from modest beginnings. In 2008, a small group of teachers, paraprofessionals, and school-related personnel formed a reading/study group. The members were dismayed by the CTU's complacence and lack of action toward Renaissance 2010. The first book they read was Naomi Klein's *The Shock Doctrine: The Rise of Disaster Capitalism*. This led them to view the Renaissance 2010 program as part of the neoliberal agenda. From this group, as well as other CTU members who were against Renaissance 2010, came the Caucus of Rank and File Educators (CORE). As Peter Brogan notes:

> Membership in CORE ran the gamut from those who were relatively new to activism or involvement in the union, including some who never saw themselves as "political," to others who were members of socialist groups like Solidarity, the International Socialist Organization (ISO), unaffiliated radicals of different stripes, as well as those teachers interested in progressive/alternative pedagogy, many of whom were members of a smaller social justice organization of educators called Teachers for Social Justice (TSJ). Thus, CORE developed from its initial formation as a multi-racial and multigenerational group.

As CORE grew from its modest beginnings, it is unlikely the group would have sought to run for office if union vice president Ted Dallas had not been forced to step down and expelled from the union due to financial improprieties, and if CTU leadership had not done very little when the Chicago Public School System threatened to fire 25 percent of teachers, increase class sizes by seven to thirty-five, and force CTU members to forego 4 percent pay increases in the final two years of the current collective-bargaining agreement. In the 2010 election, five groups were contending for power. No group received an outright majority in the first round. However, fed up with the continued assault on teachers, paraprofessionals, and school-related personnel, the CORE caucus received 60 percent of the vote in the runoff against the UPC, and Karen Lewis became president of the CTU.[41]

Lewis and the CTU's new-found militancy were clearly demonstrated in her acceptance speech, in which she stated:

> Today marks the beginning of the end of scapegoating educators for all the social ills that our children, families and schools struggle against every day. . . . This election shows the unity of 30,000 educators standing strong to put business in its place—out of our schools. Corporate America sees K–12 public education as 380 billion dollars that, up until the last 10 or 15 years, they didn't have a sizeable piece of. This so-called school reform is not an education plan. It's a business plan, and mayoral control of our schools, and our Board of Education, is the linchpin of their operation."[42]

The CTU was ready for the challenge ahead.

One of the most crucial decisions of the CORE-led CTU was not to focus on so-called bread-and-butter issues, such as wages and working conditions, but to focus more broadly on political and community issues. The CTU believed (and continues to believe) that a self-interested approach with a focus on wages and working conditions would not help itself, its members, or the wider community. A strong union in which its members are adequately rewarded for their efforts is part-and-parcel with a vibrant local community. A healthy public school system is a benefit to everyone concerned; quite simply, it is difficult to have a robust teachers' union without a strong school system. This being the case, one area the union concentrated on was public school closures. Before the formation of CORE, current leaders of the group had had ties with social movements, such as Kenwood Oakland Community Organization and Action Now, that protested privatization of public schools and school closures. These ties continued with the formation of CORE. The wider community thus did not see the CORE-led CTU as interested only in improving union members' wages and working conditions. They cared about and were part of the wider community. For example, "[r]elationships were built with other groups like Stand Up Chicago, a coalition of unions, community groups, and others, whose bold actions targeting corporations like Bank of America, the Chicago Board of Trade, and the Hyatt Hotels highlighted how money was diverted from the city budget through the use of Tax Increment Financing zones (TIF's) and given to wealthy and profitable corporations. One protest brought several hundred people to a luxury car dealership that was the recipient of TIF funds; the crowd entered the showroom and disrupted their business, demanding the return of the TIF money. Similar actions were directed at Bank of America branches throughout the city and outside the Mercantile Exchange and Hyatt hotels." Indeed, through TIF, in return for agreeing to build a hotel in Hyde Park, the Hyatt group was given $5.2 million, even though without the public money the group would have almost certainly still built the hotel. Also, Penny Pritzker of the Hyatt group was a member of the Chicago Board of Education.[43]

The CTU, other unions, and social movements involved in Stand Up Chicago were demonstrating that money was being spent to benefit already profitable Chicago businesses and multinationals rather than being spent on schools, hospitals, and other public necessities. In many ways, it was an easy message to sell; after all, to an ordinary person living in Chicago an improved school system would be much more of a benefit than the city spending money helping a luxury car dealership.

A focus on what was happening in the wider community does not mean that the CORE-led CTU ignored workplace issues and what was happening within its ranks. The rank-and-file were concerned that under previous leadership the union took a top-down approach, with union leaders dictating the direction in which the union would go. This usually involved political lobbying instead of mobilizing the membership. The rank-and-file had little say in the affairs of their union. As we have constantly seen, unions that have a primary political focus in trying to elect "friendly" political parties in an attempt to change their fortunes have repeatedly failed to get austerity policies overturned. This was certainly true for the Wisconsin Workers' Movement, which had a mobilized membership that was basically demobilized by union leadership to focus on a political strategy that ended in abject failure. The CTU did not follow the same path. In an attempt to be more beholden to the rank-and-file in the lead up to the 2012 collective-bargaining negotiations, the CTU decided that a larger bargaining committee was necessary—over sixty members were on the committee. As Robert Bartlett notes:

> The union structured a large bargaining team, which represented the broad demographic of union membership—elementary and high schools, regular and special education teachers, Paraprofessionals and School-Related Personnel (PSRP), and other non-certified staff; there were representatives across lines of race and ethnicity, seniority, and from all caucuses within the

union. This expanded the number of people who understood and debated the issues that were being bargained over and the counterposed positions of Board, and also made it harder for political opponents of CORE to oppose the contract from the outside.[44]

Basically, the CTU leadership was ensuring that all segments of the union membership had a voice in the bargaining. This is, in general, a great way to ensure unity, as all segments of the union feel they have had a say in the direction of the union. Moreover, it was a militant voice that wanted change throughout the entire community.

This new-found militancy of the CTU worried the Illinois government. In response, the government enacted the Illinois Senate Bill 7 (SB 7). Under SB 7, the Chicago Public School System could more easily fire teachers and lengthen the school day. In addition, SB 7 had a number of anti-CTU measures. These measures included that "any union in a school district with a population of more than five hundred thousand (in other words, only Chicago) must submit to arbitration before striking, strike only over wage and compensation issues, and receive support from 75 percent of the total union membership to authorize a strike." As we saw earlier, politicians often attempt to enact antiunion legislation to weaken the power of organized labor. This in turn makes it easier for them to enact neoliberal and austerity policies. Considering that it is often difficult for a union to receive a simple majority to undertake strike action, the provision in SB 7 on the surface seemingly made it exceeding unlikely that the CTU would be able to muster enough support to authorize a strike. Even then, the CTU would only be legally able to strike in regards to wages and other compensation. The corporate sector, not surprisingly, were very pleased with SB 7. For example, John Edelman, CEO of the right-wing advocacy group Stand for Children, stated: "The unions cannot strike in Chicago. . . . They will never be able to muster the 75 percent threshold necessary to strike."[45] The Illinois government was trying to ensure that the CTU's democratic militancy would not progress to result in strike action that would potentially galvanize the community against austerity.

In collective-bargaining negotiations for a new contract in spring 2012, the school system initially proposed that the school day be increased by 14 percent, there would be no limits on class size, and a large increase in family health care costs would take effect. In return, teachers would receive a one-off 2 percent wage increase. The Chicago

Public School System was thus proposing that teachers work longer hours with only a one-time small increase in pay. In an informal poll conducted by the CTU, 90 percent of its members rejected such a change. Nonetheless, even if the CTU was able to get 75 percent of its membership to agree to a strike, the public was not initially behind the union. As we have seen, the public believes—and in many cases are justified in this belief—that unions are self-interested and are thus less likely to support striking workers. However, getting public support is essential for a union in any industrial dispute, especially when it involves the education sector. It is very easy for politicians and the media to claim that striking teachers are selfish and do not care about children's education. Indeed, in January 2011, 78 percent of respondents to a *Chicago Tribune* poll were in favor of a longer school day, with only 17 percent against it. However, in a similar poll in May 2011, support for a longer school day was down to 62 percent, with 32 percent opposed. Moreover, 40 percent of people favored the CTU and its approach to approve education, compared to only 17 percent supporting Mayor Rahm Emanuel, a Democrat. As for parents with children in the public school system, 48 percent supported the CTU over Mayor Emanuel. This is another example of a so-called left-wing Mayor and political party being advocates of austerity. In an attempt to sway public opinion further to its side, the CTU publicly released its bargaining proposals. The CTU "proposed smaller class sizes; increased instruction in art, music, and world languages; air conditioning, libraries, and playgrounds for all schools (many schools currently go without); and protections against school closings." The CTU did not attempt to hide its militancy when it came to class and race issues. The union publicly highlighted the deep segregation occurring at Chicago schools, that millions of dollars were to be spent on charter schools with less funding going to schools in African American communities, and experienced African American teachers would be replaced by less experienced White teachers.[46]

Not helping the negotiations with the city was that other unions were not united with the CTU. For example, the "mayor was able to get IFT Local 1600, that represents Cook County College faculty, to agree to an early contract that specifically agreed to merit pay. The building trade-dominated Chicago Federation of Labor kept a hands-off attitude, hoping to avoid angering the mayor and jeopardizing projects that benefit the trades." Basically, other unions put their own self-interest above the interest of other unions, their members, and the wider community. Such displays of self-interest just reinforce the notion that unions care only about themselves and their members, which negatively affects all unions and workers. However, the CTU was not to be deterred. On May 23, 2011, the CTU held a ten-thousand-person-strong demonstration—the largest teacher protest in Chicago's history. Despite the show of force, the Chicago Public School System was sure that the CTU would never receive strike authorization. They thus "agreed to the negotiations' time-line proposed by the teachers union which would allow a strike to occur in September." Such confidence—some would say arrogance—was badly misplaced. On June 4, 23,780 of a possible 26,250 CTU members voted to give the union strike authorization. Only 482 members voted against the strike authorization, with 2,240 not voting (which counted toward the "no" vote under regulations imposed by SB 7). It was an overwhelming endorsement of the CORE leadership of the union. In contrast, there was a reduction in public support for Emanuel. For example, it was revealed that at a campaign in favor of an increased school day, people were bused to the protest and paid anywhere between $25 and $50 to attend and pretend to be parents of public school children.[47]

Further helping the CTU was that an independent arbitrator appointed under the provisions of SB 7 released a report stating that teachers should receive a 35.74 percent increase over four years. It was not a surprise that that mayor rejected the arbitrator's report. However, somewhat stunningly, so did the CTU. While the CTU's members would certainly welcome such a large pay increase, as Peter Brogan put it,

> the CTU rejected these recommendations because the report did not speak to any of the broader demands and issues that the union had raised to improve the school system, a fact which would go a long way towards bolstering public support and serving as evidence that, despite CPS and Emanuel's claims, the teachers and their union were not concerned with their own narrow economic interests.

The CTU was not interested only in bread-and-butter issues for its members, but with helping the entire community. It could not do so simply through higher wages for its members. The CTU was putting others' interests ahead of its own. A healthy public school system was more important than a simple pay rise. As the two sides could not come to an agreement, the teachers went on strike on Monday, September 10.[48]

The tone was set on the first day of the strike, when fifty thousand CTU members and supporters held a rally and marched in downtown

Chicago. After a few days, the CTU decided to move the rallies and marches to the west and south sides of Chicago, where the public schools had suffered the most neglect. Doing so demonstrated that the union was not only concerned with power politics represented by downtown Chicago, but with the entire community. In addition, CTU members manned picket lines at schools from 6:00 in the morning until 10:30 at night. Despite the best efforts of the mayor and some sections of the media to portray the CTU as self-interested, the community was solidly behind the teachers. The numerous efforts by the union to identify itself as part of the wider community paid dividends during the strike. However, while the CTU obtained community support, support from other unions was not entirely forthcoming. As Brogan notes: "while the two other unions with contracts with CPS, UNITE HERE Local 1 and Service Employees International Union (SEIU) Local 73, have been supportive of the CTU, by the time the teachers went out on strike both unions had already settled their contracts. Why they did so rather than bargain in parallel with the CTU is not an easy question to answer. Indeed, their failure to do so surprised many labour activists in Chicago because of the progressive reputation of these unions as well as their extensive support and collaboration with the CTU."[49] Irrespective of the reason, the lack of solidarity hurt CTU's bargaining efforts and was another example that some unions were willing to put their own interests ahead of other unions, their members, and the wider community. It is actions such as these that result in the public believing that unions care only about themselves and are willing to undermine the bargaining efforts of other unions. Additionally, unions' self-interest makes it all the more difficult for unions to win community support the next time they go out on strike or engage in an industrial struggle. Such action could thus have badly undermined the CTU's efforts.

Nonetheless, after a week of strike action, the public school system made concessions, including "[m]ore than six hundred new positions in art, music, and physical education. . . . A freeze on health-care payments (CPS originally had proposed a 40 percent increase for families and couples). . . . Teacher evaluation percentage kept at state legal minimum. . . . Raise of 7 percent over three years. . . . Antibullying language to protect teachers from abusive principals. . . . Annual supply reimbursement increased from $100 to $250. . . . Contract language to promote racial diversity in CPS hiring." The CTU was relatively happy with the proposal, and it was expected that the teachers would return to work on Monday, September 17. However, union leadership wanted to give its membership enough time to review the new proposal. The CTU leadership wanted all of its members to be informed about the proposed contract. Thus, the union stayed out on strike. It was not unusual to see members huddling in groups in the picket lines, reviewing the proposal. On September 18, the membership agreed to return to work the following day. It was a victory for both the union and the rank-and-file. Nonetheless, the CTU did agree to some concessions, such as pay guarantees for laid-off teachers decreasing from two years to one year, but there was a creation of a "Teacher Quality Pool of veteran laid-off teachers from which 50 percent of all new hires must come (the district was not obligated to hire any laid-off teachers before this settlement)."[50]

In the end, the CTU overcame overwhelming odds to even be able to go out on strike, let alone to force the public school system into concessions. The CORE-led CTU is a great example of the benefits of social movement unionism. As I have explained, social movement unionism occurs when unions are militant, with the rank-and-file playing an active role; when they have alliances with social movements and community groups; and when they care not just about bread-and-butter issues but about anything affecting the wider community. (I discuss the benefits of social movement unionism in Chapter 5). As we have seen, the CTU fit all these criteria. Another aspect of social movement unionism is that unions are not self-interested—they believe an injury to one is an injury to all. Unity is essential—not just among unions but among the rank–and-file, social movements, and the wider community. This is the only way that positive change can occur.

Buoyant following the successful strike, the CTU's membership re-elected the CORE leadership by an overwhelming margin (79 percent in favor). This should have been a period when the entire Chicago labor movement followed the CTU's lead to adopt social movement unionism, or at the very least to engage in solidarity with fellow unions and the local community. There is a limit to what one union can do by itself. While a coalition of unions was moderately successful in March 2013 in preventing the closure of four public schools, later that year fifty schools were condemned to be closed by the Chicago Board of Education. In June 2013, 855 teachers and other school employees were fired, with another 2,000 job losses (including over 1,000 teachers) announced one month later. The school system blamed budgetary decisions for the layoffs, primarily the increasing costs of pensions. In other words, they wanted the CTU to accept pension reform, meaning vastly reduced pensions for its members. Likewise, in June 2014, 1,150 public school employees (including 550 teachers) were fired. While the city is "forced" to fire teachers because of budgetary pressure, Mayor Emanuel is still able to find enough public funds to bid for President Obama's library and a Star War's museum. As Lewis asked, "Do we want Star Wars museums or public, neighborhood schools? Do we want presidential libraries or librarians for every child?"[51]

Overall, despite the strength of the CTU, at best it can only mitigate school closures and job losses because it is a single union. There is a limit to what one union can achieve without support from the entire labor movement. Nonetheless, unlike any other labor movement and/or union around the globe that I have discussed, the CTU was able to force concessions from an austerity-minded government. When victories are few and far between, the success of the CORE-led CTU in forcing concessions from the public school system, along with changing the culture of the union, should rightfully be applauded.

What Can Be Done?

In Greece, Spain, and Ireland a major economic downturn and governments seemingly unable to solve their country's economic woes led to austerity policies and EU–IMF bailouts. In the United Kingdom the Conservative Party did, and still does, believe austerity is an economic cure to a large extent. As noted in the previous chapter, the UK government has adopted an austerity-lite agenda, as pensioners and hospitals are not included in austerity measures. In contrast, this chapter has highlighted how the global economic crisis, the alleged failure of an economic stimulus, and an ideological agenda has led to austerity being implemented virtually by stealth at the federal level across the United States. Moreover, while it is often assumed that it is Republicans pushing the austerity agenda, many Democrats also firmly believe in the benefits of austerity. As noted above, Erskine Bowles claimed that a fiscal crisis "is going to happen, like the former chairman of the Fed said or Moody's said, this is a problem we're going to have to face up to. It may be two years, you know, maybe a little less, maybe a little more. . . . The markets will absolutely devastate us if we don't step up to this problem. The problem is real, the solutions are painful and we have to act." Likewise, the head of the Senate Budget Committee Patty Murray seemingly triumphed a press release revealing a nearly unprecedented level of austerity at the federal level. Indeed, only during the aftermath of World War II has there been such a slowdown of spending at the federal level.

If one was hoping that austerity was to be the cure to the US economic malaise, only in late 2014 did the economy show signs of life. However, as Krugman forcefully claims, the US "would have had a vastly healthier economy but for the de facto victory of disastrous austerity policies." In addition to austerity policies slowing economic growth and leading to a higher unemployment rate than otherwise would be the case, there is increasing inequality across the country. While one would be mistaken to blame *only* austerity for rising inequality, the simple fact of the matter is that austerity has led to the poor and most vulnerable suffering further pain in the US and across the globe. Indeed, that even federal reserve chairperson and austerity advocate Janet Yellen is concerned about the rising levels of inequality clearly indicate it is a major problem.

Considering the impact of austerity and neoliberalism more generally on people across the US, one would assume that the labor movement would be out in full force protesting against these economic policies. However, at the national level, the labor movement, despite criticizing austerity, has done very little to protest it becoming in many ways the de facto economic policy. The labor movement used to be at the forefront of struggles affecting the well-being of its members and the wider community. Now, at the national level, organized labor hopes the Democrats will be elected and abandon austerity. Of course the likelihood that the Democrats would abandon austerity and implement pro-labor economic policies is, at best, highly unlikely. The lack of protests at the national level is in stark contrast to national labor movements in Greece, Spain, Ireland, the UK, and many other countries where austerity policies have been implemented. The lack of national protests has played a role in austerity being implemented by stealth, as the negative impact of such policies have not been highlighted to any great extent by organized labor.

However, there have been anti-austerity protests by the labor movement at the state and local levels. This chapter highlighted the two most high-profile demonstrations: the Wisconsin Workers' Movement and the Chicago Teachers Union strike. In Wisconsin, after initially taking to the streets in an impressive show of force against draconian antiunion laws and deep austerity cuts, the labor movement concentrated on a political strategy of ousting Scott Walker as governor and electing a Democrat instead. This strategy was largely doomed to fail because the labor movement could not convince people that the unions were not self-interested. The alleged self-interest of unions was not helped by union leaders being willing to accept austerity measures if Governor Walker would agree to abandon the antiunion legislation. Unions were trying to convince the voting public that the collective-bargaining rights of public sector workers was more important than the austerity measures that would negatively affect nearly every sector of the community. As we have seen repeatedly in the preceding chapters, a self-interested union movement is a recipe for disaster because the general public believes that unions do not care about the wider community and put their own interests above others. Similar situations were present in Greece, Spain, Ireland, and the UK. In each case, organized labor put its own interests ahead of the wider community, and each time this led to austerity policies being implemented, causing hardship within the wider community, especially among the poor and vulnerable. As Wisconsin unions followed this same path, it was no surprise that organized labor could not convince the electorate that a strategy of austerity and antiunionism was wrongheaded, even though austerity had been shown to lead to below-average job growth and wage increases. Indeed, a substantial minority of union households and nonunion members who live in union households voted for Walker and his antiunion austerity agenda not once, but twice. This clearly demonstrates that the general public did not believe that what is best for unions and their members is best for all. As noted above, only 25 percent of Americans want unions to have more influence, an almost record low, while 42 percent want unions to have less influence, and a substantial majority believes that unions are indeed self-interested. Thus, the unions' failure and Walker's re-election should have come as no surprise. As demonstrated in Chapter 1, a strong union movement is beneficial to most, if not all, segments of society. When unions are self-interested, or are perceived to be, they lose their support and become detrimental to communities. Wisconsin unions caused hardships in nearly all segments of society.

A different story unfolded in Chicago, where the CTU under the leadership of CORE was an active part of the community. The union was not self-interested; indeed, the union rejected an arbitrator's findings that proposed large wage increases for teachers because the report did not make mention of school closures and wider community issues. That the union was seemingly willing to put the interests of the wider community ahead of itself and its members led to it gaining considerable support. Without such support, the union would have likely failed in its campaign. Unlike all other unions we have analyzed thus far, the CTU was partly successful in overturning austerity measures and in securing concessions from the Chicago Public School System. A large part of the CTU's success was a result of its social movement union strategy, which values alliances with the local community and social activism, supports causes that affect working people in the workplace and in the community, and believes that an injury to one is an injury to all. Unity is essential among unions, workers, and the wider community. This is why social movement unionism benefits everyone concerned. However, there is a limit to what one union can do alone, irrespective of the ideology it embraces. Following the CTU's success, the Chicago mayor and board of education fired thousands of teachers in subsequent years and closed many public schools. This does not diminish the accomplishments of the CTU. Unlike any other union around the world, the CTU was partly successful in its fight against austerity.

The apparent inability of labor movements in the US and around the globe to overcome austerity has led to an increasing number of people to argue that social movements are more suited to the fight. In Chapter 5 we look at whether this is true.

Chapter 5

Social Movements, Political Parties, and Social Movement Unionism: Hope for the Future?

The previous chapters have highlighted how austerity has become almost a de facto go-to economic policy when a country is struggling economically. Austerity has not been successful in solving a country's economic woes and has led to suffering across the globe, with the poor and vulnerable bearing the most pain. The chapters have also described how the labor movement has been seemingly unable to prevent austerity policies from being implemented, let alone overturning them. Only the Chicago Teachers Union has had any success in forcing a government to mitigate such policies without agreeing to major concessions. At the same time that the labor movement has been unsuccessfully fighting against austerity, there have been many high-profile social movements also battling austerity, as well as neoliberalism more generally. This chapter provides an overview and analysis of the Occupy Movement, 15M in Spain, and the Quebec student movement. Like the labor movement, social movements have generally had limited impact against austerity. However, the Quebec student movement was partly successful in its fight in 2012, while from the ashes of 15M rose the political party Podemos (We Can).

In contrast to the UK and US, where no effective left-wing political party has formed, in both Greece, with Syriza, and in Spain, with Podemos, mainstream leftist parties have become electorally popular and have an opportunity to make a difference. Thus, this chapter will also examine Podemos and the rise of Syriza, as well as its capitulation to the EU.

I will also argue that labor movements around the world still have the power in the battle against austerity. However, they need to move away from so-called left-wing political parties that embrace austerity. The labor movement needs to be independent of such political parties. While in theory it is easier for the labor movements in Spain and Greece, for example, to link to parties—because they have viable left-wing alternatives to traditional mainstream political parties that at least publicly preach anti-austerity—this is not the case in the UK and US. In each country, no left-wing political party has arisen (although in the UK a far right-wing party, UKIP, with some economic popular policies is becoming an electoral force). Thus, one would assume that it is much more difficult for labor movements in the UK and the US to limit the impact of austerity and neoliberal policies, let alone overturn them.

I will conclude the chapter and the book by arguing that irrespective of whether a viable left-wing, anti-austerity political party exists or not, the labor movements in the UK and the US must embrace social movement unionism, which has had success across the globe in a variety of situations. Most recently, the Chicago Teachers Union triumphed (in part) largely because it embraced social movement unionism. If the labor movement in the UK and the US do not adopt social movement unionism, or make some other drastic changes, they will continue to fade into irrelevance, the general public will continue to suffer from austerity policies and from neoliberalism more generally, and far-right political parties with populist economic policies will see further gains. In other words, if the labor movement continues on the same path in the UK and the US, it will be a sad state of affairs.

The Occupy Movement

Much has been written in mainstream media, alternative media, and academia on the Occupy Movement—known initially as Occupy Wall Street before it spread across the US and worldwide. Nonetheless, an analysis and overview of the Occupy Movement is important here because many believe that this kind of social movement will be at the forefront of anti-austerity and neoliberalism protests in the future.

The Occupy Movement, like many successful groups, formed from very modest beginnings. The Canadian bimonthly magazine *Adbusters* called for an encampment and occupation of Zuccotti Park in New York City beginning on September 17, 2011. *Adbusters* "depicts the developed world as a nightmare of environmental collapse and spiritual hollowness, driven to the brink of destruction by its consumer appetites. *Adbusters'* images—a breastfeeding baby tattooed with corporate logos; a smiling Barack Obama with a clown's ball on his nose—are combined with equally provocative texts and turned into a paginated montage."[1]

On September 17, between one and two thousand people gathered in the park, with somewhere between one hundred and three hundred electing to stay overnight. The choice of Zuccotti Park was strategic because it is a privately owned park. The city government can close public parks in New York City at sunset and/or impose curfews if it so desires. However, Zuccotti Park is required to be open twenty-four hours a day due to zoning laws. Writing in *The New Yorker*, Mattathias Schwartz notes that

> In the next few weeks, the encampment became more established, with tents, desks, walkways, wireless Internet, a kitchen, and an extensive lending library. A sort of organization took shape, with people forming a seemingly endless array of working groups: Structure, Facilitation, Sanitation, Food, Direct Action, Safe Spaces. A mid-October balance sheet from the occupation's Finance Working Group reported that it had received four hundred and fifty thousand dollars in donations, which it was keeping in two accounts at Amalgamated Bank. Almost every afternoon for two months, depending on the weather, hundreds of people gathered in the park. Some were drawn to the cameras and the spectacle; some came for the free food, shelter, and medical care; and some showed up for the earnest political conversation and because they believed that this might be the beginning of a revolution."[2]

Within a couple of months, the hope and energy displayed in the New York City protest had spread across the globe. There were Occupy Movement protests in over 1,600 cities. Quite simply, the protest resonated with many. Almost all of the Occupy Movement protests around the world followed the same formula as the general assembly (in which anyone could join and participate) at Zuccotti Park—namely, no leaders and no set demands. At Zuccotti Park, "Occupy Wall Street was serving more than 3,000 meals every day from its free kitchen, stocked mostly with donated food. At night, a rotating cast of as many as 500 bed down in the park, many of them using blankets and sleeping bags provided by the occupation. There's a library with some 4,500 cataloged volumes—

everything from the *Communist Manifesto* to *He's Just Not That Into You*—
an all-volunteer medical staff to provide free health care, a station that
gives out hand-rolled cigarettes if you want them." The movement was
spreading, and the protest in New York City got larger. However, what
were the protesters' demands? As the Occupy Movement did not have
predefined leaders, the list of demands was vague. The general assembly
at the New York City protest formed a "Declaration of Occupation" that
stated: "We write so that all people who feel wronged by the corporate
forces of the world can know that we are your allies. . . . No true democracy is attainable when the process is determined by economic power."
The Declaration of Occupation was more like a laundry list of grievances, claiming that corporations and its supports cause everything from
inequality to poisoning the food supply. To overcome these grievances
people needed to "Exercise your right to peaceably assemble; occupy public space; create a process to address the problems we face; and generate
solutions accessible to everyone." The Occupy Movement's demands and
grievances were vague, but to them this was a positive, not a negative.[3]

One might wonder why a movement like this would spread across
the US and the globe. Simply put, the Occupy Movement had an inge-
nious political slogan that tapped into people's beliefs. The slogan was
"We are the 99%"—a clear reference to the idea that the richest and most
powerful 1 percent of people control the world, politically, economically,
and otherwise. The other 99 percent live in the world controlled by the
1 percent. Such vagueness is a positive because anyone who feels that
life is outside of their control can identify with the slogan and the Occupy Movement. Long-time labor writer Michael Yates claims that "[t]he
imprecise nature of political slogans is a virtue. Actual political programs
do not derive from words alone but from the balance of class forces that
exist at a particular point in time. What slogans do is clarify the most
basic political cleavages; they help people develop the mindset most suited
to active participation in whatever struggles are at hand." Yates goes on
to argue that "[w]hether we speak of income or wealth, power resides
in the households of the 1%. They own our workplaces and control our
labor. They construct nearly every aspect of society—government, media,
schools, culture—to maintain and increase their dominance over us. What
the slogan, 'We are the 99%' has done is bring power into the open and
help change the political landscape."[4]

This feeling that 1 percent of the population dominated society
resonated greatly with the public because the Occupy Movement protests came on the heels of the global economic crisis, bank bailouts, and

austerity policies in many countries in an attempt to cure a country's economic woes. Many people felt the 99 percent were being forced to pay the price of the excesses of the 1 percent. Moreover, the 1 percent was not being punished—they had caused the economic crisis, caused banks to incur astronomical debt, but only in rare cases did politicians hold the 1 percent accountable for their "crimes."

The slogan "We are the 99%" and the laundry list of grievances galvanized widespread support across the globe, but at the same time because the list of demands was so vague, the practical impact of the movement was limited. While people felt a sense of solidarity in being part of the protest and being one of the 99-percenters, that sense of solidarity was limited. As Sara Ahmed eloquently stated, "[s]olidarity does not assume that our struggles are the same struggles, or that our pain is the same pain, or that our hope is for the same future. Solidarity involves commitment, and work, as well as the recognition that even if we do not have the same feelings, or the same lives, or the same bodies, we do live on common ground."[5] The Occupy Movement protesters and its supporters encompassed almost all of this, but a shared vision and sharp focus on what should be done was lacking.

Moreover, the lack of leadership was problematic. Writing for *Wired*, Quinn Norton, who visited fourteen Occupy Movement protests across America, noted at the New York city protest, as the general assembly "had no way to reject force, over time it fell to force. Proposals won by intimidation; bullies carried the day. What began as a way to let people reform and remake themselves had no mechanism for dealing with them when they didn't. It had no way to deal with parasites and predators. It became a diseased process, pushing out the weak and quiet it had meant to enfranchise until it finally collapsed when nothing was left but predators trying to rip out each other's throats."[6] I will return below to the issue of a lack of leadership and decentralized structure in social movements.

Eventually, in November 2011, the New York City police forcefully removed the protestors from Zuccotti Park. Police also forcefully removed protesters in many cities worldwide, with the police response in Oakland being particularly vicious. Over time, other Occupy Movement sites across the globe faded away. Partly because of such a wide array of people sleeping outside, there had been issues. Norton wrote that "[o]ccupiers were often poor, struggling, sick, even at times deranged, but in every camp I stayed in the residents poured huge effort into trying to keep things clean, under the circumstances. . . . The tents were each their own world once you were inside. Some of them were perfect little homes, some were shooting galleries stained with feces. Most were just what a tent looks like when you're trying to live in it." The Occupy Movement was not built to last, nor could it last, but then again it was not meant to. Indeed, the *Adbusters* team who initially formed the Occupy Wall Street protest had planned on suggesting that the physical occupation of parks and the like end in December 2011.[7]

While the Occupy Movement in its occupation form could not last—and one could argue that it led to no meaningful change—what it did do was galvanize people to the idea that a certain segment of the population had (and still has) too much power. In the fight against austerity, and neoliberalism more generally, such galvanization is invaluable. Ideas are important.

In addition, since the initial occupations around the world, the Occupy Movement has made practical improvements in people's lives, such as through Rolling Jubilee's Strike Debt program. The Rolling Jubilee involves "Occupy Wall Street activists fundraising to buy cut price debt on secondary markets, but then instead of suing for it, simply cancelling it. Donations of over $500,000 have led to millions of dollars worth of debt being written off. Now the movement is contacting all the people they have cancelled the debts of, and telling them that Occupy Wall Street did it." As of January 6, 2015, the Rolling Jubilee had raised $701,317 and abolished $14,734,569.87 in debt from unpaid medical bills and student loans. The Strike Debt movement notes that

> Debt is a tie that binds the 99%. With stagnant wages, systemic unemployment, and public service cuts, we are forced to go into debt for the basic things in life—and thus surrender our futures to the banks. Debt is a major source of profit and power for Wall Street that works to keep us isolated, ashamed, and afraid. Using direct action, research, education, and the arts, we are coming together to challenge this illegitimate system while imagining and creating alternatives. We want an economy in which our debts are to our friends, families, and communities—and not to the 1%.[8]

Thus, while the physical occupation of Zuccotti Park and other parks, squares, and other locations around the world has ended, the slogan "We are the 99%" endures, as does the notion that the richest and most powerful 1 percent of people have too much power. In addition, while the Strike Debt initiative is unlikely to undermine the capitalist system, it has helped thousands of the poor and vulnerable struggling under a mountain of debt. And this is a very good thing.

15M in Spain

As noted in Chapter 2, the Indignados movement, or by its better known name, 15M, formed in 2011 and was largely compromised of students, the unemployed, and underemployed young people. Following in the footsteps of the uprising across Egypt, 15M occupied public spaces and engaged in mass protests against austerity. Like the Occupy Movement, 15M grew from somewhat modest beginnings. In addition to drawing inspiration from the Egypt uprising, the formation of 15M was triggered by youth involvement in the September 29, 2010, general strike. The strike "saw the involvement of a layer of youth outside the majority union structures in local assemblies that organised pickets and direct action. Platforms against the cuts continued to exist in some localities after the strike, mainly sustained by the anti-capitalist left." In addition, the movement was galvanized by the "publication of the much heralded short book by veteran French activist Stéphane Hessel *Indignez-vous!* at the end of 2010 and the 'Sinde Law' (associated with the minister for culture Ángeles González-Sinde), passed in January 2011 with the aim of stopping illegal internet downloads," as well as the 250,000-strong youth protest in Lisbon in March. The protest in Lisbon led to the formation of *Jóvenes Sin Futuro* (Youth Without a Future) in Madrid, which held a protest under the slogan, "Without a job, without a home, without a pension: without fear" that saw five thousand people take part. As the protest was much larger than expected, and following an also larger-than-expected protest against austerity by trade unions in Barcelona, *Jóvenes Sin Futuro*, in conjunction with *Democracia Real Ya* (Real Democracy Now; as its name implies, members wanted electoral reform and the elimination of corruption), decided to hold a protest on May 15 in the lead-up to the Spanish general election. May 15 saw twenty thousand people protest in Barcelona and fifteen thousand in Madrid. Neither the organizers nor the political establishment had expected such a large turnout. As Andy Durgan and Joel Sans note,

> The following day there was a small occupation of the central Puerta del Sol in protests over arrests on the Madrid demonstration. When the participants were violently evicted by

the police, hundreds responded to calls for solidarity and the first camp was established. By the end of the week there were an estimated 120 such camps round the country. Daily mass assemblies ran the camps, with decisions, in most cases, being taken on the basis of consensus. Commissions were established to organise everything from food, medical assistance and cleaning through to legal advice, the spreading of the movement and the drawing up of demands. The numbers involved were far greater than any previous local assemblies or platforms: in Barcelona and Madrid there were meetings of over 10,000.[9]

Like the Occupy Movement, 15M had no official leadership and no political agenda. Initially, 15M was hostile to the union movement, especially its collaboration with the government. Nonetheless, many rank-and-file workers were part of the protests, and 15M called for a general strike, not a strike led by unions. While such a strike did not occur, 15M "coordinated online campaigns and targeted specific issues, such as banking and electoral reform. 15-M is about a bottom-up, networked approach, in direct contrast to the vertical power structures of the main parties that have dominated Spanish political life since 1978." Essential to 15M is the power of social networking. Initially, the movement used Facebook and Twitter to spread its message. However, as the movement grew, other forms of communication were necessary. It began using Mumble, "an open-source voice chat application," to hold meetings in a particular city, region, and/or nationally; "Vibe, an anonymous broadcast messaging service used to announce dates and times of actions; and Bambuser, a live video technology . . . has been adopted to stream video of people and events that matter to the movement."[10]

In June, the majority of camps were voluntarily disbanded (although the police forcibly evicted the protesters at some sites), as the activists understood the camps were not self-sustainable long term, and it was more important to form links with local communities away from city centers. As in the Occupy Movement protests across the US, the participatory democracy of the 15M Movement has limitations, especially with a large group of disparate people. Writing in *Counterpunch*, Peter Gelderloos states:

Ironically, while demanding 'real democracy now,' the protestors recreated a new democracy, just like the old democracy, much sooner than they had anticipated. Everywhere that the occupations grew to include more than a thousand people, the central assemblies that were used as a supreme organizational body became totally inoperative. Even the most experienced moderators to come out of the European antiglobalization movement had to admit that in the assemblies, real debate and meaningful consensus was impossible. Nonetheless, they continued to try to address the situation with more and better moderation.

Gelderloos goes on to note that the "central principles of the Real Democracy platform, such as nonviolence, were imposed, sometimes by force, and shielded from debate; minorities were silenced; people in certain committees were accused of corruption; the ability to make populist speeches and sway the masses outweighed real debate; people with critical views or ideas falling outside the dominant progressive-democratic ideology were excluded, silenced, or even ejected, while in some cities fascists were allowed to participate in the name of unity."[11] I discuss below whether participatory democracy is necessarily a good aspect for social movements and trade unions to embrace.

One can question the success of the 15M movement, as its initial protests did not sway voters who elected the center-right People's Party to office in the Spanish national elections. Political analyst Miguel Murado claimed that "[p]olitical movements have to be measured against their demands, and I can't think of a single measure the government has taken or the opposition proposed that meets their demands. So you have to say it's a failure. . . . It doesn't matter if they gather 70,000 people or 100,000—if there's no impact, there's no impact." Likewise, an article in *The Economist* argued that "[t]he indignants, who claim to have no leaders, are themselves unclear what they stand for. Their assembly-based, consensus-seeking debates are painfully slow. Manuel Chaves, a minister, likens their meetings to those of the bickering Peoples' Front of Judea in the Monty Python film 'Life of Brian.'" However, like the Occupy Movement, 15M tapped into people's thoughts that the austerity and suffering they were enduring was wrong. Opinion polls saw up to 80 percent of Spaniards supporting the 15M Movement.[12] Moreover, 15M had developed a plan similar to the Occupy Movement's Strike Debt initiative.

Following the abandonment of the camp protests, 15M began working closely with Plataforma de Afectados por la Hipoteca (Platform for People Affected by Mortgages; PAH) to help people who lost their jobs due to the economic crisis and were unable to meet their mortgage payments.

In many countries, if people are unable to pay their mortgage they will simply abandon their property to the banks (as happened in Detroit, for example). However, under Spanish law, abandoning your home does not cancel your debt. PAH and 15M have prevented over eight hundred homes from being foreclosed. 15M has also been helpful in creating a network so the group can more effectively help those in need. In addition, PAH and 15M "have managed to get some banks, such as Bankinter, to accept the solution [the bank forgiving debt in exchange for a person's property] to all mortgage loans, while Banco Santander has offered a three-year mortgage payment suspension for clients who have lost their jobs or families who have seen a 25-percent drop in monthly income." While it may not seem like much, and its initial protests had limited effect at best in overcoming austerity, the 15M Movements partnership with PAH have benefited thousands. In the end, the 15M Movement, like the Occupy Movement, has made a difference. As Jaime Ferri, professor of political science at of Madrid's Complutense University claimed, "[o]f course the movement has achieved some things. . . . The most significant of which is that there is a new collective awareness of the importance of the fact that a large part of the population is demonstrating its discontent and taking action."[13]

Moreover, while it may not have initially had a political platform and was unable to prevent the election of the right-wing People's Party, the 15M Movement has begun to have a large impact on electoral politics via the political party Podemos. We will look at the formation and rise of Podemos later in the chapter.

Quebec Student Movement

The Quebec student movement has a long history of militancy and strike action, beginning in the 1960s with the "quiet revolution." The quiet revolution demanded that a majority of francophone students be able to go to university. In the past, francophone students were unlikely to go to university because of the costs involved. The uprising was successful in that the "government created nine new university campuses and a free college system that was intended to open up higher education to those not part of the political and economic elite or clergy who then dominated Quebec. While tuition was initially justified to help cover the costs of the expanding campuses, students believed it would eventually be phased out." Since then, there have been numerous strikes to ensure that tuition charges do not rise, and also to ensure education remain free. In contrast to countries such as the UK and Australia, where the student unions are lobbying groups representing students, in Quebec, the student unions are more akin to that of a trade union. Every student "is a member of the union and pays dues, and there is a closed shop; by law you have to certify a student union in Québec. So student unions are not just action groups. This organizational model forms the basis for a fairly stable and institutionalized movement which gives the student union financial autonomy, and provides the basis for certain forms of direct democracy."[14]

In March 2011, Jean Charest's Liberal government proposed to increase student tuition by 75 percent—an extra $1,625 ($325 per year for a five-year course). Under the proposed changes, tuition would increase from approximately $2,168 to $3,793. The government argued that the increase in tuition would result in more money flowing to universities and that 35 percent of the new revenue would go to student aid. In addition, the government hoped that an increase in tuition would limit student influence on higher education policy. The universities were in favor of the tuition increase, and indeed were hoping for a further increase than was announced. Not surprisingly, the majority of students were against the proposed policy. For them, it was not simply about a fee increase, but also about the austerity measures being imposed throughout the region. A student union spokesperson argued that the government's "strategy to try and destroy the welfare system in Quebec, to destroy the public services, the idea of the tuition freeze and public education system is very central." In November 2011, approximately 200,000 students went out on a two-day strike across the Quebec region, with 20,000 of them marching to Premier Jean Charest's office. Likewise, another 36,000 post-secondary students went out on strike in February 2012. While the second strike was considerably smaller than the November 11 protest, more large-scale protests were to follow.[15] This was due in large part to the formation of Coalition Large de l'Association pour une Solidarité Syndicale Étudiante (CLASSE).

CLASSE formed in December 2011 with the express purpose of preventing the increase in tuition. Not only did CLASSE demand no increase in tuition but also claimed there should be free education with a tax on banks covering the loss of revenue. CLASSE eventually grew to have sixty-five local affiliates and 100,000 members, or 25 percent of Quebec's student population. CLASSE's first major demonstration occurred on March 22, 2012, and included a march that stretched 1.8 kilometers and involved over ten thousand students and their supporters, a sit-in at a government office, and a protest in downtown Montreal. Rather than respond to the students, the government claimed that the tuition increase was inevitable and would improve the region's universities. From the March 22, protest the movement grew to a peak of hundreds of thousands of students and their supporters, and included students going out on strike and not attending classes.[16]

In late April, the government slightly amended the policy, proposing that, among a range of measures, the tuition increase would be spread over seven years rather than the initially proposed five. The student groups rejected the attempted compromise. One student leader claimed that "Mr. Charest was not talking to students, he was talking to Quebec's population trying to convince them that he wanted to solve the crisis, but he still refuses to talk about the amount of tuition fee—it's still a 75 per cent tuition hike." Likewise, the CLASSE spokesperson noted, "I think it's probably closer of an insult than an offer because Mr. Charest was at a very arrogant tone. He was telling the students to go back in class, that his offer was reasonable." In response, Premier Charest stated, "[w]e said from the beginning that we would listen, we would work, we would sit down and examine the whole framework of polices with regards to post-secondary education. . . . We are maintaining the increase in tuition fees. It's $1,625. It's over seven years instead of five."[17]

Aiding the students was support from the local community and the labor movement. The students sought alliances with Rio Tinto workers locked out from their jobs, public sector workers who were facing their own austerity battle, and many others. While a number of union federations agreed with CLASSE's proposal for a joint strike involving students and workers, the union bureaucracy prevented such a strike from occurring, and the militant rank-and-file lacked the support to push the issue. Nonetheless, many workers marched and protested with the students. As for the support in the local community, writing in *The Nation*, Jesse Rosenfeld described that in Montreal "people of all ages don red squares—the symbol of solidarity with the strike, originating from French expression of being 'squarely in the red' financially. The balconies of the city's distinctive townhouses are dotted with red banners, and nightly pots-and-pans protests ring out through Montreal neighborhoods as they bring thousands into the streets." In addition to alliances with sections of the labor movement and local community, benefitting the students was that they were united. When the government attempted to sideline CLASSE from negotiations, the other student groups responded by walking out of the negotiations until CLASSE was included in the dialogue.[18]

In an attempt to stop the student protests, on May 18 the government passed a law making it illegal to hold a rally involving more than fifty people unless the protesters consulted with police on the planned route and timing. It was up to the police to agree to the route, and they could modify it if they so chose. The bill also banned any protest held "within 50 meters of a college or university." In response, the students and their supporters staged a five-thousand-strong person protest without informing the police. This led to approximately three hundred people being arrested. In addition, a major event was planned to be held on May 22 to mark one hundred days of protest. When the police demanded to know the route of the march, the student leaders sent the police a "route outline that looked decidedly like a fist holding a middle finger aloft." While one might call this action childish, it clearly demonstrated that the students would not be beholden to a law designed to stop them from protesting and thereby ease the pressure on the Charest government.[19]

The May 22 protest went ahead. In a mass showing of civil disobedience, approximately 400,000 people protested across the Quebec region. While approximately 1,000 people were arrested, the mass protest clearly demonstrated that the students were not going to quit. The CLASSE spokesperson claimed, "[i]f the government wants to apply its law, it will have a lot of work to do. That is part of the objective of the protest today, to underline the fact that this law is absurd and inapplicable." In response, Quebec's public safety minister argued that many "[o]ther societies with rights and freedoms to protect have found it reasonable to impose certain constraints, first of all to protect protesters, and also to protect police."[20] Despite the law, students were not going to stop protesting, and the government seemed powerless to stop them from doing so, as the support the students were receiving was not abating. The government thus decided on a new tactic.

Charest called for a general election on September 4. He was hoping that an electoral victory would help him and his government in its fight against the student movement. He was mistaken. The Liberal Party lost power, with a 10 percent swing against them. Despite a swing against them also, Parti Québécois won the election and "the leftist party, Québec solidaire, increased its share of the vote to over 6 per cent, becoming the fourth parliamentary party and gaining an extra parliamentary seat." The incoming government eliminated most of the anti-protest legislation and eventually modified the tuition increases by making any increase in line with inflation. Thus, while the student unions did not attain all of their demands, they achieved a partial victory. As we have seen, in the fight against austerity measures, even partial victories are few and far between. The student movement succeeded because it had broad support throughout the community and engaged in effective civil disobedience. In addition, the students were successful because they were militant and did not rely on trying to elect a political party to overturn the fees. As Seymour argues:

> Inevitably, fighting and winning tactical battles on the parliamentary terrain was a crucial part of their victory. The existence of a radical left, anti-neoliberal party, *Québec solidaire*, helped polarise the parliamentary battle more to the left than would have otherwise been the case. To this extent, the battle was fought both inside and outside the state. But the starting point for the protesters was to work on the terrains where they were strongest, not where they had least strategic advantage, and this meant emphasising their disruptive capacity."[21]

In Quebec, the students' battle against austerity continues. In partnership with unions, they have been protesting against austerity policies implemented by the Liberal government, who returned to power in April 2014. In the fight against austerity, partial victories (tuition fees are currently $2,550, well below the $3,793 proposed by the Charest government) such as this must be celebrated, as applying austerity policies as a cure to economic woes remains the prevalent strategy in many countries and regions.

Podemos Party in Spain

As we have seen, a number of high-profile social movements have arisen in the fight against austerity. Unfortunately, like the majority of unions, these movements have been generally unsuccessful in forcing governments to overturn or modify austerity policies. However, despite the lack of success of movements thus far, there is another potential way to overcome such policies—if an anti-austerity party is elected to office. On the surface, electing a true left-wing anti-austerity political party to office would be the "easiest" way to overcome austerity. As we saw in the previous two chapters, both the union movement in the UK and the US believe that by electing the Labour Party and the Democrats, respectively, austerity will be overcome. While I have criticized the idea that either party would in fact abandon austerity as the dominant economic policy, anti-austerity political parties are now rising up in Europe to contest the notion that there is no alternative. As I highlighted in Chapter 3, in the UK, with the main political parties wedded to austerity, it is the far-right political party UKIP that has begun to adopt some economic populist measures in an attempt to gain increased support. Now, whether the party believes in such measures is open to debate, but by adopting them it has helped UKIP electorally, especially in gaining working-class support. In contrast to UKIP, in Spain and Greece it is left-wing parties that are benefitting the most by embracing anti-austerity as an economic platform.

As noted in Chapter 2, Podemos formed in Spain in 2014 and registered only 0.2 percent support from the electorate. However, in the May European elections, ther Party received 1.2 million votes and managed to elect five of its members to the European Parliament. If such an impressive showing for a new party was not enough, by December 2014 Podemos overtook both the Socialists and the People's Party in the polls. Among Podemos's main platforms is an end to corruption; ceasing mass privatization of government-owned assets, especially in relation to the health and education system; and eliminating austerity.

Podemos has its roots in the 15M Movement. A number of university lecturers decided to participate in the mass media to heighten class consciousness. The 15M Movement was a perfect opportunity to do so: "Its online programme of political debate, *La Tuerka*, became the mouthpiece of the 15-M, providing daily coverage of what was happening in the squares. More importantly, it served as a launch pad for its charismatic presenter, Pablo Iglesias, onto national television. Iglesias, a political science teacher at the Complutense, rapidly acquired fame and notoriety with his inflexible, albeit didactic, confrontations on popular chat shows with representatives of the political establishment." In January 2014, the group decided to form a political party to contest the European elections. Within three days the group received more than fifty thousand signatures in support of the new political party.[22]

Apart from *La Tuerka*, Podemos has further roots from 15M. Writing in *Newsweek*, Dan Hancox notes that following the abandonment of the camps across Spain, "small groups continued to meet on Saturday mornings in town squares, campaigning on local issues, organising to help families facing evictions, or struggling to feed themselves. This grassroots organisation gave Podemos a ready-made, experienced activist base, and the electoral success in May saw many more local circulos (circles) start up, even in the smallest of villages. Some are organised by neighbourhood, others by political or professional theme: there are circulos for feminism, arts and culture, disabilities, public health and so on." There are circulos across Spain and even in other cities throughout Europe, such as in London and Manchester. However, it would be mistaken to assume that Podemos has a decentralized structure. In October 2014, Podemos held a citizens assembly in part to formulate the structure of the party. Pablo Iglesias and his allies wanted a centralized power structure with the party headed by one leader. As he told the assembly, "You don't defeat [Prime Minister] Rajoy or [PSOE leader] Pedro Sanchez with three general secretaries . . . 'only one.'" In contrast, the circulos wanted the party to have three leaders, with the circulos having power to formulate Podemos policy. Drawing largely on the popularity of Iglesias, his platform overwhelmingly won the support of Podemos members. This is not to argue that Podemos is a top-down party, but the central leadership has much more power than the circulos and ordinary members. As described by Barriere, Durgan and Robson, the Party's structure is as follows:

> the general secretary chooses an executive of 15, while a citizens' council, a political leadership consisting of 62 people, would be elected online by all those listed as "members" on the basis of both individual candidates and open lists which could be voted for as a block or separately. The council in turn would endorse the executive and interpret the mandates of a national assembly that meets every three years. While the general secretary can call assemblies at any level and propose or remove members of the executive at will, in order for the membership to do the same, 25 percent of those registered, over sixty thousand people at the time of writing, or 30 percent of the circles, need to support such a move.

Thus, while the circulos have some power, the citizens council and, moreover, the general secretary have the majority of power in Podemos.[23]

In addition to criticism that Podemos has moved to a centralized structure, there are concerns that the party's political platform has moved away from the Left. One can get a sense of the direction Podemos is heading from a November 2014 policy paper. The paper abandons many of Podemos's policies it campaigned on for the May 2014 European elections. Podemos no longer wants a "basic universal wage for all citizens (instead there will be more state aid to those in poverty), the nationalisation of 'strategic sectors of the economy,' the lowering of the retirement age to 60 (instead it will drop from 67 back to 65) and, what was the centrepiece in May, the cancellation of the Spanish state's debt. Instead the debt will be 'renegotiated' from the position of a defence of 'national interests.'" In regards to debt, while previously Podemos was arguing that the European Union and the IMF should "forgive" the debts, now Podemos is arguing that Spain should repay the debt, but the repayment system should be renegotiated. Moreover, while the party once called for the working week to be thirty-five hours, this is no longer Podemos policy. The policy paper further argues that there will have to be "costs and sacrifices" due to the previous government's economic policies and obligations under political agreements, such as to the European Union. Podemos has also been criticized for allegedly having a "male bias," as its grassroots elections in January 2015 for leadership positions in the party led to the election of men in the top position in eight of the ten largest Spanish cities. That *The Guardian* reported on this demonstrates that Podemos is of interest to readers of the paper worldwide, and even seemingly insignificant internal party events become headline news.[24]

Podemos should have more females in leadership positions. However, this is not unique to Podemos. The majority of political parties should have more women in positions of power. Now, whether one should criticize Podemos for this turn from the far-left is open to debate. However, the Podemos leadership obviously believes that the best chance for it to be elected and implement meaningful change is to appeal to more centrist voters. Such a strategy was reinforced following the July 2015 Greece bailout referendum (see below). Iglesias stated that the referendum result was "good news for Europeans and Greek citizens. . . . The people of Greece have said they want change, they support a government who says that things can be done in a different way." However he also made it clear that whatever the outcome in Greece, Podemos would not consider leading Spain out of the euro or any other drastic measures. He noted that Podemos "have a great friendship with Syriza, but luckily, Spain is not Greece. . . . We're an economy with much more weight in the euro-zone, we're a country with a stronger administration and with a better economic situation. The circumstances are different and I think it makes no sense to draw parallels."[25] Time will tell if the Podemos strategy is the best approach. Nonetheless, Podemos's policy platform, with its basis in Scandinavian and social democracy political ideology, is still to the Left of the "mainstream" political parties in Spain, and a lot further to the Left of any mainstream political party in the UK and the US.

By July 2015, Podemos was leading in the polls, but there has been a history of newly formed political parties surging in the polls, yet come election time, people go with the political parties they know. Indeed, in the lead-up to the December General election the Party began to fade in popularity. By mid-November Podemos was projected to finish a distant fourth in the election behind the ruling Popular Party, Ciudadanos (Citizens) a kind of Podemos of the center-right, and the PSOE. One potential reason for the decline of Podemos is that the European Union forced the Greek people to accept more austerity irrespective of their wishes (see below). Pablo Bustinduy, who leads international relations for the party, claims the EU "were so harsh on Greece in order to teach Spain a lesson. . . . Certainly what has happened in Greece has been difficult for our voters because the message that Europe wanted to project is: 'There is no alternative, there is nothing else you can do to solve these problems.' "[26]

The rise of Podemos gives the Spanish people a real choice between parties that have continued to follow the austerity orthodoxy despite very little improvement in the economy, and a party that despite its move away from the far-left is still anti-austerity. In the end, irrespective of what party the Spanish people vote for, having a real choice is a good in itself. Of course, whether Podemos would have been allowed to implement anti-austerity policies and followed through with its promises if elected is another matter. This leads us to Greece and Syriza's rise to power.

Syriza's Rise to Power in Greece
and Its Capitulation to Austerity and the EU

While Podemos has been an "overnight sensation," the Greek left-wing political party Syriza has had a slightly longer journey to the political mainstream. As noted in Chapter 2, in 2004, its first year of contesting a general election, Syriza received 3.3 percent of the vote (six seats), while in 2007 it received 5.04 percent of the vote. Even by 2009, only 4 percent of the electorate supported the party. However, by the 2012 election, Syriza became the main opposition party, receiving 27 percent of the vote (seventy-two seats in Parliament). Moreover, at the 2014 Greece European Parliament elections, Syriza finished first, gaining 26.6 percent of the vote (six seats). This was the first time that a far-left party finished first in any election in Greece. The party also did very well in local elections in 2014.

Syriza formed via a coalition of ecologist groups, socialist parties, and euro-communists. If elected, it promised a "radical agenda." Its policies include increasing the "minimum wage [to 751 euros], reintroduce[ing] collective bargaining, and repeal[ing] the measures that have led to economic collapse and a humanitarian crisis. It will ask for a substantive haircut of the debt to make it viable—at the start of the crisis, the debt was 120% of GDP[;] after four years of austerity it stands at 175%—and will peg repayment of the rest on economic growth." In addition, Syriza's policies include higher taxes for the rich, the most recent property tax being abolished, 300,000 new jobs, a new national development bank, and the reintroduction of public radio and television stations closed by the previous Greek government.[27] Simply put, if Syriza implemented all or even some of these policies it would be a radical departure from what Greece has experienced since successive governments have applied austerity policies in an attempt to cure the country's economic woes and to receive bailout packages from the EU and the IMF.

The opportunity for Syriza to potentially govern came earlier than expected. In December 2014, the Samaras government was unable to muster enough votes in Parliament to elect its preferred candidate, Stavros Dimas, a former European commissioner, as president. Dimas needed 180 votes from the three-hundred-seat Parliament to get elected. However, he could gain only 168 votes. Under Greek law, if a president cannot be elected, the parliament is forced to dissolve within ten days and a general election to be held within thirty days. Greece Prime Minister Antonis Samaras stated, "I will go to the president of the republic to request snap polls as early as possible on 25 January. It is the hour of democracy, which means truth and responsibility, not populism." He further noted, "We did whatever we could for a president to be elected by today's parliament and to avert early elections which hold serious dangers and which the majority of Greeks don't want . . . unfortunately a minority of 132 parliamentarians are dragging the country to snap polls." In contrast, the leader of Syriza, Alexis Tsipras, claimed, "In a few days the Samaras government, which pillaged the country, will belong to the past, as will the memoranda of austerity."[28]

Not surprisingly, the financial markets reacted negatively to the failure to elect a new president and moreover to the prospect of a Syriza victory. Immediately following the announcement that there would be new elections, the Greek stock exchange fell by as much as 10 percent, while the interest rate on Greece's three-year debt increased to over 12 percent. There were also major concerns that Greece would default on its loans—20 billion euros were scheduled to be repaid in 2015—as the bailout funds extended only until February, 2015. In addition, there was a fear that a Syriza-led Greece would abandon the euro and, in effect, the European Union. However, Syriza's shadow finance minister, Euclid

Tsakalotos, argued that the "[s]olution to Greece's problems lies within the European context but the first thing we will say is that the programme has failed because it was badly planned and didn't see the pitfalls that were coming. . . . Then we will address the priorities of austerity and debt." Tsakalotos also repeatedly stated that, if elected, Syriza would keep the euro. Nonetheless, the German finance minister Wolfgang Schäuble forcefully stated that no matter who was elected in Greece, the government must abide by the bailout conditions: "The tough reforms are bearing fruit and there is no alternative to them." For Schäuble, the Greek GDP growing by 1.9 percent in 2013, after losing almost 30 percent in just over the five years preceding, is "bearing fruit." To put it another way, the size of the Greek economy was $341.6 billion in 2009. In 2013 it had shrunk to $241.72 billion.[29] Of course, people have different definitions of progress, but to claim that austerity in Greece is bearing fruit is equivalent to taking solace in one remaining apple tree after a whole orchard has been destroyed.

While Syriza potentially remains committed to the euro and the European Union, its leader Alexis Tsipras was consistently inconsistent in the lead-up to the January 25 election. Manfred Ertel and Christoph Schult, writing in *Der Spiegel*, note that Tsipras "says one thing, at others something entirely different. His contradictory positions are also a product of the fact that Syriza was only formed as a formal party year and a half ago, the product of an electoral alliance among highly diverse left-wing splinter groups. 'Our party as a whole wants to see the country in the euro,' Tsipras has said, for example. But he qualified that statement by adding: 'on the condition that social cohesion isn't threatened.' On another occasion, he said the euro was 'not a fetish' and that Greece was 'nobody's hostage,' whatever that might mean." In addition, the leader of the left-wing faction of Syriza, Panagiotis Lafazanis, claimed that Syriza wants Greece "to exit the euro and a complete break with the totalitarian EU." The inconsistency was also evident in regards to Greece's debt:

> Tsipras has spoken of freeing "Europe from the straightjacket of debts" through a further radical debt haircut and a moratorium on debt repayments for euro-zone crisis countries. He is calling for a European debt conference like the one in London in 1953 that was called in order to address the debt problems of postwar Germany. But other comments have been less statesman-like. Such as Tsipras' promise that he would simply

> "tear up" existing agreements on austerity measures and loans
> and cease making interest payments overnight.[30]

Certainly it would be preferable for Syriza to have a consistent policy platform; however, what the party and Tsipras were doing was no different than most political parties across the globe. They were trying to appeal to as many people as possible and hope that people hear only what they want to hear. Moreover, the strategy was working. Syriza was consistently ahead in all polls in the lead-up to the election. In mid-January, Syriza had a 4 percent lead over Samaras's New Democracy party. Political pundits were no longer arguing whether Syriza would form a new government, but how large a majority the Party would have.

In addition, the threat of Syriza gaining power led to a policy shift by Samaras and his New Democracy party. New Democracy initially campaigned on a strategy of fear if Syriza was elected. However, such a strategy had no effect on reducing Syriza's lead in the polls. As a result, two weeks before the January 25 election, Samaras promised that if re-elected New Democracy would ease the austerity measures. He stated, "[t]here won't be any further pension and wage cuts. . . . The next breakthrough in our growth plan includes tax cuts across the board which can happen gradually, step by step." Samaras also vowed to reduce the rate of the newly introduced property tax. Of course, Samaras did not claim that if re-elected his government would raise wages and pensions, but he did promise businesses that a New Democracy government would gradually reduce the corporate tax rate from 26 percent to 15 percent.[31]

However, after years of austerity, the Greek people did not believe Samaras and his New Democracy party would truly abandon austerity policies. In a stunning triumph, especially considering that the overwhelming majority of mainstream media was against it, Syriza secured 36.3 percent (an increase of 9.4 percent over the previous general election) of the vote to win 149 out of a possible 300 seats in Parliament, just two seats short of an absolute majority. New Democracy secured 76 seats (29.7 percent of the vote—a 1.9 percent decline), with Golden Dawn coming in third, with 17 seats (6.3 percent—a 0.6 percent decline). After years of suffering, the Greek people had finally had enough of austerity. In a potentially ominous note for the stability of the government, Syriza decided to form a coalition with the right-wing Independent Greeks Party, which secured 13 seats in Parliament. The Independent Greeks are a nationalist, xenophobic party; the only thing they have in common with Syriza is that both are anti-austerity.[32] At the very least, the coalition government with the Independent Greeks Party clearly demonstrates that overturning austerity is Syriza's primary goal. In the end, at the very least, outside of a war, it is difficult to imagine a future for Greece as painful as during the austerity years. The Greek people seemingly showed the world that there is an alternative to austerity.

For the suffering that the Greek people have endured, one would have hoped that the incoming government lived up to its promises and the EU, IMF, and international creditors allow the Greek government to follow an austerity-free economic policy. Of course, if history is any guide, such a thing will not occur without an almighty struggle. And this is a struggle that those opposing austerity lost.

Following five months of failed negotiations between Syriza and its European lenders, the EU ended Greece's bailout, and the country refused (was unable) to pay a €1.5bn debt installment to the IMF. In response, Tsipras organized a referendum on a proposed new bailout package. The referendum was basically a vote on whether Greece should accept more austerity. In a stunning result, "Greeks voted by more than 60% to 40% in support of the prime minister, spurning the extra austerity demanded—mainly by Germany and the International Monetary Fund—in return for an extension of bailout funds." Greece's finance minister Yanis Varoufakis stated, "[t]oday's no is a big yes to democratic Europe. A no to a vision of the eurozone as a boundless iron cage for its people. From tomorrow, Europe, whose heart tonight beats in Greece, starts healing its wounds, our wounds." However, the wounds were not healed; they were made worse. In response to the referendum, the EU issued an ultimatum: accept even harsher austerity measures or else they would let Greece collapse and expel the country from the single currency bloc. One senior EU official claimed that the EU's response was triggered by Tsipras calling the referendum and encouraging the people to vote no: "He was warned a yes vote would get better terms, that a no vote would be much harder." Rather than fight, Tsipras capitulated and accepted the harsh austerity policies just over one week from the referendum. These austerity measures include up to €50bn of Greek assets that will eventually be privatized so as to "contribute to the recapitalisation of the country's banks," further pension reforms, increases in the VAT, spending cuts, a reduction in the Greek state (which will lead to further job losses), and a general liberalization of the economy. The austerity measures were so great that even the IMF stated that the austerity agreement went too far and argued that the country needed a thirty-year moratorium on its debt or a large write-off.

Nonetheless, the Greek Parliament passed the austerity bill. For Syriza, it came at a cost: there were deep divisions as forty Syriza MPs voted against the bill.[33]

While the Greek Parliament passed the austerity bill, it was a resounding defeat for the people who elected Syriza on an anti-austerity platform and those who voted no in the referendum. Neither Tsipras nor the EU adhered to the wishes of the Greek people. What resulted is indeed a new constitutionalism. Even when people are able to elect a government that goes against the economic orthodoxy, in the end the public are subjected to more of the same. For the Greek people there is seemingly no alternative. Austerity is what the EU wanted, and austerity is what it achieved, democracy be dammed.

Social Movements as the Cure for Austerity Woes?

Electing a political party to government that vows to end austerity policies and actually follows through on those promises, and for those countries who have accepted EU–IMF bailouts to be allowed to live up to the promises—this would be a good way to overcome the current economic orthodoxy. However, such a strategy is not the best option if a country and its people have to suffer through years of crippling austerity before realizing that there is indeed a possible alternative to austerity, as was the case in Greece. One could reasonably suggest that the Greek people would have preferred it if austerity could have been overcome without the years of suffering. Moreover, they may well have preferred that an anti-austerity party was never elected to govern, considering that Syriza failed and was unable to live up to its promises.

At this stage there are no viable left-wing parties in the UK or the US. However, the rise of UKIP demonstrates that there is the potential for a left-wing anti-austerity political party to make a difference. There needs to be a catalyst of change for the general public to believe that there is indeed an alternative to austerity. The success of the Quebec student movement and the high-profile nature of social movement, such as the Occupy Movement and the 15M Movement, have led some to embrace the idea that social movements are best suited to right the wrongs of society, including the challenge of overcoming austerity and neoliberalism.

But this is not a new idea. Indeed, following the wave of protests against international economic institutions beginning with the World Trade Organization protest in Seattle in 1999, it was thought by some that new social movements would be at the forefront of the fight against capitalism, inequality, and the like. Indeed, for all the media that the WTO protests in Seattle received, the coverage was only about 10 percent of that received by the Occupy Movement in the first two months of its existence. For some, social movements are the cure to almost all ills of society. It has been argued that social movements "nurture both heroes and clowns, fanatics and fools. They function to move people beyond their mundane selves to acts of bravery, savagery, and selfless charity. Animated by the injustices, sufferings, and anxieties they see around them, men and women in social movements reach beyond their customary resources of the social order to launch their own crusade against the evils of society. In doing so they reach beyond themselves and become new men and women."[34] While this is obviously hyperbole, the message is clear: social movements can greatly help society, while helping people better themselves.

In her analysis of the Occupy Movement, Jacquelien van Stekelenburg argues that social movements are becoming more popular because

> Solid societal patterns are eroding and we are moving towards a more liquid society . . . in which bonds between people are becoming looser and more flexible. People are becoming increasingly connected as individuals rather than as members of a community or group. Traditional "greedy" institutions such as trade unions and churches which made significant demands on members' time, loyalty and energy . . . are replaced by "light" groups and associations that are loose, easy to join and easy to leave. Despite this process of individualization people are still committed to collective causes. Underlying this . . . people feel a personal sense of political responsibility rather than feeling restricted or obliged to a community or group.[35]

Thus, in this vision, social movements are more preferable to trade unions in the fight against austerity and neoliberalism because even though people still feel a sense of political responsibility they would rather join social movements because one can devote less time to them and people can join and leave such movements easily.

It is certainly easier to join and leave a social movement than a trade union, but because it is easier to leave when times get tough or participants have better things to do, this can result in the social movement fading away rather quickly. Indeed, considering the mass number of people at the height of the Occupy Movement, it did fade quite dramatically. If such a thing happened to a trade union there would be an astonishing number of stories in the mainstream media highlighting the union's demise. Moreover, for those truly committed to a social movement, such as its leaders, the amount of time devoted to it would be comparable to union leaders. The people truly committed to the Occupy Movement were sleeping in public places and were constantly trying to ensure that the protest ran smoothly. This would involve the same amount of time commitment as a union leader when his or her union is out on strike.

Nonetheless, van Stekelenburg argues that "[i]n traditional demonstrations, participants are offered ready-made claims. What the protest is about is decided from the top, as well as who the opponent is, and what the organization forwards as a possible solution. This 'pre-fab frame' ensures sharedness. . . . In the occupy movement this process of consensus mobilization takes place in the open, bottom up rather than top-down fashion." In other words, social movements such as Occupy and 15M are not top-down but bottom-up, in that members decide the goals and everyone can participate and have their voice heard. However, as I highlighted, both the 15M Movement and the Occupy Movement had issues with strong, powerful groups within them dominating the proceedings and pushing their agenda. So much so that dissenting or minority opinions were shouted down and ignored. This is a common problem for social movements that have an absence of leaders. Participatory democracy can certainly be beneficial if everyone contributes equally, or at least relatively equally. If everyone has a say and has their voice heard, this can lead to people being more committed to the cause. This was true for the CTU, which had an expanded bargaining committee to ensure that all sections of the union had a say in the upcoming struggle against the public school system. The difference between the CTU and social movements like 15M and Occupy is that the CTU had a clear leadership structure. The structure ensured that everyone's voice could be heard. Moreover, another problem for social movements is that if there is no clear hierarchy in place it is difficult to deal with drawn-out protests because there is an absence of a clear institutional structure. Likewise, as historian Barbara Epstein argues, "[a]nti-leadership ideology cannot eliminate leaders, but it can lead a movement to deny that it has leaders, thus undermining democratic constraints on those who assume the roles of leadership, and also preventing the formation of vehicles for recruiting new leaders when the existing ones become too tired to continue."[36] These issues were clearly seen with both the Occupy Movement and the 15M Movement. Of course not all social movements have these issues. The Quebec student unions have a clear institutional structure in place, one that is modeled on trade unions, and have clearly defined leaders; this helped them in their long battle against the Quebec government.

Social movements have a major role to play in the fight against austerity and neoliberalism. However, a strong labor movement is *essential* if such economic ideologies are to be overcome. This is clearly understood by political parties, as austerity-minded governments continually try to weaken the influence of organized labor; they understand that a weakened labor movement means the austerity agenda is more easily achieved. Quite simply, as Francis Mulhern argues, the "working class is revolutionary, Marxists have maintained, because of its historically constituted nature as the exploited collective producer within the capitalist mode of production. As the exploited class, it is caught in a systematic clash with capital, which cannot generally and permanently satisfy its needs. As the main producing class, it has the power to halt—and within limits redirect—the economic apparatus of capitalism, in pursuit of its goals. And as the collective producer it has the objective capacity to found a new, non-exploitative mode of production. This combination of interest, power and creative capacity distinguishes the working class from every other social or political force in capitalist society."[37] It is for this reason that governments intent on an austerity path enact antiunion legislation.

This of course does not mean that social movements have no role in the battle against austerity. Indeed, social movements such as Occupy, 15M, and the Quebec student movement demonstrate that austerity and the neoliberal society in a range of countries have negatively affected so many. They have been—and in the case of the Quebec student movement, still are—incredibly important social movements and have generally achieved as much as the labor movement in overcoming austerity. However, as highlighted, just like organized labor outside of the Chicago Teachers Union, social movements have not achieved much at all in the fight against austerity, or neoliberalism more generally. Nonetheless, the Quebec student movement was partly successful, and the Occupy Movement has benefited thousands with its debt elimination program, as has 15M with its anti-foreclosure partnership. 15M also has the opportunity to indirectly make a difference to Spanish politics if Podemos continues its rise. In the end, though, at the time of this writing (late 2015) austerity is still dominant in the United States, United Kingdom, Greece, Ireland, Spain, and many other places around the world. If organized labor, in alliance with social movements, is going to have even a small chance to successfully combat austerity and neoliberalism around the world it needs to change path from its current trajectory.

Social Movement Unionism: A Beacon of Light?

While there are many strategies and theories on how to revive the labor movement, one that has been successful in both the developed world and the developing world is social movement unionism.[38] The most influential definition of social movement unionism comes from long-time labor activist and writer Kim Moody:

> Social movement unionism is one that is deeply democratic, as that is the best way to mobilize the strength of numbers in order to apply maximum economic leverage. It is militant in collective bargaining in the belief that retreat anywhere only leads to more retreats—an injury to one is an injury to all. It seeks to craft bargaining demands that create more jobs and aid the whole class. It fights for power and organization in the workplace or on the job in the realization that it is there that the greatest leverage exists, when properly applied. It is political by acting independently of the retreating parties of liberalism and social democracy, whatever the relations of the union with such parties. It multiplies its political and social power by reaching out to other sectors of the class, be they other unions, neighborhood organizations, or other social movements. It fights for all the oppressed and enhances its own power by doing so.[39]

The crucial aspects of social movement unionism are that there is rank-and-file involvement in all aspects of the union, and union democracy leads to strong progressive unions; unions should organize the unorganized; there needs to be militancy in collective bargaining; unions need alliances with social movements and community groups; the labor movement needs to undertake independent political action; and, most crucially, an injury to one is an injury to all. In other words, unions do not care only about their own and their members' interests but about everything that affects the wider community. This is in sharp contrast to business unions that care only about themselves and so-called bread-and-butter issues such as the wages and working conditions of its membership.

Social movement unionism has been successful throughout the world. For example, the formation of the Congress of South African Trade Unions (COSATU) and its embrace of social movement unionism played a major role in overthrowing the apartheid system. COSATU, which formed in the mid-1980s, fights for everything that affects working people, both in the factory and in the wider community. It launched a living wage campaign for all workers, not just union members; it advocated for full employment, and COSATU workers funded programs for the unemployed.[40]

COSATU has alliances with social movements and community groups. Philip Hirschsohn claimed that "COSATU's Executive Committee encouraged affiliates to strengthen their community ties, arguing that the problems faced at work and in their communities were inextricably linked to the struggle for democratic control of their lives. To address problems with rent, transport and poor living conditions, workers were urged to take the lead in establishing street committees in the townships to build democratic organization, unity and strength."[41]

COSATU does not just concentrate on workplace issues, but makes the link between workplace issues and the economic structure of society. COSATU has an alliance with the African National Congress (ANC). While this alliance has always been somewhat controversial, during the first few years of the alliance, the ANC fought for democracy and for the overthrow of apartheid, which were also among COSATU's goals. Moreover, the first few years under an ANC government was beneficial to the working class: South Africa's Bill of Rights incorporated workers' rights, and the ANC "ratified several international labour conventions."[42]

In the UK, while not necessarily social movement unions, as noted in Chapter 1, the labor movement grew in the 1960s and 1970s because it had alliances with social movements and fought for "nontraditional" labor issues such as nuclear disarmament and saving the environment. The labor movement was also militant and engaged in a number of wildcat strikes. Crucially, organized labor was not self-interested; it cared about everything that affected worker people and their families in the wider community. Indeed, the labor movement was considered *part* of the local community; it was generally understood that what benefited the community benefited unions and its members. This is in sharp contrast to organized labor in the UK and the US today where they are often considered *separate* from the community; there is a perception that what benefits unions and its members do not benefit the wider community. The perception is that unions are only, or primarily, self-interested. Unfortunately, as we have seen, this perception is not aided by unions in a number of cases exhibiting self-interest and putting the interests of the community well behind their own. Such cases have badly damaged the anti-austerity movement.

Social movement unionism has also been successful in the US through fighting not just for increased wages and improved working conditions for its members. For example, in the 1930s and 1940s, the United Electrical Workers (UE) organized the unorganized, forged alliances with community groups, embraced union democracy and rank-and-file involvement in all affairs of the union, and was at the forefront of fighting for all workers and their families. UE membership grew from less than 50,000 in 1939 to 432,000 during the middle of World War II, and by VJ day the UE had 750,000 members. The UE was also more successful than its rival business unions in collective bargaining and improving the well-being of the local community.[43]

As it organized thousands of new members, the UE built links with the local community, another important aspect of social movement unionism. For example, in St. Louis during the 1930s and 1940s, UE Local President William Senter claimed that while the UE was interested in the livelihood of its members, it was also "interested in the effects of their economic status on our community."[44] In other words, when workers received higher wages, this would result in a healthy vibrant local community. The UE Local's belief in the benefit of labor-community alliances helped in a campaign to prevent the Emerson Electrical Company moving its production plant from St. Louis in late 1939 to early 1940. The *St. Louis Star-Times* claimed that the UE "deserves a full measure of credit for its civic spirit and initiative in starting a campaign to keep Emerson . . . from leaving St. Louis. . . . Its attitude, as shown in its literature, is intelligent, sympathetic and constructive." The UE's campaign was eventually successful. As a result, this led to the UE becoming a respected part of the community. This helped the Local during a five-month strike at Century Electric in 1940, which led to a good settlement for the union. Likewise, during World War II, the Local hosted a convention involving UE members, business representatives, and noted St. Louis dignitaries that debated the course industrial relations should take following the end of the war.[45] Simply put, the UE was a valued member of the St. Louis community.

The UE's social movement unionism was also very beneficial to its members. Judith Stepan-Norris and Maurice Zeitlin argued that the

UE contracts were more pro-labour than other unions for the period 1938 to 1955.[46] For example, they concluded that an "examination of the local agreements of each of these Big 3 Internationals [UE, UAW, USWA] reveals that those won by UE Locals were more systematically pro-labor . . . than were the UAW's; the USWA was a distant third in pro-labor provisions. The same pattern appears in these unions' national contracts . . . [T]he agreements between UE and General Electric over the years were consistently pro-labor; those between UAW and General Motors less so; and those between the USWA and Carnegie-Illinois (which became US Steel in late 1950) were the least pro-labour."[47] Thus, the UE's social movement unionism was valuable to its members and the community. It was a win-win for all concerned.

The UE's campaign to keep Stewart-Warner's Chicago plant open in the 1980s demonstrates the extent to which social movement unions are willing to fight for their members and the local community, even when it is a fight they ultimately cannot win. The UE gained certification at the plant in 1980 following dissatisfaction with the International Brotherhood of Electrical Workers.[48] In 1985, following financial difficulties, the UE formed the Coalition to Keep Stewart-Warner Open (CKSWO). Among its members were the UE, as well as a range of other social movements and community groups. In 1986, Stewart-Warner announced that it was to transfer 150 jobs to its Johnson City plant. However, the UE demonstrated that 2,500 jobs were at risk due to the company's financial mismanagement. In 1987, Stewart-Warner merged with the British multinational British Thermoplastics and Rubber. Reverend Jesse Jackson urged all Chicago workers to help in the fight to keep Stewart-Warner in Chicago. He forcefully claimed that the reduction of US jobs was "just another form of economic violence that must be ended the same way we ended racial violence about 20 years ago."[49] However, later that year the company stated that it would fire almost 25 percent of its Chicago workforce in 1988. In June 1989, the company revealed that its Chicago plant may be closed due to high operational costs. Andrew Jonas noted that the "campaign to save Stewart-Warner was built around a well-organized community base and linked to a wider political movement to transform economic policy in Chicago. In this respect, the CKSWO's concerns and goals fed into a broader program of action to protect inner-city neighborhoods from manufacturing displacements. . . . Opportunities to link with political movements beyond the city limits also came up during the course of the struggle."[50] Not only was the UE part of the community struggle to keep the Stewart-Warner plant open, it was part of the community.

In an attempt to keep the plant operational, Stewart-Warner workers agreed to concessions amounting to $2.5 million per year; management viewed the concessions as inadequate. In November 1989, Stewart-Warner announced that it was shutting its Chicago plant and moving to Mexico two years later. However, the Stewart-Warners' Chicago plant remained open until the middle of 1995. During this time, the UE managed to achieve a contract without concessions, as well as raises in wages for the remaining employees.[51] Nevertheless, despite alliances with the local community and politicians, the UE was unable to keep Stewart-Warner's Chicago plant open.

The Stewart-Warner campaign demonstrates that social movement unions will not only fight for its members, but for the community at large. The UE's attempt to keep Stewart-Warner open utilized labor-community alliances, as well as alliances with politicians, and even offered wage concessions because the plant remaining in Chicago would have benefitted workers and the local community. A never-say-die attitude and the belief that an injury to one is an injury to all are needed in the fight against austerity, and neoliberalism more generally. Not every site of struggle will be a success, as was the case at Stewart-Warner, but social movement unions' ideology and unwillingness to simply accept the decline of unions is desperately needed and can potentially help in future battles. This was seen with the UE in St. Louis during the 1940s. It has held especially true as business unionism and alliances with politicians (Labour Party in the UK, Democrats in the US) have left unions docile for decades, in many ways accepting their near demise while holding out hope that pro-labor politicians will one day enact favorable legislation. As we saw in Chapter 1, unions appear to be in a terminal decline and have been unable or unwilling to do enough about it. They talk about change, but they make only minor changes at best, and this is simply not good enough.

In contrast, as I argue in *Unions in Crisis?*, while social movement unionism "is not currently widely practiced in America, it has been successful in a number of situations throughout the world. In America, by fighting for workplace (such as higher wages) and nonworkplace issues (such as adequate childcare or the fight against racism), social . . . [movement] unions have improved society for all. On purely bread-and-butter issues, social . . . [movement] unions have achieved better collective-bargaining agreements than their rival business unions, as well as organized more new workers per capita." In addition to the UE, social movement unionism has been an effective strategy for the Canadian Auto Workers

and the Teamsters: "with respect to wages, working conditions, and organizing new members, social . . . [movement] unions achieve better wages
and working conditions and organize more new members per capita than
their rival business unions. Likewise, the Teamsters achieved its greatest
success in recent years [the 1997 United Parcel Service strike/collective-
bargaining agreement] when it implemented a contract campaign that
had a definite social movement unionism flavor."[52]

In other words, social movement unionism benefits workers in
regards to so-called bread-and-butter issues like wages and working
conditions. It also helps unions because such an approach leads to an
increase in members. Social movement unionism also helps communities, as unions that embrace such an approach care about everything that
affects working people, their families, and their friends in the wider community. Thus, everyone benefits. It is a win for everyone concerned.

As highlighted in the previous chapter, the Chicago Teachers Union
has the hallmarks of a social movement union. The CTU is a democratic
union that encourages rank-and-file involvement throughout the union.
This was demonstrated when the CTU expanded the bargaining committee
to ensure that more sections of the union were represented. The CTU is
clearly militant in collective bargaining. The CTU has alliances with many
social movements and community organizations. Moreover, the CTU does
not care only about wages and working conditions; this was clearly illustrated when the union rejected an arbitrator's report that recommended
teachers should receive higher wages without mention of preventing school
closures. Higher wages would benefit teachers, but would do nothing for
the decaying public schools system if schools were continued to be closed.
The social movement unionism nature of the CTU clearly helped it in its
struggle with the Chicago Public School System, especially as it was seen
as part of the local community. The CTU was partly successful in combat-
ing austerity measures. Conversely, no other union or labor federation in
Greece, Spain, Ireland, the UK, or the US has had any success in the fight
against austerity without agreeing to major concessions.

There is a clear contrast between the social movement unionism
of the CTU and the strategy adopted by the Wisconsin Workers' Movement. Both groups had to battle against politicians determined to impose
austerity measures, and in the case of Scott Walker in Wisconsin, a governor wanting to impose anti-collective-bargaining policies for public sector unions. The CTU did not rely on an electoral strategy. It mobilized
its members and had (and still has) longstanding alliances with social
movements and community groups. The Chicago community generally

supported the CTU. The public did not see the CTU as self-interested, but perceived it as a group that cared about and was part of the local community. In contrast, the Wisconsin Workers' Movement, after initially demonstrating impressive power in militant mass mobilization, settled on an electoral strategy of electing a Democrat as Governor in the hope that he would overturn the public sector collective-bargaining laws. In addition, Wisconsin union leaders were willing to support Walker's austerity cuts as long as his government did not implement antiunion collective-bargaining laws. Such an action was clearly seen by the wider community as self-interested. This was demonstrated in the 2012 Wisconsin recall election: 30 percent of union members voted for Walker, and 48 percent of people living with union members also voted for Walker. The Wisconsin labor movement was unable to convince a sizeable minority of its own members and nearly 50 percent of people living with a union member not to vote Walker. Thus, it was no surprise that 61 percent of nonunion households voted for Walker and his antiunion policies. The CTU cared about its members and the local community, while union leaders in Wisconsin largely cared only about their members. The end result was that the CTU managed to overcome some austerity policies, while the Wisconsin Workers' Movement was unable to overcome austerity policies and antiunion collective-bargaining laws.

Of course, there is no guarantee that social movement unions will continue along a "radical" path. As has happened with other unions and social movements, there is always the chance they will be co-opted. For example, while COSATU's partnership with the ANC was relatively uncontroversial when the ANC was fighting to overthrow apartheid, the same was not true when the ANC rose to political power. Following their election victories, the ANC moved from a radical left-wing party to one that began embracing neoliberalism. Rather than question their alliance, COSATU accepted the ANC's rightward turn, thus implicitly supporting the implementation of neoliberal policies in South Africa.[53] A union adopting a social movement unionism strategy is no guarantee it will remain militant. However, through having an active and mobilized rank-and-file, social movement unions are less likely to be co-opted than are business unions because the rank-and-file in social movement unions is more likely to hold leadership accountable. However, as the COSATU example demonstrates, even with a mobilized and active rank-and-file, the chance that social movement unions will abandon their ideals always remains.

Likewise, there is no guarantee that social movement unionism will succeed where other theories or strategies have failed. As we have seen, both the UE and CTU, while partly successful in their struggles against Stewart-Warner and the Chicago Public School System, respectively, were unable to secure lasting victories. In the end, there is a limit to what one union can do by itself. Moreover, as Ian Robinson argues: social movement unions often take a militant approach, and this means that

> government and employers often target them with higher levels of repression than rival union types. We have seen this dynamic recur in U.S. labor history, and the result was clear: SMUs were marginalized except during the great economic crises of the 1930s. The lesson, it seems, is that even with superior mobilization capacity, SMUs will be crushed by the superior power resources of the state, employers, and more conservative unions—if they are willing and able to cooperate. Less inclusive and radical forms of unionism will thus come to dominate unless such a coordinated repressive response proves impossible.

In a similar vein, J.M. Barbalet argues that "[e]very time that radical unionism has flourished in the USA, it has been destroyed or severely damaged by political repression. In addition, the 'mainstream' labour movement came under special attack when it showed signs of becoming radical.' In particular, state repression had the effect of totally removing the radical element form the labour movement, and of providing a strong incentive away from the radical end of the political and industrial organisational spectrum." Indeed, the UE is a classic example of a union that was subjected to continued repression by the US government, employers, and conservative unions due to its left-wing ideology in the late 1940s and beyond. Although the UE is still in existence, it has been decimated by repression. Likewise, in the UK, the labor movement was becoming too militant in the eyes of politicians in the 1960s and 1970s. A conservative government thus passed several Acts of Parliament that severely curtailed the power of unions.[54] Militant unionism, such as the one that social movement unionism entails, is not welcome when the majority of politicians around the world embrace neoliberalism.

While it is not necessarily the case that the government and employers will attempt to destroy "radical" unionism or legislate against them, in this era of austerity it is more likely to occur. This was clearly seen when the Illinois government implemented a new law that required any union in a school district with a population of more than 500,000 to have 75 percent of its members agree to a strike. Moreover, the law also included counting non-voting union members automatically as "no" votes in strike ballots. Plus, the union must submit to arbitration before any strike, and can strike only over wage and compensation matters. The law was solely aimed at the CTU, as the only school district with a population of more than 500,000 in Illinois is Chicago. The Illinois government was attempting to control the militancy of the CTU. The CTU still managed to overcome these odds and achieve partial success. This further highlights the benefits of social movement unionism. Moreover, as we have seen, in a number of countries, governments have been enacting legislation in an attempt to weaken organized labor so that austerity policies can be more easily implemented.

Unfortunately, it is not realistic to expect that unions across the globe will suddenly change their union culture and embrace social movement unionism. Even if they do, there is no guarantee that this will lead to the revitalization of the labor movement and that austerity and neoliberalism will be overcome. However, something must be done. Bluntly speaking, the labor movement has been almost totally ineffectual in the fight against austerity and neoliberalism. If the labor movement follows its current path, it will only continue its downward trend, with millions of people suffering hardship as a result.

A Look Back and a Look into the Future: Concluding Thoughts

This book has looked at austerity around the globe. In Greece, Spain, Ireland, the United Kingdom, and the United States, the pattern is largely the same. When the country ran into economic problems, the government, after initially trying to resist austerity policies, began to embrace them, whether in the hope of receiving an EU–IMF bailout (as was the case in Greece, Spain, and Ireland) or because they believed in the ideology (the UK) or because of a perceived failure of a Keynesianism economic stimulus (as seen in the US). This did not lead to an economic recovery and well-being, but only to further pain being inflicted on the economy and, by extension, the people. While the labor movement may once have been in a position to force a government who implemented austerity from power and/or to modify the harshest austerity policies, in each country

highlighted in this book, the labor movement has seemingly been powerless to stop the spread of austerity and the resulting hardships on the
poor and most vulnerable.

In Greece, despite massive protests, including numerous general
strikes, successive governments remained on the austerity path. The same
was true in Spain. Although the entire country seemed to be suffering, and
after wave after wave of protests, even a change in government kept Spain
on the austerity road. In Ireland, while there were a few large protests,
the labor movement was generally in a weak position, and certain unions
decided it would be best to agree to austerity policies in an attempt to
prevent even harsher policies being forced on its members. In the UK,
following the election of the Conservative Party–Liberal Democrat government and the implementation of numerous austerity policies, the labor
movement struck in force in 2011. However, while it was an impressive
show of power, the protest could not get the government to change its
austerity path. Moreover, rather than continuing to be militant, a number
of unions decided it would be better for their members to cut deals with
the government. The UK labor movement was pinning its hopes on a
Labour victory in the 2015 general election. However, the Labour leader at
the time, Ed Miliband, promised that a future Labour government would
keep many austerity policies in place. Thus, at best, there could have been
only some respite for the UK people. In the US, austerity was adopted
almost by stealth. Nonetheless, the decline in federal government spending is almost unsurpassed in US history. Only the decline in government
spending after World War II was larger. Lest one make the mistake that
it was only the Republicans driving austerity, a number of Democrats, as
noted in Chapter 4, also believe that austerity is the best course of action.
In response, the labor movement at the national level has been seemingly mute. While there have been condemnations of austerity policies,
no large-scale protests have occurred. Only at the state and local level was
the labor movement out in force against austerity. The Wisconsin Workers'
Movement began as an impressive show of force against austerity policies and anti-collective-bargaining laws. However, the union bureaucracy
believed the best course of action was through electoral politics and was
willing to accept austerity measures as long as there were no antiunion
laws. This strategy led to an abject failure. Thus far, only the Chicago
Teachers Union and its social movement unionism ideology has been able
to force a government to modify its austerity policies.

As is true of the labor movement, anti-austerity social movements,
while often being higher in profile, have had no impact in forcing govern-

ments to abandon or modify austerity policies. That said, both the Occupy Movement and the 15M Movement succeeded in reinforcing people's beliefs that a tiny minority of the population has too much power. One social movement that did have success was the Quebec student movement. Structured along the lines of a traditional trade union, the movement was prepared for a long battle, following the announcement of a large rise in tuition fees in 2012. The students were militant, formed alliances with workers, reinforced the idea that their struggle was the same as the struggle of other groups against austerity measures, and was largely supported by the local community. In the end, like the CTU, the Quebec student movement was partly successful in its fight. Considering victories against austerity are few and far between, any success is to be celebrated. While social movements, like the labor movement, have generally failed in their anti-austerity struggles, the 15M Movement helped pave the way for the political party Podemos.

In a sign of hope that the people of Greece and Spain have finally had enough, anti-austerity political parties in both these countries surged to the lead in opinion polls; as the 2015 general elections approached, there was a feeling of optimism that austerity could finally be overcome. In Spain, Podemos had a meteoric rise after its formation in 2014. It started the year polling only a miniscule amount in the opinion polls. However, by May, it finished first in the Spanish European Parliament election, did well in local elections, and ended the year regarded as the most likely winner of the 2015 Spanish general election. There was the feeling that the dominant two-party political system in Spain may finally be coming to an end. However, arguably because of what had happened in Greece, the Spanish people in the end voted for more of the same. In the December 2015 National election Podemos received over 20.5 percent of the vote. The ruling People's Party gained the most support with almost 29 percent, with the Socialist Workers' Party (PSOE) coming in second with just over 22 percent. At the time of this writing (March 2016), Spanish political parties were still in discussions to form a coalition government. In the end, while Podemos was not elected to power, it has become an established political party and may well have ended the two-party system in Spain. For Spaniards, this is a good thing in itself—as long as Podemos does not follow the same path as Syriza.

In Greece, following years of successive governments implementing painful austerity policies, it seemed in 2014 that the population had finally had enough. Austerity had become increasingly unpopular. Following the failure of the government to elect its preferred choice as president, a general election was held on January 25, 2015. The main opposition party, Syriza, which is anti-austerity, was favored to become the ruling party. Political pundits believed Syriza would surely be elected—it was only a matter of how large the margin of victory would be. The popularity of Syriza led to the ruling New Democracy party to promise no more austerity policies if it was re-elected. The pundits were indeed correct, as Syriza was elected to government. Unfortunately, Syriza did not live up to its promises. Because the country was reliant on the EU for a bailout, the Greek government was "forced" to accept even harsher austerity measures. The major capitalist states wanted austerity, and they pushed it through, flying in the face of democracy.

Although the Greek government was "forced" to accept further austerity measures, since neither the UK nor the US is beholden to bailouts, it seems on the surface that it should be much easier for anti-austerity parties to gain a foothold. However, in the US, with its dominant two-party system, the choice between the Democrats and Republicans is in many ways no choice at all when it comes to which party will further embrace austerity. After all, it was a Democrat in Chicago, Rahm Emanuel, who ushered in austerity policies for the public schools system. Federally, Democrat Patty Murray, the head of the Senate Budget Committee, has appeared to support austerity by trumpeting an almost unprecedented decline in federal spending. In the UK, the Conservative Party promised the "age of austerity" would continue, while the Labour Party stated that, if elected to office, a number of austerity policies would remain in place and that further cuts to spending may occur.

A new party rising up to challenge the dominance of the main political parties in the UK is much more likely than an anti-austerity party coming to prominence in the US, due to the huge costs of running for office in the US and the entrenchment of the two-party system. Unfortunately, the economic malaise in the UK has led to the far-right, anti-immigrant, anti-EU party UKIP gaining popularity. In an attempt to gain more support with working-class voters, UKIP has begun hinting at some anti-austerity policies as part of its policy platform. That a far-right party has begun to adopt such measures should be a wake-up call to the Labour Party to modify, if not drop, some of its pro-austerity positions. Indeed, following Syriza's election victory, a number of Labour MPs began urging Ed Miliband to abandon the Party's pledge to implement further spending cuts and instead, in the Keynesianism tradition, to spend money to kick-start the economy.[55] Moreover, the Syriza victory lends credence to the idea that it is possible for a left-wing, anti-austerity party in the UK to form and perhaps even gain considerable support. However, the Labour leadership did not follow a path of anti-austerity and, as noted in Chapter 3, were soundly defeated in the general election. The UK labor movement's electoral strategy in overturning austerity was an abject failure. Considering that even if it had been elected to govern, the Labour Party planned to continue austerity measures, organized labor's strategy would have failed regardless. That the Party is beholden to austerity and neoliberalism is clearly seen following the popular election of left-wing Jeremy Corbyn to the Labour Party leadership. A number of MPs resigned from the Shadow cabinet and attempted to undermine Corbyn at every possible opportunity. They were aided by the mainstream media, including the "left-wing" *Guardian*, as a number of anti-Corbyn articles ran before his election and continued afterward. The organic intellectuals do not want a truly left-wing, anti-austerity politician leading the main opposition party, even though he was overwhelmingly voted into the position by Labour voters. As Tariq Ali notes, a "serving General in the British Army publicly threatened mutiny and a possible coup if Jeremy Corbyn were to be elected Prime Minister and attempted to carry through his policies. He was mildly rebuked by the Ministry of Defence."[56] Quite simply, the organic intellectuals and political establishment are happy with the new constitutionalism and do not want an alternative to neoliberalism and austerity, nor even for the idea of an alternative to take hold.

All considered, the labor movements in the US and UK have been ineffectual in the fight against austerity, and against neoliberalism more generally. Changes must take place. It says a lot about the state of the US labor movement that the Wisconsin Workers' Movement was lauded by so many even though it failed to overcome, or even reduce, austerity policies and antiunion laws, and that a right-wing Republican was elected, and then re-elected, to govern Wisconsin. In both the US and the UK, the union bureaucracy has repeatedly promised change for a number of years, while membership declines, or at best remains stagnate, and while the power of the labor movement to influence government policies continues to wane. This holds true despite the fact that unions have aided in Labour politicians being elected in the UK, and Democrats in the US.

I have argued that the labor movement in both countries should embrace social movement unionism. Social movement unionism has been successful in a variety of situations in both developed and developing countries since at least the 1930s. The social movement unionism of the CTU was instrumental in the union's success—one of the few success stories in the anti-austerity struggle. At this time, the labor movement in both countries remains strong enough to effect meaningful change for both its members and their wider communities. How much longer this will hold true remains to be seen.

In the end, the labor movement must do something if it wants to be more than an organization trying to protect the wages and working conditions of its ever-dwindling membership (and even here unions are continually accepting lower wages and worse working conditions for their members). This might mean embracing social movement unionism, and/or forming an independent political party, and/or forging alliances with the local community and anti-austerity social movements, or just simply doing *something* different. Doing more of the same is not working. The status quo is a detriment not only to union members but to almost all members of society. Even if political parties in the UK and the US no longer continue to embrace austerity, the Tories, large sections of Labour, Republicans, and Democrats still believe in neoliberalism, which is an economic system in which a select minority benefits to the detriment of the majority. But while there is life, there is hope, and if history has taught us anything it is that change can happen when one least expects it. Let the changes begin with the labor movement in the UK and the US. For if change does not occur, not only will austerity fail to lead to a buoyant economy, as this book has repeatedly highlighted, it may result in the far-right gaining more power, and austerity will lead to further suffering for the majority of the population, with the poor and vulnerable hit hardest. It is a sad state of affairs indeed.

Notes

Chapter 1.
Austerity and the Labor Movement

1. Mark Blyth, *Austerity: The History of a Dangerous Idea* (Oxford: Oxford University Press, 2013), 2.

2. "What is Austerity?" *The Economist*, May 20, 2015, http://www.economist.com/blogs/buttonwood/2015/05/fiscal-policy

3. Stephen Gill, "Neo-Liberalism and the Shift Towards a US-Centred Transnational Hegemony' in Henk Overbeek (ed.) *Restructuring Hegemony in the Global Political Economy.* (London: Routledge, 1993): 256–257.

4. Stephen Gill, "Finance, Production and Panopticism: Inequality, Risk and Resistance in an Era of Disciplinary Neo-liberalism" in Stephen Gill (ed.) *Globalization, Democratization and Multilateralism* (NY: St. Martin's Press, 1997): 54; Stephen Gill and David Law, "Global Hegemony and the Structural Power of Capital," *International Studies Quarterly*, vol 33: 4 (1989), 485.

5. Stephen Gill, "Structural Change and Global Political Economy: Globalizing Elites and the Emerging World Order" in Y. Sakamoto (ed.) *Global Transformation* (Japan: United Nations University 1994) 182, 192. Stephen Gill, *American Hegemony and the Trilateral Commission* (Cambridge: Cambridge University Press, 2009), 217; Stephen Gill "Knowledge, Politics, and Neo-Liberal Political Economy" in Richard Stubbs and Geoffery Underhill (eds.) *Political Economy and the Changing Global Order,* 2nd edition (Canada: Oxford University Press, 2000): 53.

6. Gill, "Neo-Liberalism and the Shift Towards a US-Centred Transnational Hegemony," 271

7. Stephen Gill, "Market Civilization, New Constitutionalism, and World Order," in Stephen Gill and A. Claire Cutler (eds.) *New Constitutionalism and World Order* (Cambridge: Cambridge University Press, 2014): 41

8. Stephen Gill, "Globalisation, Market Civilisation, and Disciplinary Neoliberalism" *Millennium*, 24, no. 3 (1995), 413; Gill, "Structural Change and

Global Political Economy: Globalizing Elites and the Emerging World Order," 190.

9. Mark Blyth, "The Austerity Delusion," *Foreign Affairs*, May/June (2013), http://www.foreignaffairs.com/articles/139105/mark-blyth/the-austerity-delusion; Blyth, *Austerity: History of a Dangerous Idea*, 119–121; Konzelmann, "The Economics of Austerity," 14.

10. Blyth, "The Austerity Delusion"; Blyth, *Austerity: History of a Dangerous* Idea; Arndt quoted in Konzelmann, "The Economics of Austerity," 14; "There Could Be Trouble Ahead," *The Economist*, December 10, 2011, http://www.economist.com/node/21541388

11. Roosevelt quoted in Marshall Auerback, "'End' of the Recession No Time to End Government Spending," *Roosevelt Institute*, n.d, http://www.rooseveltinstitute.org/new-roosevelt/end-recession-no-time-end-government-spending

12. Blyth, *Austerity: History of a Dangerous Idea*, 122–123; Baldwin quoted in Blyth, *Austerity: History of a Dangerous Idea*, 123; Hawtrey quoted in Konzelmann, "The Economics of Austerity," 10.

13. Blyth, *Austerity: History of a Dangerous Idea*, 123–125; Sally Hills and Ryland Thomas, "The UK Recession in Context—What Do Three Centuries of Data Tell Us?" *Bank of England*, http://www.bankofengland.co.uk/publications/Documents/quarterlybulletin/qb100403.pdf; "There could be trouble ahead."

14. Churchill quoted in Konzelmann, "The Economics of Austerity," 11–12.

15. "Austerity Britain: It's Déjà Vu All Over Again," *University of Cambridge*, January 16, 2013, http://www.cam.ac.uk/research/news/austerity-britain-its-d%C3%A9j%C3%A0-vu-all-over-again; Blyth, *Austerity: History of a Dangerous Idea*; Nicholas Crafts, "How Housebuilding Helped the Economy Recover: Britain in the 1930s," *The Guardian*, April 19, 2013, http://www.theguardian.com/housing-network/2013/apr/19/1930s-house-building-economic-recovery

16. Richard Seymour, *Against Austerity: How We Can Fix the Crisis They Made* (London and New York Pluto Press, 2014). Kindle Edition; Michael Spear, "In the Shadows of the 1970s Fiscal Crisis: New York City's Municipal Unions in the Twenty-First Century," *WorkingUSA*, September (2010). For an excellent analysis of how New York became more beholden to neoliberalism, see Kim Moody, *From Welfare State to Real Estate* (New York: The New Press, 2007).

17. Seymour, *Against Austerity*.

18. Spear, "In the Shadows of the 1970s Fiscal Crisis."

19. Spear, "In the Shadows of the 1970s Fiscal Crisis."

20. Spear, "In the Shadows of the 1970s Fiscal Crisis"; Moody, *From Welfare State to Real Estate*.

21. Michael Eisenscher, "Is the Secret to Labor's Future in Its Past?" *WorkingUSA* 5, no. 4 (2002): 62.

22. Richard W. Hurd, "Contesting the Dinosaur Image: The Labor Movement's Search for a Future," *Labor Studies Journal* 22, no. 4 (Winter 1998): 11.

23. Rick Fantasia and Kim Voss, *Hard Work* (Berkeley: University of California Press, 2004), 65. For an analysis of concession bargaining in American sports, see Michael Schiavone, *Sports and Labor in the United States* (Albany, NY: SUNY Press, 2015).

24. Eric Helleiner, "Freeing money: Why Have States Been More Willing to Liberalize Capital Controls Than Trade Barriers?" *Policy Science,* 27(4), 1994: 306–307, 301–302.

25. John Williamson, "A Short History of the Washington Consensus," paper commissioned by Fundación CIDOB for the conference "From the Washington Consensus towards a New Global Governance," Barcelona, September 24–25 (2004): 1–3.

26. Williamson, "A Short History of the Washington Consensus," 1–3; Blyth, *History of a Dangerous Idea,* 161.

27. Blyth, *History of a Dangerous Idea,* 163; "Mexico External debt," *Index Mundi,* http://www.indexmundi.com/mexico/debt_external.html; "Brazil External Debt," *Index Mundi,* http://www.indexmundi.com/brazil/debt_external.html

28. Philip Dine, *State of the Unions* (New York: McGraw Hill, 2008), xix.

29. Robert Hoxie, *Trade Unionism in the United States.* 2nd edition (New York: Appleton, Century, Crofts Inc., 1966), 62.

30. Dan Swinney, "Strategic Lessons for Labor from Candyland," *New Labor Forum* 55 (Fall/Winter 1999).

31. Michael Schiavone, *Unions in Crisis? The Future of Organized Labor in America* (Westport CT: Praeger Publishers, 2008): 1.

32. Table 2. Median weekly earnings of full-time wage and salary workers by union affiliation and selected characteristics, *Bureau of Labor Statistics,* 2015, http://www.bls.gov/news.release/union2.t02.htm

33. Table 4. Median weekly earnings of full-time wage and salary workers by union affiliation, occupation, and industry, 2013–2014 annual averages, *Bureau of Labor Statistics,* 2015, http://www.bls.gov/news.release/union2.t04.htm

34. "Employee Benefits in the United States—March 2014," *Bureau of Labor Statistics,* 2014, http://www.bls.gov/news.release/pdf/ebs2.pdf; "Better Pensions, Health Care," *AFL-CIO,* 2014, http://www.aflcio.org/Learn-About-Unions/What-Unions-Do/The-Union-Difference/Better-Pensions-Health-Care

35. Elise Gould and Will Kimball, " 'Right-to-Work' States Still Have Lower Wages," *Economic Policy Institute,* April 22, 2015, http://www.epi.org/publication/right-to-work-states-have-lower-wages/; " 'Right to Work' Laws: Get the Facts," *Minnesota AFL-CIO,* n.d., http://www.mnaflcio.org/news/right-work-laws-get-facts

36. Table 4. Median weekly earnings of full-time wage and salary workers by union affiliation, occupation, and industry, 2013–2014 annual averages.

37. Table 4. Median weekly earnings of full-time wage and salary workers by union affiliation, occupation, and industry, 2013–2014 annual averages.

38. Nina Fishman, "The Union Makes Us Strong," *TUC Online,* n.d. http://www.unionhistory.info/timeline/1960_2000.php; Lowell Turner, "Reviving the labor movement: A comparative perspective" [Electronic version],

Cornell University, ILR School site, 2003, http://digitalcommons.ilr.cornell.edu/articles/756/

39. Dave Lyddon, "The Union Makes Us Strong," *TUC Online*, n.d. http://www.unionhistory.info/timeline/1960_2000_Narr_Display.php?Where=NarTitle+contains+%27Anti-Union+Legislation%3A+1980-2000%27+

40. Dave Lyddon, "The 1984-85 Miners' Strike," *TUC Online*, n.d. http://www.unionhistory.info/timeline/1960_2000_Narr_Display_2.php?Where=NarTitle+contains+%27The+1984-85+Miners+Strike%27+; Dave Lyddon, "Industrial Relations," *TUC Online*, n.d. http://www.unionhistory.info/timeline/1960_2000_7.php; Turner, "Reviving the labor movement."

41. "Trade Union membership 2014," *Department for Business, Innovation & Skills*, June 2015, https://www.gov.uk/government/statistics/trade-union-statistics-2014; "The Union Advantage," *TUC*, 2014, http://strongerunions.org/wp-content/uploads/2014/09/TUC_UnionADV_A5_16pp_FINAL-LO1.pdf

Chapter 2.
Austerity in Modern-Day Europe

1. Constantinos Alexiou and Joseph Nellis, "Is There Life After 'Death' for the Greek Economy?," *International Journal of Economics and Financial Issues*, 3, no. 4 (2013): 864–866; Asbjørn Wahl, "Political and Ideological Crisis in an Increasingly More Authoritarian European Union," *Monthly Review*, 65, issue 8 (2014), http://monthlyreview.org/2014/01/01/european-labor/; Neil Irwin, *The Alchemists: Three Central Bankers and a World on Fire.* (NY: Penguin, 2013), 203–204.

2. Irwin, *The Alchemists*, 203–205; Blyth, *History of a Dangerous Idea*, 64; Vassilis Monastiriotis, "A Very Greek Crisis," *Intereconomics* (2013), http://www.intereconomics.eu/archive/year/2013/1/austerity-measures-in-crisis-countries-results-and-impact-on-mid-term-development/

3. Irwin, *The Alchemists: Three Central Bankers and a World on Fire*, 207–208; Paul Krugman, "How the Case for Austerity Has Crumbled," *The New York Review of Books*, June 6 (2013), http://www.nybooks.com/articles/archives/2013/jun/06/how-case-austerity-has-crumbled/?pagination=false

4. Philip R. Lane, "The European Sovereign Debt Crisis," *Journal of Economic Perspective*, 26, no. 3 (2012): 56.

5. Carmen Reinhardt and Kenneth Rogoff, "Growth in a Time of Debt," *National Bureau of Economic Research* working paper 15639, Cambridge, MA, January (2010), http://www.nber.org/papers/w15639.pdf; Robert Pollin and Michael Ash, "Debt and Growth: A Response to Reinhart and Rogoff," *The New York Times*, April 29, 2013, http://www.nytimes.com/2013/04/30/opinion/debt-and-growth-a-response-to-reinhart-and-rogoff.html?_r=0; Peter Coy, "FAQ: Reinhart, Rogoff, and the Excel Error That Changed History,"

Businessweek, April 18, 2013, http://www.businessweek.com/articles/2013-04-18/faq-reinhart-rogoff-and-the-excel-error-that-changed-history

6. Irwin, *The Alchemists: Three Central Bankers and a World on Fire*, 214.

7. "Eurozone approves massive Greece bail-out," *BBC News*, May 2, 2010, http://news.bbc.co.uk/2/hi/business/8656649.stm; Thomas L. Friedman, "Greece's Newest Odyssey," *The New York Times*, May 12, 2010, http://www.nytimes.com/2010/05/12/opinion/12friedman.html; Thomsen quoted in "Europe and IMF Agree €110 Billion Financing Plan With Greece," *IMF Survey Magazine*, May 2, 2010, http://www.imf.org/external/pubs/ft/survey/so/2010/car050210a.htm; Irwin, *The Alchemists: Three Central Bankers and a World on Fire*.

8. Annika Breidthardt and Jan Strupczewski, "Europe Seals New Greek Bailout But Doubts Remain," *Reuters*, February 21, 2012, http://www.reuters.com/article/2012/02/21/us-greece-idUSTRE8120HI20120221; Stephen Castle, "With Details Settled, a 2nd Greek Bailout Is Formally Approved," *The New York Times*, March 14, 2012, http://www.nytimes.com/2012/03/15/business/global/greece-gets-formal-approval-for-second-bailout.html; "Financial Assistance to Greece," *European Commission*, October 20, 2014, http://ec.europa.eu/economy_finance/assistance_eu_ms/greek_loan_facility/

9. Quotes in this paragraph from Harry Papachristou, "Factbox: Greek Austerity and Reform Measures," *Reuters*, February 19, 2012, http://www.reuters.com/article/2012/02/19/us-greece-austerity-idUSTRE81I05T20120219

10. Charlie Cooper, "Tough Austerity Measures in Greece Leave Nearly a Million People with No Access to Healthcare, Leading to Soaring Infant Mortality, HIV Infection and Suicide," *The Independent*, February 21, 2014, http://www.independent.co.uk/news/world/europe/tough-austerity-measures-in-greece-leave-nearly-a-million-people-with-no-access-to-healthcare-leading-to-soaring-infant-mortality-hiv-infection-and-suicide-9142274.html

11. "Unemployment Rate by Sex and Age Groups—Monthly Average, %," *Eurostat*, November 18, 2014, http://appsso.eurostat.ec.europa.eu/nui/show.do?dataset=une_rt_m&lang=en

12. Savas Michael-Matsas, "Greece at the Boiling Point," *Critique*, 41, no. 3 (2013): 438; Landon Thomas Jr., "Money Troubles Take Personal Toll in Greece," May 15, 2011, http://www.nytimes.com/2011/05/16/business/global/16drachma.html?_r=3&pagewanted=all&

13. European Economic and Social Committee Workers' Group, *The Impact of Anti-Crisis Measures, and the Social and Employment Situation: Greece* (2012), http://www.ictu.ie/download/pdf/greceen.pdf

14. "Greece GDP Annual Growth Rate," *Trading Economics*, 2015, http://www.tradingeconomics.com/greece/gdp-growth-annual; "Greece GDP," *Trading Economics*, 2015, http://www.tradingeconomics.com/greece/gdp; IMF, "Greece: Ex Post Evaluation of Exceptional Access under the 2010 Stand-By Arrangement," *IMF Country Report No. 13/156*, June (2013): 2; Howard Schneider, "An amazing mea culpa from the IMF's chief economist on austerity," *The Washington Post*,

January 3, 2013, http://www.washingtonpost.com/blogs/wonkblog/wp/2013/01/03/an-amazing-mea-culpa-from-the-imfs-chief-economist-on-austerity/; Thomsen quoted in Matina Stevis and Ian Talley, "IMF Concedes It Made Mistakes on Greece," *The Wall Street Journal*, June 5, 2013, http://online.wsj.com/articles/SB10001424127887324299104578527202781667088

15. Seymour, *Against Austerity: How We Can Fix the Crisis They Made*.

16. Wolfgang Rüdig and Georgios Karyotis, "Who Protests in Greece? Mass Opposition to Austerity," *British Journal of Political Science*, 44 no:3 (2014): 491–492, 503, 507, 508.

17. Seymour, *Against Austerity: How We Can Fix the Crisis They Made*.

18. Horen Voskeritsian, "Whither Greek Trade Unionism?," *Better Together*, July (2013): 2; Markos Vogiatzoglou, "Trade Unions in Greece: Protest and Social Movements in the Context of Austerity Politics," 4-6 translated from Markos Vogiatzoglou," Die griechische Gewerkschaftsbewegung: Protestund Sozialbewegungen im Kontext der Austeritätspolitik," *WSI-Mitteilungen*, 2014; George Harissis, "Unions in the Firing Line," *The Institute of Employment Rights*, August 22, 2014, http://www.ier.org.uk/blog/unions-firing-line

19. Voskeritsian, "Whither Greek Trade Unionism?" 2.

20. Harissis, "Unions in the Firing Line."

21. Demertis Nellas and Elena Becatoros, "Greek Election Results: New Democracy Wins," *The World Post*, June 16, 2012, http://www.huffingtonpost.com/2012/06/17/greek-election-results-new-democracy-wins_n_1603971.html; Rachel Donadio, "Supporters of Bailout Claim Victory in Greek Election," *The New York Times*, June 18, 2012, http://www.nytimes.com/2012/06/18/world/europe/greek-elections.html?pagewanted=all&_r=0; "Leftist Syriza wins Greek EU poll, requests early general election," *Euractiv*, May 26, 2014, http://www.euractiv.com/sections/eu-elections-2014/leftist-syriza-wins-greek-eu-poll-requests-early-general-election-302396

22. Blyth, *History of a Dangerous Idea*, 66–68; Luis Buendía, "Crisis, Austerity and Labor Reactions—Spain in the Spotlight," *ZNet*, October 20, 2010, http://zcomm.org/znetarticle/crisis-austerity-and-labor-reactions-spain-in-the-spotlight-1st-part-by-luis-buend-a/; Irwin, *The Alchemists: Three Central Bankers and a World on Fire*.

23. Blyth, *History of a Dangerous Idea*, 66; "Timeline: Spain's Economic Crisis," *Reuters*, December 30, 2011, http://www.reuters.com/article/2011/12/30/us-spain-cuts-economy-idUSTRE7BT0RL20111230; Irwin, *The Alchemists: Three Central Bankers and a World on Fire*.

24. "Timeline: Spain's economic crisis"; J. Ignacio Conde-Ruiz and Carmen Marín, "The Fiscal Crisis in Spain," *Intereconomics* (2013), http://www.intereconomics.eu/archive/year/2013/1/austerity-measures-in-crisis-countries-results-and-impact-on-mid-term-development/; Buendía, "Crisis, austerity and labor reactions—Spain in the spotlight."

25. "Timeline: Spain's Economic Crisis."

26. Daniel Woolls and Ciaran Giles, "Spain's Austerity Plan Aims to Shave $79 Billion Off The State Budget," *The Huffington Post*, September 10, 2012, http://www.huffingtonpost.com/2012/07/11/spain-austerity-plan_n_1664443.html; "Spain Budget Imposes Further Austerity Measures," *BBC News*, September 27, 2012, http://www.bbc.com/news/business-19733995; "Timeline: Spain's Economic Crisis"; Rajoy quoted in Woolls and Giles, "Spain's Austerity Plan Aims to Shave $79 Billion Off The State Budget."

27. "Spain Unemployment Rate," *Trading Economics*, http://www.trading-economics.com/spain/unemployment-rate; "Spain GDP Growth Rate," *Trading Economics*, http://www.tradingeconomics.com/spain/gdp-growth; "Spain Government Debt to GDP," Trading Economics, http://www.tradingeconomics.com/spain/government-debt-to-gdp; "Spain's debt-to-GDP ratio to top 100% in 2015," *RTÉ News*, September 30, 2014, http://www.rte.ie/news/business/2014/0930/649073-spain-gdp-2015/

28. Joseph Choonara, "The Class Struggles in Europe," *International Socialism*, 138 (2013), http://www.isj.org.uk/?id=883#138choonara52; Angie Gago, "Trade Unions' Strategies and Austerity Politics in Southern Europe: The Role of Labour in Spain, Italy and Portugal vis-à-vis Austerity Measures," Paper prepared for the ECPR General Conference 2014, Glasgow Panel: Anti-Austerity Protest in Southern Europe Section: Reshaping State and Society in Southern Europe 3–6 September 2014, University of Glasgow: 16; Angie Gago, "Spanish Trade Unions Must Change with the Times If They Are to Offer a Coherent Voice Against Austerity Policies," *The London School of Economics and Political Science*, August (2013), http://blogs.lse.ac.uk/europpblog/2013/08/19/spanish-trade-unions-must-change-with-the-times-if-they-are-to-offer-a-coherent-voice-against-austerity-policies/

29. Michael D. Yates, "Does the U.S. Labor Movement Have a Future?" *Monthly Review*, 48, no. 9 (1997): 4–5.

30. Choonara, "The Class Struggles in Europe"; Peter Gelderloos, "Spain Fights Austerity," April 3, 2012, http://www.counterpunch.org/2012/04/03/spain-fights-austerity/; Gago, "Trade Unions' Strategies and Austerity Politics in Southern Europe," 17.

31. Giles Tremlett, "Spain: The Pain of Austerity Deepens," *The Guardian*, January 1, 2013, http://www.theguardian.com/world/2013/jan/01/spain-pain-austerity-deepens; Kate Kelland, "Spanish Austerity Cuts Put Lives at Risk, Study Finds," *Reuters*, June 13, 2013, http://www.reuters.com/article/2013/06/13/us-austerity-spain-idUSBRE95C0DB20130613

32. "Spain," *Center for Economic and Social Rights*, January 2015, http://www.cesr.org/downloads/FACTSHEET_Spain_2015_web.pdf

33. Raphael Minder, "Saying No to Austerity, Spain Unveils Tax Cuts," *The New York Times*, June 21, 2014, http://www.nytimes.com/2014/06/21/business/international/spain-stepping-back-from-austerity-plans-to-cut-taxes.html?_r=0; "Spain's Reform Example," *The Wall Street Journal*, October 29, 2014, http://

online.wsj.com/articles/spains-reform-example-1414539336; Amelia Smith, "Radical Spanish Party Podemos Lead Polls for First Time," *Newsweek*, November 3, 2014, http://www.newsweek.com/radical-spanish-party-podemos-lead-polls-first-time-281699; Dan Hancox, "Podemos: The Radical Party Turning Spanish Politics on Its Head," *Newsweek*, October 31, 2014, http://www.newsweek.com/2014/10/31/podemosradical-party-turning-spanish-politics-head-279018.html

34. Blyth, *History of a Dangerous Idea*, 208; Stephen Kinsella, "Is Ireland Really the Role Model for Austerity?" *Cambridge Journal of Economics* 36, 1 (2012).

35. Blyth, *History of a Dangerous Idea*, 207–208; Arthur L. Centonze, "The Irish Banking Crisis," *Review of Business and Finance Studies*, 5, no. 2 (2014): 86, 90–92.

36. Blyth, *History of a Dangerous Idea*, 65–66, 235; Centonze, "The Irish Banking Crisis," 86, 90, 91, 92; Stephen Kinsella, "Is Ireland Really the Role Model for Austerity?" *UCD Geary Institute Discussion Paper Series*, September (2011): 3–6.

37. Niamh Hardiman, Aidan Regan, "The Politics of Austerity in Ireland," *Intereconomics* (2013): 11–12; Stephen Bach and Alexander Stroleny, "Public Service Employment Restructuring in the Crisis in the UK and Ireland: Social Partnership in Retreat," *European Journal of Industrial Relations*, 19, no. 4 (2013): 352; Peter Rigney, *The Impact of Anti-crisis Measures and the Social and Employment Situation: Ireland* (Dublin: European Economic and Social Committee Workers' Group, 2012), http://www.ictu.ie/download/pdf/impact_of_austerity_on_ireland_eesc_paper.pdf

38. Liz Alderman, "Ireland Unveils Austerity Plan to Help Secure Bailout," *The New York Times*, November 25, 2010, http://www.nytimes.com/2010/11/25/world/europe/25ireland.html?_r=0; Anthony Faiola, "Ireland Agrees to $90 Billion Bailout Terms," *The Washington Post*, November 28, 2010, http://www.washingtonpost.com/wp-dyn/content/article/2010/11/28/AR2010112804133.html; "ECB threatened to cut off emergency funding for banks in 'secret' Nov 2010 letter," *Breaking News.ie*, November 6, 2014, http://www.breakingnews.ie/ireland/ecb-threatened-to-cut-off-emergency-funding-for-banks-in-secret-nov-2010-letter-649969.html; Anthony Faiola, "Irish Government, Seeking Bailout, Unveils $20 Billion in Spending Cuts, Taxes," *The Washington Post*, November 24, 2010, http://www.washingtonpost.com/wp-dyn/content/article/2010/11/24/AR2010112401510.html; Liz Alderman, "In Ireland, Austerity Is Praised but Painful," *The New York Times*, December 6, 2011, http://www.nytimes.com/2011/12/06/business/global/despite-praise-for-its-austerity-ireland-and-its-people-are-being-battered.html?pagewanted=all

39. Henry McDonald, "Ireland Budget Imposes More Austerity," *The Guardian*, December 5, 2012, http://www.theguardian.com/world/2012/dec/05/ireland-austerity-budget; "Ireland Budget: More Austerity Measures," *Sky News*, December 5, 2012, http://news.sky.com/story/1021182/ireland-budget-more-austerity-measures; Graeme Wearden, "Ireland Austerity Budget Announced as

Markets Cling to Debt Ceiling Deal Hopes—As It Happened," *The Guardian*, October 16, 2013, http://www.theguardian.com/business/2013/oct/15/us-debt-ceiling-deal-hopes-push-markets-higher-live; "Ireland's 'Final Austerity Budget' Unveiled," *Sky News*, October 15, 2013, http://news.sky.com/story/1154987/ire-lands-final-austerity-budget-unveiled; "Budget 2015 'Marks End of Austerity' as Welfare Hikes, Tax Cuts Announced," *RTÉ News*, October 14, 2014, http://www.rte.ie/news/budget/2014/1014/652098-budget-morning/; "Irish Water: Domestic Water Charges Scheme to Begin," *BBC News*, September 30, 2014, http://www.bbc.com/news/world-europe-29423564

40. "Ireland Unemployment Rate," *Trading Economics*, 2014, http://www.tradingeconomics.com/ireland/unemployment-rate; Liz Alderman, "Hardships Linger for a Mending Ireland," *The New York Times*, December 12, 2013, http://www.nytimes.com/2013/12/12/business/international/as-bailout-chapter-closes-hardships-linger-for-irish.html?pagewanted=1&_r=0; "Ireland Has the Highest Birth, Lowest Death and Greatest Emigration Rates in Europe," *The Journal*, November 21, 2013, http://www.thejournal.ie/emigration-figures-ireland-1185157-Nov2013/; Ciara Kenny, "Emigration of Irish Nationals Falls 20% in Year to April," *The Irish Times*, August 26, 2014, http://www.irishtimes.com/news/social-affairs/emigration-of-irish-nationals-falls-20-in-year-to-april-1.1908275; Julien Mercille, "Ireland Under Austerity," *Counterpunch*, April 3, 2014, http://www.counterpunch.org/2014/04/03/ireland-under-austerity-2/

41. Mercille, "Ireland Under Austerity"; "Irish Healthcare Suffers Most in Europe from Austerity," *Breaking News.ie*, November 21, 2014, http://www.breaking-news.ie/ireland/irish-healthcare-suffers-most-in-europe-from-austerity-651885.html; "The True Cost of Austerity and Inequality," *Oxfam*, September 2013, https://www.oxfamireland.org/sites/default/files/upload/pdfs/austerity-ireland-case-study.pdf; Eoin Burke-Kennedy, "'Married or co-habiting women 'hit harder by austerity,'" *The Irish Times*, October 3, 2014, http://www.irishtimes.com/business/economy/married-or-co-habiting-women-hit-harder-by-austerity-1.1950132

42. Blyth, *History of a Dangerous Idea*, 236; Malone quoted in Blyth, *History of a Dangerous Idea*, 236.

43. Tilford quoted in Alderman, "Hardships Linger for a Mending Ireland"; Mody quoted in "Reliance on Austerity is Counterproductive, Says Former IMF Mission Chief," *RTÉ News*, April 11, 2013, http://www.rte.ie/news/business/2013/0411/380836-too-much-austerity-in-bailout-imf-mission-chief/

44. Gavan Reilly, "Here's What's Contained in the New 'Haddington Road' Public Pay Deal," *The Journal*, May 23, 2013, http://www.thejournal.ie/hadding-ton-road-agremeent-922129-May2013/; Christina Finn, "ASTI Accepts Latest Haddington Road Agreement," *The Journal*, December 19, 2013, http://www.the-journal.ie/asti-accept-haddington-road-agreement-1232561-Dec2013/; Bach and Stroleny, "Public Service Employment Restructuring," 348, 352–353

45. Ronald Erne, "Let's Accept a Smaller Slice of a Shrinking Cake. The Irish Congress of Trade Unions and Irish Public Sector Unions in Crisis," *Transfer: European Review of Labour and Research*, 19, no. 3 (2013): 427.

46. Irwin, *The Alchemists: Three Central Bankers and a World on Fire*, 284.

47. Bach and Alexander Stroleny, "Public Service Employment Restructuring," 348, 352–353; Séamus A. Power and David Nussbaum, "The Fightin' Irish? Not When it Comes to Recession and Austerity," *The Guardian*, July 24, 2014, http://www.theguardian.com/science/head-quarters/2014/jul/24/the-fightin-irish-not-when-it-comes-to-recession-and-austerity; Laurence Cox, "Why Are the Irish Not Resisting Austerity?" *Open Democracy*, October 11, 2013, https://www.opendemocracy.net/can-europe-make-it/laurence-cox/why-are-irish-not-resisting-austerity; Patrick Counihan, "Irish Labour Party Vote Collapses in Local and European Elections," *Irish Central*, May 24, 2014, http://www.irishcentral.com/news/politics/Irish-Labour-Party-vote-collapses-in-local-and-European-elections.html?showAll=y; David McKittrick, "Election Results 2014: Sinn Fein Profits as Voters Reject Austerity Policies," *The Independent*, May 26, 2014, http://www.independent.co.uk/news/uk/politics/election-results-2014-sinn-fein-profits-as-voters-reject-austerity-policies-9434210.html; Fionnan Sheahan and John Downing, "Sinn Fein 'Backs Austerity in North and Rejects it in South,' " *Irish Independent*, February 8, 2014, http://www.independent.ie/irish-news/politics/sinn-fein-backs-austerity-in-north-and-rejects-it-in-south-29990949.html; Michael Lee-Murphy, "Ireland's Resurgent Left," *Jacobin*, January 2015, https://www.jacobinmag.com/2015/01/ireland-water-charges-sinn-fein/

Chapter 3.
Austerity and the Labor Movement in the United Kingdom

1. "Long-term Profile of Gross Domestic Product (GDP) in the UK," *Office for National Statistics*, August 23, 2013, http://www.ons.gov.uk/ons/rel/elmr/explaining-economic-statistics/long-term-profile-of-gdp-in-the-uk/sty-long-term-profile-of-gdp.html; "United Kingdom Government Debt to GDP, 1980–2014," *Trading Economics*, 2014, http://www.tradingeconomics.com/united-kingdom/government-debt-to-gdp

2. Seymour, *Against Austerity: How We Can Fix the Crisis They Made*; Cameron quoted in Deborah Summers, "David Cameron Warns of 'New Age of Austerity,' " *The Guardian*, April 26, 2009, http://www.theguardian.com/politics/2009/apr/26/david-cameron-conservative-economic-policy1; Osborne quoted in "UK to Dodge Greek Fate with Tough Budget—Osborne," *Reuters*, June 20, 2010, http://uk.reuters.com/article/2010/06/20/uk-britain-osborne-budget-idUK-TRE65J0UX20100620; Osborne quoted in John Cassidy, "The Reinhart and Rogoff Controversy: A Summing Up," *The New Yorker*, April 26, 2013, http://www.newyorker.com/news/john-cassidy/the-reinhart-and-rogoff-controversy-a-summing-up

3. Blyth, *Austerity: History of a Dangerous Idea*, 60; Jeffrey Sachs, "Time to Plan for Post-Keynesian Era," *The Financial Times*, June 7, 2010, http://www.ft.com/intl/cms/s/0/e7909286-726b-11df-9f82-00144feabdc0.html#axzz3KghUVntJ; Jean-Claude Trichet, "Stimulate No More—It Is Now Time for All to Tighten," *The*

Financial Times, July 22, 2010, http://www.ft.com/intl/cms/s/0/1b3ae97e-95c6-11df-b5ad-00144feab49a.html#axzz1rw5D7xpm

4. King and Barker quoted in Irwin, *The Alchemists: Three Central Bankers and a World on Fire*, 241; Johnson quoted in "UK Economy 'Faces Crisis' Warns Former IMF Economist," *BBC News*, February 7, 21010, http://news.bbc.co.uk/2/hi/8503090.stm

5. Elliot quoted in Seymour, *Against Austerity: How We Can Fix the Crisis They Made*.

6. Seymour, *Against Austerity: How We Can Fix the Crisis They Made*.

7. Cameron quoted in Paul Hoggett, Hen Wilkinson, and Pheobe Beedell, "Fairness and the Politics of Resentment," *Journal of Social Policy*, 42, no:3 (2013): 583

8. Seymour, *Against Austerity: How We Can Fix the Crisis They Made*; "Election 2010," *BBC News*, 2010, http://news.bbc.co.uk/2/shared/election2010/results/; Cabinet office spokesperson and O'Donnell quoted in Alex Stevenson, " 'God' Denies Coalition Meddling," *Politics.co.uk*, October 28, 2010, http://www.politics.co.uk/news/2010/10/28/god-denies-coalition-meddling; Cable quoted in Kirsty Walker, "Vince Cable Admits Previously Opposing VAT Rise to 'Score Points' " *Daily Mail*, June 28, 2010, http://www.dailymail.co.uk/news/article-1290176/Vince-Cable-admits-previously-opposing-VAT-score-points.html#ixzz3KlAO6gtg

9. Osborne quoted in Paul Krugman, *End This Depression Now!* (London and New York: W. W. Norton & Company, 2013), 200; "Budget 2010: Key Points," *The Guardian*, June 22, 2010, http://www.theguardian.com/uk/2010/jun/22/budget-2010-key-points; "Britain's emergency budget Ouch!," *The Economist*, June 22, 2010, http://www.economist.com/blogs/newsbook/2010/06/britains_emergency_budget?zid=295&ah=0bca374e65f2354d553956ea65f756e0; Osborne quoted in Larry Elliott and Hélène Mulholland, "Budget 2010: VAT to Rise to 20% as Osborne Seeks to Balance Books by 2015," *The Guardian*, http://www.theguardian.com/uk/2010/jun/22/budget-2010-vat-rise-osborne

10. Barber quoted in Elliott and Mulholland, "Budget 2010"; Chris Giles, "Poor to Be Hit Most by Service Cuts," *Financial Times*, June 23, 2010, http://www.ft.com/intl/cms/s/0/47b05ac2-7efe-11df-8398-00144feabdc0.html#axzz3KsPKGHFC

11. Julia Werdigier, "Its Growth Slowing, Britain Extends Austerity Measures," *The New York Times*, November 29, 2011, http://www.nytimes.com/2011/11/30/business/global/britain-lowers-economic-growth-forecast.html?_r=0; "Budget 2012 at a glance: George Osborne's Key Points," *BBC News*, March 22, 2012, http://www.bbc.com/news/uk-politics-17449501; Katie Allen, "Budget 2012: The Key Points in Summary," *The Guardian*, March 22, 2012, http://www.theguardian.com/uk/2012/mar/21/budget-2012-summary; "Budget 2013 at a Glance: George Osborne's Key Points," *BBC News*, March 20, 2013, http://www.bbc.com/news/uk-politics-21851965; Paul Owen, "Budget 2013–The Key Points," *The Guardian*, March 20, 2013, http://www.theguardian.com/uk/2013/mar/20/budget-2013-key-points-live

12. Osborne quoted in James Kirkup, "Osborne: We've Saved the Economy and Proved Labour Wrong," *The Telegraph*, September 9, 2013, http://www.telegraph.co.uk/news/politics/georgeosborne/10295060/Osborne-Weve-saved-the-economy-and-proved-Labour-wrong.html; Greenspan quoted in Hugo Duncan, "Top Central Banker Alan Greenspan Praises Osborne's Austerity Measures as Economic Recovery Continues to Gather Speed," *Daily Mail*, October 22, 2013, http://www.dailymail.co.uk/news/article-2471132/Banker-Alan-Greenspan-praises-George-Osbornes-austerity-measures.html

13. Osborne quoted in Fraser Nelson, "We'll Balance the Books!! (By 2020) George Osborne Speech Analysis," *The Spectator*, http://blogs.spectator.co.uk/coffeehouse/2013/09/tory-conference-2013-well-balance-the-books-by-2020-george-osbornes-speech-analysis/; "United Kingdom Government Debt to GDP, 1980–2015."

14. John Cassidy, "By George, Britain's Austerity Experiment Didn't Work!," *The New Yorker*, December 5, 2013, http://www.newyorker.com/news/john-cassidy/by-george-britains-austerity-experiment-didnt-work; John Lanchester, "Let's Call It Failure," *London Review of Books*, 35, no. 1, January 3, 2013, http://www.lrb.co.uk/v35/n01/john-lanchester/lets-call-it-failure; Ambrose Evans-Pritchard, "Britain to Have Worst 2014 Trade Deficit in Industrial World on EU Forecasts," *The Telegraph*, November 5, 2013, http://www.telegraph.co.uk/finance/economics/10427783/Britain-to-have-worst-2014-trade-deficit-in-industrial-world-on-EU-forecasts.html; Rowena Mason, "Clegg Backs Osborne's Timetable for Eliminating UK's Structural Deficit," *The Guardian*, February 11, 2014, http://www.theguardian.com/politics/2014/feb/10/clegg-backs-osborne-timetable-eliminate-uk-structural-deficit

15. "Economy Tracker: Unemployment," *BBC News*, November 12, 2014, http://www.bbc.co.uk/news/10604117; "UK Wages Rise More Than Expected, Unemployment Rate Stays Unchanged," *Reuters*, November 12, 2014, http://uk.reuters.com/article/2014/11/12/uk-britain-jobs-idUKKCN0I-W0VJ20141112; Cassidy, "By George, Britain's Austerity Experiment Didn't Work!"; David Blanchflower and Stephen Machin, "Falling Real Wages," *CentrePiece*, Spring 2014, http://cep.lse.ac.uk/pubs/download/cp422.pdf; Will Hutton, "Inequality Has Become a Challenge to Us as Moral Beings," *The Guardian*, January 25, 2015, http://www.theguardian.com/books/2015/jan/25/inequality-has-become-challenge-how-good-we-can-be-extract-will-hutton

16. Katie Allen, "UK on Track to be Fastest Growing G7 Economy Despite Slowdown," *The Guardian*, October 25, 2014, http://www.theguardian.com/business/2014/oct/24/uk-economic-growth-slows; "GDP growth (annual %)"; Mark Gilbert, "Britain's Austerity Finally Leads to Economic Growth," *Bloomberg*, May 1, 2014, http://www.bloomberg.com/bw/articles/2014-05-01/britains-austerity-finally-leads-to-economic-growth

17. Larry Summers, "Britain's Economic Growth Is Not a Sign That Austerity Works," *The Washington Post*, May 4, 2014, http://www.washingtonpost.com/opinions/britains-economic-growth-is-not-a-sign-that-austerity-works/2014/05/0

4/26b345e8-d204-11e3-937f-d3026234b51c_story.html; Allen, "UK on Track to be Fastest Growing G7 Economy Despite Slowdown"; Cassidy, "By George, Britain's Austerity Experiment Didn't Work!"; Simon Wren-Lewis, "How Much Has Austerity Cost (So Far)?" *Mainly Macro*, July 21, 2013, http://mainlymacro.blogspot.com.au/2013/07/how-much-has-austerity-cost-so-far.html; Simon Wren-Lewis, "Recovery Rhetoric and Reality," *Mainly Macro*, April 29, 2014, http://mainly-macro.blogspot.com.au/2014/04/recovery-rhetoric-and-reality.html

18. Lanchester, "Let's Call It Failure."

19. Krisnah Poinasamy, *The True Cost of Austerity and Inequality* (Oxford: Oxfam GB for Oxfam International. September 2013), http://www.oxfam.org/sites/www.oxfam.org/files/cs-true-cost-austerity-inequality-uk-120913-en.pdf

20. Poinasamy, *The True Cost of Austerity and Inequality*; Patrick Butler and Amelia Gentleman, "Benefit Cuts Putting 200,000 Children in Poverty Must be Stopped, Experts Say," *The Guardian*, March 27, 2013, http://www.theguardian.com/society/2013/mar/27/benefit-cuts-poverty-stopped-experts

21. Owen Jones, "It's Socialism for the Rich and Capitalism for the Rest of Us in Britain," *The Guardian*, August 29, 2014, http://www.theguardian.com/books/2014/aug/29/socialism-for-the-rich; Dina Rickman, "More than 100 Mentally Ill People a day Have Their Benefits Sanctioned," *The Independent*, January 21, 2015, http://i100.independent.co.uk/article/more-than-100-mentally-ill-people-a-day-have-their-benefits-sanctioned--gky3O8Nmsl

22. Jones, "It's Socialism for the Rich and Capitalism for the Rest of Us in Britain"; Oliver Wright, "Tory Attitudes to Poverty under Fire amid Benefit Sanctions and Baroness Jenkin Comment That Poor 'Don't Know How to Cook,'" *The Independent*, December 9, 2014, http://www.independent.co.uk/news/uk/politics/tory-attitudes-to-poverty-under-fire-amid-benefit-sanctions-and-baroness-jenkin-comment-that-poor-dont-know-how-to-cook-9911580.html; Nigel Morris, "Benefit Cuts Sends Number of Food Bank Users Soaring," *The Independent*, July 11, 2013, http://www.independent.co.uk/news/uk/politics/benefit-cuts-sends-number-of-food-bank-users-soaring-8701367.html; Rose Troup Buchanan, "Almost 50% of Referrals to Food Banks in the UK Are Due to 'Issues with the Welfare System,'" *The Independent*, December 9, 2014, http://www.independent.co.uk/news/uk/home-news/almost-50-of-referrals-to-food-banks-in-the-uk-are-due-to-issues-with-the-welfare-system-9910973.html; McAuley quoted in Buchanan, "Almost 50% of Referrals to Food Banks in the UK Are Due to 'Issues with the Welfare System.'"

23. Wright, "Tory Attitudes to Poverty Under Fire"; Evan Bartlett, "Lords Refuse to Cut Costs Because 'Champagne Quality Would Suffer,'" *The Independent*, December 7, 2014, http://i100.independent.co.uk/article/lords-refuse-to-cut-costs-because-champagne-quality-would-suffer-gkRgp-6Cux

24. Susan Pashkoff, "Women and Austerity in Britain," *New Politics*, Winter (2014), http://newpol.org/content/women-and-austerity-britain

25. Poinasamy, *The True Cost of Austerity and Inequality*; Pashkoff, "Women and Austerity in Britain"; "Benefits," *Fawcett Society*, February, 2013, http://www.fawcettsociety.org.uk/2013/02/benefits/

26. Simpson quoted in "Trade Union Responses to the Emergency Budget," *Trade Union Solidarity*, June 22, 2010, http://solidaritymagazine.org/2010/06/trade-union-responses-to-the-emergency-budget/; Crow quoted in "Call for Emergency TUC Meeting," *Express*, June 21, 2010, http://www.express.co.uk/news/uk/182086/Call-for-emergency-TUC-meeting

27. Choonara, "The Class Struggles in Europe"; Simon Rogers, "Major UK Demonstrations and Protests Listed: Which One Was Biggest?," *The Guardian*, March 28, 2011, http://www.theguardian.com/news/datablog/2011/mar/28/demonstrations-protests-uk-list; Mark Townsend, Tracy McVeigh, Jamie Doward, and David Sharrock, "Anti-Cuts March Draws Hundreds of Thousands as Police Battle Rioters," *The Guardian*, March 27, 2011, http://www.theguardian.com/society/2011/mar/26/anti-cuts-march-police-rioters; Prentis and McCluskey quoted in Mauro Galluzzo, "Anti-Cuts March: 500,000 Protest Against Cuts," *Express*, March 26, 2011, http://www.express.co.uk/news/uk/236958/Anti-cuts-march-500-000-protest-against-cuts; Paul Mason, "A Snapshot of the 26 March Demo," *BBC News*, March 26, 2011, http://www.bbc.co.uk/blogs/legacy/newsnight/paulmason/2011/03/a_snapshot_of_the_26_march_dem.html

28. For example, following the announcement of a range of austerity measures in Australia, the union movement went on the offensive in an attempt to prevented them from being implemented. Helped by the parliamentary system, the union movement was largely successful because it highlighted the effects austerity would have on the general public and hence made austerity an electorally unpopular course of action for the government to take.

29. Michael White, "Public Sector Strikers Clean up after Giving Dressing Down to Government," *The Guardian*, June 30, 2011, http://www.theguardian.com/society/2011/jun/30/public-sector-pensions-policy; Miliband quoted in Patrick Wintour and Allegra Stratton, "Ed Miliband Sets Out Reform Agenda and Says: Labour Cannot Go on Like This," *The Guardian*, June 25, 2011, http://www.theguardian.com/politics/2011/jun/24/labour-ed-miliband-reform; Blair quoted in Patrick Wintour, "Strikes a Mistake, Insists Ed Miliband—But Signs of Dissent in Shadow Cabinet," *The Guardian*, June 27, 2011, http://www.theguardian.com/politics/2011/jun/26/strikes-mistake-miliband-dissent-cabinet

30. Severin Carrell, Dan Milmo, Alan Travis, and Nick Hopkins, "Day of Strikes as Millions Heed Unions' Call to Fight Pension Cuts," *The Guardian*, November 30, 2011, http://www.theguardian.com/society/2011/nov/30/public-sector-workers-strike-uk; Cameron quoted in Hélène Mulholland, "David Cameron Admits Day of Action Was 'Obviously a Big Strike,'" *The Guardian*, December 1, 2011, http://www.theguardian.com/society/2011/dec/01/david-cameron-obviously-big-strike?newsfeed=true; Seumas Milne, "This Strike Could Start to Turn the Tide of a Generation," *The Guardian*, December 1, 2011, http://www.theguardian.com/commentisfree/2011/nov/30/strike-turns-tide-of-generation

31. Tony Robson, "UK: TUC Moves to Sell Out Fight Against Public Sector Pension Cuts," *World Socialist Web Site*, December 22, 2011, http://www.wsws.org/en/articles/2011/12/tucp-d22.html; "Public Sector Pensions: Most Unions Agree

Some Changes," *BBC News*, December 19, 2011, http://www.bbc.co.uk/news/business-16243824

32. McAnea quoted in Robson, "UK: TUC Moves to Sell Out Fight Against Public Sector Pension Cuts"; Robinson quoted in "Teaching Unions Accept Pension Deal," *The Guardian*, January 31, 2012, http://www.theguardian.com/society/2012/jan/30/association-teachers-accepts-pension-reforms

33. Dan Milmo and Jessica Shepherd, "Public Sector Workers Prepare to Strike Over Cuts and Pension Reforms," *The Guardian*, May 10, 2012, http://www.theguardian.com/society/2012/may/09/public-sector-workers-strike-cuts; Richard Seymour, "How to Protest in the Age of Austerity," *The Guardian*, October 22, 2013, http://www.theguardian.com/commentisfree/2013/oct/22/how-to-protest-austerity-left-social-movements-union; Shane Croucher, "UK Strikes: Number of Working Days Lost Rockets 78% in 2013," *International Business Times*, July 17, 2014, http://www.ibtimes.co.uk/uk-strikes-number-working-days-lost-rockets-78-2013-1457055

34. "50,000 Attend Manchester Protest Against Austerity," *The Guardian*, September 29, 2013, http://www.theguardian.com/uk-news/2013/sep/29/thousands-protest-manchester-austerity; Matthew Taylor, Rowena Mason, Helena Horton and Rebecca Maguire, "Public-Sector Strikes: Hundreds of Thousands Join Rallies in Pay Protest," *The Guardian*, July 11, 2014, http://www.theguardian.com/society/2014/jul/10/public-sector-strikes-rallies-francis-maude-frances-ogrady; Natasha Culzac, "Teachers' Strike: Mass Public Sector Walk-Out as Thousands Protest Against Pay and Working Conditions," *The Independent*, July 10, 2014, http://www.independent.co.uk/news/uk/teachers-strike-mass-public-sector-walk-out-as-thousands-protest-against-pay-and-working-conditions-9596547.html

35. "Labour Won't Reverse Tory Public Spending Cuts, Miliband Will Announce," *Huffington Post*, June 22, 2013, http://www.huffingtonpost.co.uk/2013/06/21/labour-spending-cuts-hars_n_3480442.html; Andrew Whitaker, "Labour Will Keep Austerity, Says Miliband," *The Scotsman*, February 11, 2014, http://www.scotsman.com/news/uk/labour-will-keep-austerity-says-miliband-1-3300839

36. Steve Coulter, "Insider Lobbying: 'New Labour and the TUC,'" *New European Trades Union Forum*, February 27, 2014, http://blogs.lse.ac.uk/netuf/2014/02/27/insider-lobbying-new-labour-and-the-tuc/

37. "Policies for People," *UKIP Website*, n.d, http://www.ukip.org/policies_for_people; "What We Stand For," *UKIP Website*, n.d, http://www.ukip.org/issues; Nigel Morris, "Nigel Farage's Suggestion of a Privatised NHS Flares Tensions Within Ukip," *The Independent*, January 21, 2015, http://www.independent.co.uk/news/uk/politics/farages-suggestion-of-a-privatised-nhs-flares-tensions-within-ukip-9991340.html; George Eaton, "How Ukip is Turning Left on the Economy," *The New Statesman*, April 22, 2014, http://www.newstatesman.com/politics/2014/04/how-ukip-turning-left-economy

38. Geoffrey Evans and Jon Mellon, "Working Class Votes and Conservative Losses: Solving the UKIP Puzzle," *The London School of Economics*

and Political Science, April 30, 2015, http://blogs.lse.ac.uk/generalelection/working-class-votes-and-conservative-losses-solving-the-ukip-puzzle/

39. Eric Kaufmann, "The 'Shy' English Nationalists Who Won It for the Tories and Flummoxed the Pollsters," *The London School of Economics and Political Science,* May 12, 2015, http://blogs.lse.ac.uk/generalelection/the-shy-english-nationalists-who-won-it-for-the-tories-and-flummoxed-the-pollsters/; "Election 2015," *BBC News,* 2015, http://www.bbc.com/news/election/2015/results

40. Tim Wigmore, "20 Seats with the Lowest Turnout Show Labour Voters Drifting to Ukip—Or Not Voting At All," *New Statesman,* May 13, 2015, http://www.newstatesman.com/politics/2015/05/20-seats-lowest-turnout-show-labour-voters-drifting-ukip-or-not-voting-all; Mark Townsend, "Five Million Votes, Two Seats: Smaller Parties Demand a Change in the Rules," *The Guardian,* May 9, 2015, http://www.theguardian.com/politics/2015/may/09/margate-ukip-greens-electoral-reform-farage

41. Len McCluskey, "Mandelson is Wrong: Labour Can't Survive Without the Unions," *The Guardian,* May 13, 2015, http://www.theguardian.com/commentisfree/2015/may/13/labour-survive-unite-unions-peter-mandelson

Chapter 4.
Austerity and the Labor Movement in the United States

1. Blyth, *The History of a Dangerous Idea,* 5; Krugman, *End This Depression Now!,* 111.

2. Blyth, *The History of a Dangerous Idea,* 48; Krugman, *End This Depression Now!,* 114.

3. Krugman, *End This Depression Now!,* 117; "United States Government Debt to GDP," *Trading Economics,* 2014, http://www.tradingeconomics.com/united-states/government-debt-to-gdp; Robert Pollin, "Austerity Economics and the Struggle for the Soul of US Capitalism," *Social Research,* 80, no. 3 (2013): 757–758.

4. "Full Page Ad," *CATO Institute,* January 9, 2009, www.cato.org/special/stimulus09/cato_stimulus.pdf

5. "Executive Order 13531—National Commission on Fiscal Responsibility and Reform," *Office of the Press Secretary: White House,* February 18, 2010, http://www.whitehouse.gov/the-press-office/executive-order-national-commission-fiscal-responsibility-and-reform; The National Commission on Fiscal Responsibility and Reform, "The Moment of Truth," *The White House,* December 2010, http://momentoftruthproject.org/sites/default/files/TheMomentofTruth12_1_2010.pdf

6. Bowles quoted in Krugman, *End This Depression Now!,* 192; The National Commission on Fiscal Responsibility and Reform, "The Moment of Truth."

7. Ryan, Camp, and Sessions quoted in Travis Waldron, "11 Republicans Who Cited a Faulty Study to Push for Drastic Spending Cuts," *Think Progress,* April 16, 2013, http://thinkprogress.org/economy/2013/04/16/1875541/11-republicans-who-cited-a-flawed-study-to-push-for-drastic-spending-cuts/

8. "Daily Treasury Long Term Rate Data," *US Department of Treasury*, May 27, 2015, http://www.treasury.gov/resource-center/data-chart-center/interest-rates/Pages/TextView.aspx?data=longtermrateAll

9. Obama quoted in Peter Baker and Jackie Calmes, "Amid Deficit Fears, Obama Freezes Pay," *The New York Times*, November 29, 2010, http://www.nytimes.com/2010/11/30/us/politics/30freeze.html?_r=0; Kellie Lunney, "Obama Signs Off On Fed Pay Freeze," *Government Executive*, March 26, 2013, http://www.govexec.com/pay-benefits/2013/03/obama-signs-fed-pay-freeze/62103/; Josh Hicks, "Obama Gives Federal Workers a 2015 Pay Raise," *The Washington Post*, December, 19, 2014, http://www.washingtonpost.com/blogs/federal-eye/wp/2014/12/19/obama-gives-federal-workers-a-2015-pay-raise/

10. Marc Labonte, and Mindy R. Levit, "Congressional Research Service: The Budget Control Act of 2011: Effects on Spending Levels and the Budget Deficit," *Council on Foreign Relations*, October 5, 2011, http://www.cfr.org/united-states/congressional-research-service-budget-control-act-2011-effects-spending-levels-budget-deficit/p26369; Kevin Drum, "How Austerity Wrecked the American Economy," *Mother Jones*, September 23, 2013, http://www.motherjones.com/kevin-drum/2013/09/obama-austerity-wrecked-american-economy; Blyth, *The History of a Dangerous Idea*, 1.

11. Drum, "How Austerity Wrecked the American Economy."

12. Patty Murray, "Ten Facts You May Not Know about the Federal Budget," *Senate Budget Committee*, 2014, http://www.budget.senate.gov/democratic/public/index.cfm/blog?ID=151019c5-2655-4530-8e6b-c7455de71dba

13. "United States Government Debt to GDP"; "GDP growth (annual %)." *World Bank*, 2014, http://data.worldbank.org/indicator/NY.GDP.MKTP.KD.ZG

14. Paul Krugman, "American Austerity, Charted Yet Again," *The New York Times*, March 1, 2014, http://krugman.blogs.nytimes.com/2014/03/01/american-austerity-charted-yet-again/?_r=1

15. "United States Unemployment Rate," *Trading Economics*, 2014, http://www.tradingeconomics.com/united-states/unemployment-rate; Mark Gongloff, "U.S. Creates 248,000 Jobs In September; Unemployment Rate Falls To 5.9%," *The Huffington Post*, October 3, 2014, http://www.huffingtonpost.com/2014/10/03/september-jobs-report-unemployment-rate_n_5922146.html

16. Drew DeSilver, "For Most Workers, Real Wages Have Barely Budged for Decades," *Pew Research Center*, October 9, 2014, http://www.pewresearch.org/fact-tank/2014/10/09/for-most-workers-real-wages-have-barely-budged-for-decades/

17. Matt Phillips, "American Families are Stuck in a Lost Quarter Century," *Quartz*, September 16, 2014, http://qz.com/265980/american-families-are-stuck-in-a-lost-quarter-century/

18. Rakesh Kochhar and Richard Fry, "Wealth Inequality Has Widened Along Racial, Ethnic Lines Since End of Great Recession," *Pew Research Center*, December 12, 2014, http://www.pewresearch.org/fact-tank/2014/12/12/racial-wealth-gaps-great-recession/

19. Credit Suisse, *Global Wealth Report 2014* (Zurich: Credit Suisse Research Institute, 2014):6; Emmanuel Saez and Gabriel Zucman, "Exploding Wealth Inequality in the United States," *Washington Center for Equitable Growth*, October 20, 2014, http://equitablegrowth.org/research/exploding-wealth-inequality-united-states/

20. Yellen quoted in Mark Gongloff, "Janet Yellen: Rising Income Inequality Could Seriously Harm the U.S. Economy," *The Huffington Post*, October 17, 2014, http://www.huffingtonpost.com/2014/10/17/janet-yellen-inequality_n_6002774.html

21. See Coalition for Health Funding, *Faces of Austerity: How Budget Cuts Hurt America's Health*, July (2014) for these and many other examples of the decline in health care funding since 2010. David Stuckler quoted in "Austerity Seriously Affecting Health in Europe, North America," *VOA News*, May 3, 2013, http://www.voanews.com/content/austerity-seriously-affecting-health-in-europe-north-america/1654291.html

22. Eric Pianin, "The Surprising Fact of Hunger in America," *The Fiscal Times*, December 19, 2014, http://www.thefiscaltimes.com/2014/12/19/Surprising-Fact-Hunger-America; Mortimer B. Zuckerman, "Mort Zuckerman: The Jobs Picture Is Far Worse Than It Looks," *US News & World Report*, February 28, 2013; http://www.usnews.com/opinion/mzuckerman/articles/2013/02/28/mort-zuckerman-the-jobs-picture-is-far-worse-than-it-looks; John Zogby, "Demography Of Hunger in America in 2014," *Forbes*, December 17, 2014, http://www.forbes.com/sites/johnzogby/2014/12/17/the-demography-of-hunger-in-america-2014-2/; Rosenbaum quoted in "The Surprising Fact of Hunger in America."

23. Rosenbaum quoted in Pianin, "The Surprising Fact of Hunger in America."

24. Richard Trumka, "Austerity Only Weakens the Economy," *The Hill*, March 19, 2013, http://thehill.com/special-reports/jobs-and-the-economy-march-2013/289143-austerity-only-weakens-the-economy

25. Rick Nagin, "Nationwide Rallies Against Austerity," *People's World*, January 31, 2013, http://peoplesworld.org/nationwide-rallies-against-austerity/

26. Andy Kroll, "Wisconsin Gov. Scott Walker: Funded by the Koch Bros.," *Mother Jones*, February 18, 2011, http://www.motherjones.com/mojo/2011/02/wisconsin-scott-walker-koch-brothers

27. Étienne Cantin, "The Politics of Austerity and the Conservative Offensive against US Public Sector Unions, 2008–2012," *Relations Industrielles*, 67 no:4 Fall (2012): 620–621; "What Most People Don't Understand About the Wisconsin Budget Repair Bill," *Daily Kos*, February 17, 2011, http://www.dailykos.com/story/2011/02/18/946466/-What-Most-People-Don-t-Understand-About-the-Wisconsin-Budget-Repair-Bill-Updated#; Andy Kroll, "What's Happening in Wisconsin Explained," *Mother Jones*, March 17, 2011, http://www.motherjones.com/mojo/2011/02/whats-happening-wisconsin-explained;

28. Erza Klein, "What is Actually Being Proposed in Wisconsin?," *The Washington Post*, February 18, 2011, http://voices.washingtonpost.com/ezra-klein/2011/02/what_is_actually_being_propose.html; Seymour, "*Against Austerity.*"

29. Tami Luhby, "Gov. Scott Walker Unveils Wisconsin budget," *CNN*, March 1, 2011, http://money.cnn.com/2011/03/01/news/economy/wisconsin_budget_walker/; Walker quoted in Luhby, "Gov. Scott Walker Unveils Wisconsin budget"; Ellis and Grigsby quoted in Jason Stein, Patrick Marley, and Lee Bergquist, "Walker's Budget Cuts Would Touch Most Wisconsinites," *Milwaukee Journal Sentinel*, March 1, 2011, http://www.jsonline.com/news/statepolitics/117154428.html

30. Cantin, "The Politics of Austerity and the Conservative Offensive"; Seymour, *Against Austerity*; Dan La Botz, "A New American Workers Movement Has Begun," *MR Zine*, February 18, 2011, http://mrzine.monthlyreview.org/2011/labotz180211.html; Stein, Marley and Bergquist, "Walker's Budget Cuts Would Touch Most Wisconsinites"; Dave Umhoefer, "Gov. Scott Walker Says He Asked Unions for Concessions and They Refused," *PolitiFact Wisconsin*, September 16, 2011, http://www.politifact.com/wisconsin/statements/2011/sep/16/scott-walker/gov-scott-walker-says-he-asked-unions-concessions-/

31. Cantin, "The Politics of Austerity and the Conservative Offensive"; Seymour, *Against Austerity*; Brian Montopoli, "Scott Walker Wins Wisconsin Recall Election," *CBS News*, June 6, 2012, http://www.cbsnews.com/news/scott-walker-wins-wisconsin-recall-election/; "Millions Spent on Wisconsin Recall Election," *The New York Times*, June 4, 2012, http://www.nytimes.com/interactive/2012/06/04/us/politics/money-spent-on-wisconsin-recall-election.html?_r=0

32. Montopoli, "Scott Walker Wins Wisconsin Recall Election"; Doug Henwood, "Walker's Victory, Un-Sugar-Coated," *LBO News from Doug Henwood*, June 6, 2012, http://lbo-news.com/2012/06/06/walkers-victory-un-sugar-coated/

33. Henwood, "Walker's Victory, Un-Sugar-Coated"; Scott Clement and Aaron Blake, "Wisconsin Recall: Union voters ≠ Union Households," *The Washington Post*, June 6, 2012, http://www.washingtonpost.com/blogs/the-fix/post/wisconsin-recall-union-voters-union-households/2012/06/06/gJQA3l6VHV_blog.html; Betsy Woodruff, "Wisconsin Three-Peat," *Slate*, November 5, 2014, http://www.slate.com/articles/news_and_politics/politics/2014/11/scott_walker_wins_wisconsin_again_why_the_conservative_governor_won_again.html; "2014 Wisconsin Governor Election Results," *Politico*, December 17, 2014, http://www.politico.com/2014-election/results/map/governor/wisconsin/#.VKC7Sv-xMw

34. "Union Membership in Wisconsin—2014," *Bureau of Labor Statistics*, 2015, http://www.bls.gov/regions/midwest/news-release/unionmembership_wisconsin.htm; Robert Samuels, "Walker's Anti-Union Law has Labor Reeling in Wisconsin," *The Washington Post*, February 22, 2015, http://www.washingtonpost.com/politics/in-wisconsin-walkers-anti-union-law-has-crippled-labor-movement/2015/02/22/1eb3ef82-b6f1-11e4-aa05-1ce812b3fdd2_story.html; Barry T. Hirsch and David A. Macpherson, "Union Membership, Coverage, Density and Employment by State, 2011," *Unionstats.com*, 2012, http://unionstats.gsu.edu/State_U_2011.htm; Barry T. Hirsch and David A. Macpherson, "Union Membership, Coverage, Density and Employment by State, 2014," *Unionstats.com*, 2015, http://unionstats.gsu.edu/State_U_2014.htm; Henwood, "Walker's victory, un-sugar-coated."

35. Lee A. Saunders, "Scott Walker's Austerity Plan: Turning Wisconsin Into the New Greece," *The Huffington Post*, May 23, 2013, http://www.huffingtonpost. com/lee-a-saunders/scott-walker-austerity_b_3326111.html; Craig Gilbert, "State Posts Largest Percentage Job Loss in U.S. Over Past Year," *Milwaukee Journal Sentinel*, April 24, 2012, http://www.jsonline.com/business/state-posts-largest-per-centage-job-loss-in-us-over-past-year-report-shows-ib54utt-148694855.html; Tim Jones, "Republican Whipping-Boy Illinois Beats Wisconsin on Jobs," *Bloomberg*, April 20, 2012, http://www.bloomberg.com/news/2012-04-20/republican-whip-ping-boy-illinois-beats-wisconsin-on-jobs.html; "Issue of the Week: Walker's Aus-terity Agenda Is Killing Job Creation," *Express Milwaukee*, March 28, 2014, http:// expressmilwaukee.com/article-23007-issue-of-the-week:-walker%E2%80%99s-austerity-agenda-is-killing-job-creation-|-expresso-|-shepherd-express.html; Tom Kertscher, "Under Scott Walker, Wisconsin Lags U.S. in Wage, Job Growth, 'Meet the Press' Host Chuck Todd Says," *Politifact*, November 28, 2014, http:// www.politifact.com/wisconsin/statements/2014/nov/28/chuck-todd/under-scott-walker-wisconsin-lags-us-wage-job-grow/; Dan Kaufman, "Scott Walker and the Fate of the Union," *The New York Times*, June 12, 2015, http://www.nytimes. com/2015/06/14/magazine/scott-walker-and-the-fate-of-the-union.html

Steven Greenhouse, "Wisconsin's Legacy for Unions," *The New York Times*, February 22, 2014, http://www.nytimes.com/2014/02/23/business/wisconsins-legacy-for-unions.html

36. Kim Moody and Charles Post, "The Politics of US Labor: Paralysis and Possibilities," in *Socialist Register* (Leo Panitch and Greg Albo eds, London: Merlin Press, 2014): 302; Keith Mann, "Resistance to Neo-Liberalism: France, Greece, Spain, and the US," *Perspectives on Global Development and Technology*, 11 (2012): 186.

37. Julian Zelizer, "How Labor Unions and Democrats Fell Out of Love," *CNN*, August 31, 2014, http://edition.cnn.com/2014/08/31/opinion/zelizer-labor-democrats/; Schiavone, *Unions in Crisis?*, 51.

38. Azam Ahmed, "CPS Faces $1 Billion Deficit, Huberman Says," *Chi-cago Tribune*, February 25, 2010, http://articles.chicagotribune.com/2010-02-25/ news/ct-met-chicago-school-cuts-20100225_1_pension-system-pension-reform-furlough-days; Joel Hood, "Chicago Teachers Union Gets a New Chance to Contest 2010 Firings," *Chicago Tribune*, February 16, 2011, http://articles.chi-cagotribune.com/2011-02-16/news/ct-met-teacher-firings-0217-20110216_1_chi-cago-teachers-union-cps-firings; "Tenure Rights Restored in Chicago," *Chicago Teachers Union*, March 29, 2011, http://www.ctunet.com/blog/appeals-court-orders-board-to-recall-unlawfully-fired-teachers

39. Peter Brogan, "Getting to the CORE of the Chicago Teachers' Union Transformation," *Studies in Social Justice*, 8, no. 2 (2014): 149–150.

40. Rob Bartlett, "Chicago Teachers' Strike Looms: Going Head to Head with 'Mayor 1%,' " *Solidarity*, August 10, 2012, http://www.solidarity-us.org/site/ node/3664; Robert Bartlett, "Creating a New Model of a Social Union," *Monthly Review*, 65, no. 2, June (2013), http://monthlyreview.org/2013/06/01/creating-a-new-model-of-a-social-union/; Micah Uetricht, "Strike for America: The CTU and

the Democrats," *Jacobin*, December 2012, https://www.jacobinmag.com/2012/12/ctu-and-dems/; Tom Atler, "It Felt Like Community": Social Movement Unionism and the Chicago Teachers Union Strike of 2012," *Labor: Studies in Working-Class History of the Americas*, 10, no. 3 (2013): 15–16.

41. Lewis quoted in Atler, "It Felt Like Community," 18.

42. Atler, "It Felt Like Community," 16–17; Brogan, "Getting to the CORE of the Chicago Teachers' Union Transformation,," 149–150.

43. Brogan, "Getting to the CORE of the Chicago Teachers' Union Transformation"; Bartlett, "Creating a New Model of a Social Union"; Atler "It Felt Like Community," 18.

44. Bartlett, "Creating a New Model of a Social Union."

45. Atler, "It Felt Like Community," 18–19; Edelman quoted in Atler, "It Felt Like Community," 19.

46. Atler, "It Felt Like Community," 19–20; Bartlett, "Chicago Teachers' Strike Looms."

47. Bartlett, "Creating a New Model of a Social Union"; Atler, "It Felt Like Community," 22; Brogan, "Getting to the CORE of the Chicago Teachers' Union Transformation," 154; Bartlett, "Chicago Teachers' Strike Looms"; Moody and Post, "The Politics of US Labor: Paralysis and Possibilities," 308.

48. Brogan, "Getting to the CORE of the Chicago Teachers' Union Transformation," 154.

49. Brogan, "Getting to the CORE of the Chicago Teachers' Union Transformation," 157–158.

50. Atler, "It Felt Like Community," 23–24; Brogan, "Getting to the CORE of the Chicago Teachers' Union Transformation," 158–159; David Kaplan, "The Chicago Teachers' Strike and Beyond," *Monthly Review*, 65, no. 2, June (2013), http://monthlyreview.org/2013/06/01/the-chicago-teachers-strike-and-beyond/

51. Brogan, "Getting to the CORE of the Chicago Teachers' Union Transformation," 159–160; Noreen S. Ahmed-Ullah and Kim Geiger, "CPS Lays Off More than 2,000, Including 1,000 Teachers," *Chicago Tribune*, July 19, 2013, http://articles.chicagotribune.com/2013-07-19/news/ct-met-cps-layoffs-20130719_1_pension-reform-cps-new-teachers-contract; Lauren Gambino, "Chicago Lays Off 1,150 Teachers and School Staff as Enrollment Dwindles," *The Guardian*, June 28, 2014, http://www.theguardian.com/world/2014/jun/28/chicago-schools-teacher-layoffs-rahm-emanuel-union; Lewis quoted in Gambino, "Chicago Lays Off 1,150 Teachers."

Chapter 5.
Social Movements, Political Parties, and
Social Movement Unionism: Hope for the Future?

1. Mattathias Schwartz, "Pre-Occupied," *The New Yorker*, November 28, 2011, http://www.newyorker.com/magazine/2011/11/28/pre-occupied; Steven Tufts and Mark P. Thomas, "Populist Unionism Confronts Austerity in Canada," *Labor Studies Journal*, 39, no. 1 (2014): 68.

2. Schwartz, "Pre-Occupied"; Jeff Sharlet, "Inside Occupy Wall Street," *Rolling Stone*, November 10, 2011, http://www.rollingstone.com/politics/news/occupy-wall-street-welcome-to-the-occupation-20111110

3. Sharlet, "Inside Occupy Wall Street"; Schwartz, "Pre-Occupied."

4. Michael D. Yates, "Occupy Wall Street and the Significance of Political Slogans," *Counterpunch*, February 27, 2013, http://www.counterpunch.org/2013/02/27/occupy-wall-street-and-the-significance-of-political-slogans/

5. "Sarah Ahmed Quotes," *Goodreads*, n.d. http://www.goodreads.com/author/quotes/11036.Sara_Ahmed

6. Quinn Norton, "A Eulogy for #Occupy," *Wired*, December 12, 2012, http://www.wired.com/2012/12/a-eulogy-for-occupy/all/

7. Norton, "A Eulogy for #Occupy"; Schwartz, "Pre-Occupied."

8. Tim Gee, "Occupy One Year On: What is the Financial System's Achilles Heel?," *The Guardian*, February 28, 2013, http://www.theguardian.com/commentisfree/2013/feb/28/occupy-one-year-on; *Rolling Jubilee*, n.d. http://rollingjubilee.org/; Paula Mejia, "Occupy Wall Street Offshoot Rolling Jubilee Wants to Pay Off Your Student Debt," *Newsweek*, September 17, 2014, http://www.newsweek.com/occupy-wall-street-offshoot-rolling-jubilee-wants-pay-your-student-debt-271273; Anya Kamenetz, "These People Can Make Student Loans Disappear," *NPR*, September 17, 2014, http://www.npr.org/blogs/ed/2014/09/17/348036877/these-people-can-make-student-loans-disappear; *Strike Debt*, n.d. http://strikedebt.org/

9. Andy Durgan and Joel Sans, ""No One Represents Us": The 15 May Movement in the Spanish State," *International Socialism*, 132, October, 2011, http://www.isj.org.uk/?id=757; Pablo Ouziel, "Spain's 'Indignant Ones,'" *Common Dreams*, June 15, 2011, http://www.commondreams.org/views/2011/06/15/spains-indignant-ones

10. Joseba Elola, "Where Did the 15-M movement Go?" *El Pais*, May 9, 2012, http://elpais.com/elpais/2012/05/09/inenglish/1336575923_876352.html; Ariana Eunjung Cha, "Occupy Movement Evolves in Spain," *The Washington Post*, September 17, 2012, http://www.washingtonpost.com/business/economy/occupy-movement-evolves-in-spain/2012/09/17/92605a86-fb66-11e1-8adc-499661afe377_story.html

11. Peter Gelderloos, "Spanish Revolution at a Crossroads," *Counterpunch*, June 7, 2011, http://www.counterpunch.org/2011/06/07/spanish-revolution-at-a-crossroads/

12. Durgan and Sans, "No One Represents Us"; Murado quoted in Sarah Rainsford, "Spain's 'Indignants' Lead International Protest Day," *BBC News*, October 14, 2011, http://www.bbc.com/news/world-europe-15315270; "Europe's Most Earnest Protesters," *The Economist*, July 14, 2011, http://www.economist.com/node/18959259

13. Elola, "Where Did the 15-M Movement Go?"

14. Seymour, *Against Austerity*; Jesse Rosenfeld, "Quebec Students Spark Mass Protests Against Austerity," *The Nation*, June 12, 2012, http://www.thenation.com/article/168355/quebec-students-spark-mass-protests-against-austerity#;

"Tuition Hike Angers Quebec Students," *CBC News*, March 18, 2011, http://www.cbc.ca/news/canada/montreal/tuition-hike-angers-quebec-students-1.990024

15. "Quebec Students Stage Massive Tuition Fee Protest," *CBC News*, November 10, 2011, http://www.cbc.ca/news/canada/montreal/quebec-students-stage-massive-tuition-fee-protest-1.1044340; "Quebec student strike grows," *CBC News*, February 20, 2012, http://www.cbc.ca/news/canada/montreal/quebec-student-strike-grows-1.1278364

16. Seymour, *Against Austerity*; Rosenfeld, "Quebec Students Spark Mass Protests Against Austerity"; "Massive Student Tuition March Paralyzes Montreal," *CBC News*, March 22, 2011 http://www.cbc.ca/news/canada/montreal/massive-student-tuition-march-paralyzes-montreal-1.1165575

17. "Quebec Offers to Stretch Tuition Hike over 7 Years," *CBC News*, April 27, 2012, http://www.cbc.ca/news/canada/montreal/quebec-offers-to-stretch-tuition-hike-over-7-years-1.1209004

18. Seymour, *Against Austerity*; Rosenfeld, "Quebec Students Spark Mass Protests Against Austerity."

19. "Montreal Protesters Defy Demo Law and Clash with Police," *CBC News*, May 21, 2012, http://www.cbc.ca/news/canada/montreal/montreal-protesters-defy-demo-law-and-clash-with-police-1.1279274; Seymour, *Against Austerity*.

20. Seymour, *Against Austerity*; "Massive Montreal Rally Ends with Police Clashes," *CBC News*, May 22, 2012, http://www.cbc.ca/news/canada/montreal/massive-montreal-rally-ends-with-police-clashes-1.1138111

21. Seymour, *Against Austerity*.

22. Manel Barriere, Andy Durgan, and Sam Robson, "The Challenge of Podemos," *International Socialism*, 145, January 2015, http://www.isj.org.uk/index.php4?id=1028; Louis Proyect, "The Rise of Podemos," *Counterpunch*, December 12–14, 2014, http://www.counterpunch.org/2014/12/12/the-rise-of-podemos/

23. Hancox, "Podemos: The Radical Party Turning Spanish Politics on Its Head"; Barriere, Durgan and Robson, "The Challenge of Podemos"; Owen Jones, "Viva Podemos: The Left Shows It Can Adapt and Thrive in a Crisis," *The Guardian*, November 16, 2014, http://www.theguardian.com/commentisfree/2014/nov/16/podemos-left-crisis-ukip-anti-immigrant; Jonathan Blitzer, "In Spain, Politics via Reddit," *The New Yorker*, October 7, 2014, http://www.newyorker.com/tech/elements/spain-politics-via-reddit

24. Barriere, Durgan and Robson, "The Challenge of Podemos"; David Alexandre, "Is Podemos Slowly Moving Towards Social Democracy?," *Telesur*, December 7, 2014, http://www.telesurtv.net/english/opinion/Is-Podemos-Slowly-Moving-Towards-Social-Democracy-20141208-0019.html; James Badcock, "Podemos under Fire after Grassroots Votes Give Eight of 10 Top Spots to Men," *The Guardian*, January 5, 2015, http://www.theguardian.com/world/2015/jan/04/podemos-municipal-votes-eight-leadership-spots-men

25. Ashifa Kassam, "Spain's Politicians Distance Themselves from Euro Crisis: 'This Isn't Greece,'" *The Guardian*, July 7, 2015, http://www.theguardian.com/world/2015/jul/06/spain-politicians-euro-crisis-greece-podemos

26. "UPDATE: Sigma Dos Poll Shows Ciudadanos Second Behind PP," *The Spain Report*, November 19, 2015, https://www.thespainreport.com/newsitems/329-151119215346-update-sigma-dos-poll-shows-ciudadanos-second-behind-pp; Bustinduy quoted in Guy Hedgecoe, "Has the Party Ended for Podemos?," *Politico*, December 4, 2015, http://www.politico.eu/article/has-the-party-ended-for-podemos-spain-syriza-general-elections/

27. Costas Douzinas, "Syriza Can Be the Future for Greece, and for Europe Too," *The Guardian*, June 3, 2014, http://www.theguardian.com/commentisfree/2014/jun/03/syriza-future-greece-europe-radical-left; Ilias Milonas, "The New Programme of SYRIZA," *The Socialist Network*, December 27, 2014, http://socialistnetwork.org/the-new-programme-of-syriza/

28. Helena Smith and Jill Treanor, "Greece Plunged into Crisis as Failure to Elect President Sets up Snap Election," *The Guardian*, December 30, 2014, http://www.theguardian.com/world/2014/dec/29/greece-crisis-president-snap-election

29. Helena Smith, "The future has begun, says leftist Alexis Tsipras as he scents power in Greece," *The Guardian*, December 30, 2014, http://www.theguardian.com/world/2014/dec/29/syriza-leading-polls-future-begun-alexis-tsipras-greece; "Greece GDP Annual Growth Rate"; "Greece GDP."

30. Manfred Ertel and Christoph Schult, "Greek Roulette: What Would Syriza's Victory Mean for Europe?," *Der Spiegel*, January 5, 2015, http://www.spiegel.de/international/europe/aims-of-greek-politician-alexis-tsipras-remain-a-mystery-in-europe-a-1011288.html

31. Helena Smith, "Greek PM Samaras Forced into U-turn as Syriza Closes in on Election Victory," *The Guardian*, January 11, 2015, http://www.theguardian.com/world/2015/jan/10/greece-election-u-turn-antonis-samaras-syriza; Angeliki Koutantou, "Greek PM Samaras Vows Tax Cuts as Leftists Hold Poll Lead," *Reuters*, January 10, 2015, http://www.reuters.com/article/2015/01/10/us-greece-election-samaras-idUSKBN0KJ0H520150110

32. Ian Traynor and Helena Smith, "Syriza's Historic Win Puts Greece on Collision Course with Europe," *The Guardian*, January 26, 2015, http://www.theguardian.com/world/2015/jan/25/syriza-historic-win-greece-european-union-austerity; Helena Smith and Ian Traynor, "Greek PM Alexis Tsipras Unveils Cabinet of Mavericks and Visionaries," *The Guardian*, January 28, 2015, http://www.theguardian.com/world/2015/jan/27/greece-alexis-tsipras-syriza-cabinet; Paul Mason, "'Hope Begins Today': The Inside Story of Syriza's Rise to Power," *The Guardian*, January 29, 2015, http://www.theguardian.com/world/2015/jan/28/greek-people-wrote-history-how-syriza-rose-to-power

33. Ian Traynor, "Tsipras's Shock Call for vote on Greek Bailout Sets Day of Destiny for Europe," *The Guardian*, June 28, 2015, http://www.theguardian.com/world/2015/jun/27/greece-bailout-referendum-ramps-up-eurozone-crisis; Ian Traynor and Jennifer Rankin, "Greek Failure to Make IMF Payment Deals Historic Blow to Eurozone," *The Guardian*, July 1, 2015, http://www.theguardian.com/world/2015/jun/30/eurozone-emergency-greece-without-financial-lifeline; Varoufakis quoted in Ian Traynor, John Hooper, and Helena Smith, "Greek

Referendum No Vote Signals Huge Challenge to Eurozone Leaders," July 6, 2015, http://www.theguardian.com/business/2015/jul/05/greek-referendum-no-vote-signals-huge-challenge-to-eurozone-leaders; EU official quoted in Ian Traynor, Jennifer Rankin, Helena Smith, "Greek Crisis: Surrender Fiscal Sovereignty in Return for Bailout, Merkel Tells Tsipras," *The Guardian*, July 13, 2015, http://www.theguardian.com/business/2015/jul/12/greek-crisis-surrender-fiscal-sovereignty-in-return-for-bailout-merkel-tells-tsipras; Graeme Wearden, "Greece Bailout Agreement: Key Points," *The Guardian*, July 14, 2015, http://www.theguardian.com/business/2015/jul/13/greece-bailout-agreement-key-points-grexit; Helena Smith, Emma Graham-Harrison, Ben Quinn, Heather Stewart, and Graeme Wearden, "Greek MPs Pass Austerity Bill as Athens Police Clash with Protesters," *The Guardian*, July 16, 2015, http://www.theguardian.com/world/2015/jul/15/greek-mps-pass-austerity-bill-as-athens-police-clash-with-protesters

34. Jacquelien van Stekelenburg, "The Occupy Movement: Product of this time," *Local/Global Encounters*, 55, no. 2 (2012): 227; Robin Cohen, "Transnational Social Movements: An Assessment," Paper to the Transnational Communities Program, 19 June, 1998, http://aix1.uottawa.ca/~rroberge/cohen.pdf

35. van Stekelenburg, "The Occupy Movement," 228

36. van Stekelenburg, "The Occupy Movement," 229; Claus Offe, "Reflections on the Institutional Self-Transformation of Movement Politics: A Tentative Stage Mode" in *Challenging the Political Order*, Russell J. Dalton and Manfred Kuechler (eds.) (NY: Oxford University Press, 1990), 238–239; Barbara Epstein, "Anarchism and the Anti-Globalization Movement," *Monthly Review*, September (2001): 8–9; Ana Cecilia Dinerstein and Juan Pablo Ferrero, "The limits of participatory democracy: social movements and the displacement of disagreement in South America," *Working Paper. Centre for Development Studies* (Bath: University of Bath, 2012).

37. Francis Mulhern, "Towards 2000, or News from You-Know-Where," *New Left Review*, 148, November–December (1984): 22. [Emphasis in Original]

38. There is a debate that there is a difference between social movement unionism in the developing and the developed world. As such, I have previously argued that such a strategy in the developed world should be called social justice unionism (see, Schiavone, *Unions in Crisis?*). However, for the sake of simplicity here I will just use the term social movement unionism.

39. Kim Moody, *Workers in a Lean World* (London and NY: Verso, 1997), 4-5.

40. Anthony W. Marx, "South African Black Trade Unions as an Emerging Working-Class Movement," *The Journal of Modern African Studies*, 27, no. 3 (1989): 393–394.

41. Philip Hirschsohn, "From Grassroots Democracy to National Mobilization: COSATU as a Model of Social Movement Unionism," *Economic and Industrial Democracy*, 19 (1998): 655.

42. Andries Bezuidenhout, "Towards Global Social Movement Unionism? Trade Union Responses to Globalization in South Africa," *International Institute*

for Labor Studies Discussion Paper (2000): 8–9. For analysis of COASTU's alliance with the ANC, see Michael Schiavone, "Social Movement Unions and Political Parties (in South Africa and the Philippines): A Win-Win Situation?" *African and Asian Studies*, 6 (2007): 373–393.

43. Robert H. Zieger, *The CIO 1935–1955* (Chapel Hill and London: University of North Carolina Press, 1995), 145; Ronald L. Filippelli and Mark D. McColloch, *Cold War in the Working Class: The Rise and Decline of the United Electrical Workers* (NY: State University of New York, 1995), 80; James J. Matles and James Higgins, *Them and Us: Struggles of a Rank-and-File Union* (NJ: Prentice-Hall, 1995), 127.

44. Rosemary Feurer, "William Senter, The UE, and Civic Unionism in St. Louis" in Steve Rosswurm (ed.) *The CIO's Left-Led Unions* (New Brunswick, NJ: Rutgers University Press, 1992), 101.

45. *St. Louis Star-Times* quoted in "How a Union Saved 1500 Jobs, a $2,000,000 Payroll and the Business they Create for St. Louis," March 1940, pp. 5–6, *United Electrical, Radio and Machine Workers of America Archive [UEA]*, University of Pittsburgh, Box 1430, FF6; Feurer, pp. 108–112; *UE News*, August 5, 1944, pp. 6–7.

46. Stepan-Norris and Zeitlin determine whether a contract is pro-labour in the following areas: management prerogatives; the right to strike; contract term; trade-off provisions; and grievance procedure, see Judith Stepan-Norris, Maurice Zeitlin, "Union Democracy, Radical Leadership, and the Hegemony of Capital,' *American Sociological Review*, 60, no. 6, December (1995): 839–840.

47. Ibid., 844.

48. Andrew E. G. Jonas, "Investigating the Local-Global Paradox," in *Organizing the Landscape: Geographical Perspectives on Labor Unionism*, edited by Andrew Herod (London: University of Minnesota Press, 1998), 333.

49. Ibid., 337.Andrew E. G. Jonas, "Labor and Community in the Deindustrialization of Urban America," *Journal of Urban Affairs*, 17, no. 2 (1995): 189; Reverend Jesse Jackson quoted in *UE News*, December 11, 1987, p. 3.

50. Jonas, "Investigating the Local-Global Paradox," 345.

51. *UE News*, January 15, 1993, p. 4; *UE News*, February 4, 1994, p. 2.

52. Schiavone, *Unions in Crisis?*, 107, 79. For greater analysis of the success of social justice/movement unionism around the globe, see Michael Schiavone, "Moody's Account of Social Movement Unionism: An Analysis," *Critical Sociology*, 33, March (2007): 279–309.

53. Schiavone, "Social Movement Unions and Political Parties," 382–385.

54. Ian Robinson, "Does Neoliberal Restructuring Promote Social Movement Unionism? U.S. Developments in Comparative Perspective." In *Unions in a Globalized Environment*, edited by Bruce Nissen, 199 (Armonk: M.E. Sharpe, 2002); J.M. Barbalet, "Social Movements and the State: The Case of the American Labour Movement." In *Politics of the Future: The Role of Social Movements,* edited by Christine Jennet and Randal G. Stewart, 237–261. (Melbourne: The MacMillan

Company of Australia, 1989), 255; Michael Schiavone, "Social Movement Unionism and the UE," *The Flinders Journal of History and Politics*, 23 (2006).

55. Jonathan Walker, "'Abandon austerity and borrow' North East Labour MPs urges Ed Miliband," *Chronicle Live*, January 28, 2015, http://www.chronicle-live.co.uk/news/north-east-news/abandon-austerity-borrow-north-east-8526379

56. Tariq Ali, "Bloody Sunday: the Combined Attack on Jeremy Corbyn," *Counterpunch*, September 22, 2015, http://www.counterpunch.org/2015/09/22/bloody-sunday-the-combined-attack-on-jeremy-corbyn/

Bibliography

"2014 Wisconsin governor election results." *Politico*, December 17, 2014, http://www.politico.com/2014-election/results/map/governor/wisconsin/#.VKC7Sv-xMw

"50,000 attend Manchester protest against austerity." *The Guardian*, September 29, 2013, http://www.theguardian.com/uk-news/2013/sep/29/thousands-protest-manchester-austerity

Ahmed, Azam. "CPS faces $1 billion deficit, Huberman says." *Chicago Tribune*, February 25, 2010, http://articles.chicagotribune.com/2010-02-25/news/ct-met-chicago-school-cuts-20100225_1_pension-system-pension-reform-furlough-days

Ahmed-Ullah, Noreen S., and Kim Geiger, "CPS lays off more than 2,000, including 1,000 teachers." *Chicago Tribune*, July 19, 2013, http://articles.chicagotribune.com/2013-07-19/news/ct-met-cps-layoffs-20130719_1_pension-reform-cps-new-teachers-contract

Alderman, Liz. "Hardships linger for a mending Ireland." *The New York Times*, December 12, 2013, http://www.nytimes.com/2013/12/12/business/international/as-bailout-chapter-closes-hardships-linger-for-irish.html?pagewanted=1&_r=0

———. "Ireland unveils austerity plan to help secure bailout." *The New York Times*, November 25, 2010, http://www.nytimes.com/2010/11/25/world/europe/25ireland.html?_r=0

———. "In Ireland, austerity is praised but painful." *The New York Times*, December 6, 2011, http://www.nytimes.com/2011/12/06/business/global/despite-praise-for-its-austerity-ireland-and-its-people-are-being-battered.html?pagewanted=all

Alexandre, David. "Is Podemos slowly moving towards Social Democracy?" *Telesur*, December 7, 2014, http://www.telesurtv.net/english/opinion/Is-Podemos-Slowly-Moving-Towards-Social-Democracy-20141208-0019.html

Alexiou, Constantinos, and Joseph Nellis. "Is there life after 'death' for the Greek economy?" *International Journal of Economics and Financial Issues*, 3: 4 (2013): 861–873.

Ali, Tariq. "Bloody Sunday: The combined attack on Jeremy Corbyn." *Counterpunch*, September 22, 2015, http://www.counterpunch.org/2015/09/22/bloody-sunday-the-combined-attack-on-jeremy-corbyn/

Allen, Katie. "Budget 2012: the key points in summary." *The Guardian*, March 22, 2012, http://www.theguardian.com/uk/2012/mar/21/budget-2012-summary

———. "UK on track to be fastest growing G7 economy despite slowdown," *The Guardian*, October 25, 2014, http://www.theguardian.com/business/2014/oct/24/uk-economic-growth-slows

Atler, Tom. "It felt like community": Social movement unionism and the Chicago Teachers Union strike of 2012." *Labor: Studies in Working-Class History of the Americas*, 10: 3 (2013), 11–25.

Auerback, Marshall " 'End' of the Recession No Time to End Government Spending," *Roosevelt Institute*, n.d, http://

"Austerity Britain: It's déjà vu all over again." *University of Cambridge*, January 16, 2013, http://www.cam.ac.uk/research/news/austerity-britain-its-d%C3%A9j%C3%A0-vu-all-over-again

"Austerity seriously affecting health in Europe, North America." *VOA News*, May 3, 2013, http://www.voanews.com/content/austerity-seriously-affecting-health-in-europe-north-america/1654291.html

Bach, Stephen, and Alexander Stroleny. "Public service employment restructuring in the crisis in the UK and Ireland: Social partnership in retreat." *European Journal of Industrial Relations*, 19:4 (2013), 341–357.

Badcock, James. "Podemos under fire after grassroots votes give eight of 10 top spots to men." *The Guardian*, January 5, 2015, http://www.theguardian.com/world/2015/jan/04/podemos-municipal-votes-eight-leadership-spots-men

Baker, Peter, and Jackie Calmes. "Amid deficit fears, Obama freezes pay." *The New York Times*, November 29, 2010, http://www.nytimes.com/2010/11/30/us/politics/30freeze.html?_r=0

Barbalet, J.M. "Social movements and the state: The case of the American Labour Movement." In *Politics of the Future: The Role of Social Movements*, edited by Christine Jennet and Randal G. Stewart, 237–261. (Melbourne: The MacMillan Company of Australia, 1989).

Barriere, Manel Andy Durgan, and Sam Robson. "The challenge of Podemos." *International Socialism*, 145, January 2015, http://www.isj.org.uk/index.php4?id=1028

Bartlett, Evan. "Lords refuse to cut costs because 'champagne quality would suffer.' "*The Independent*, December 7, 2014, http://i100.independent.co.uk/article/lords-refuse-to-cut-costs-because-champagne-quality-would-suffer-gkRgp-6Cux

———. "Creating a new model of a social union," *Monthly Review*, 65:2 (June 2013), http://monthlyreview.org/2013/06/01/creating-a-new-model-of-a-social-union/

Bartlett, Rob. "Chicago Teachers' Strike Looms: Going Head to Head with 'Mayor 1%.' " *Solidarity*, August 10, 2012, http://www.solidarity-us.org/site/node/3664

"Benefits." *Fawcett Society*, February, 2013, http://www.fawcettsociety.org.uk/2013/02/benefits/

"Better Pensions, Health Care." *AFL-CIO*, 2014, http://www.aflcio.org/Learn-About-Unions/What-Unions-Do/The-Union-Difference/Better-Pensions-Health-Care

Bezuidenhout, Andries. "Towards global social movement unionism? Trade union responses to globalization in South Africa." *International Institute for Labor Studies Discussion Paper*, (2000).

Blanchflower, David, and Stephen Machin, "Falling real wages." *CentrePiece*, Spring 2014, http://cep.lse.ac.uk/pubs/download/cp422.pdf

Blitzer, Jonathan. "In Spain, politics via Reddit." *The New Yorker*, October 7, 2014, http://www.newyorker.com/tech/elements/spain-politics-via-reddit

Blyth, Mark. *Austerity: The History of a Dangerous Idea*. (Oxford: Oxford University Press, 2013). Kindle Edition.

———. "The Austerity Delusion." *Foreign Affairs*, May/June (2013), http://www.foreignaffairs.com/articles/139105/mark-blyth/the-austerity-delusion

Botz, Dan La. "A New American Workers Movement has begun." *MR Zine*, February 18, 2011, http://mrzine.monthlyreview.org/2011/labotz180211.html

"Brazil External Debt." *Index Mundi*, http://www.indexmundi.com/brazil/debt_external.html

Breidthardt, Annika, and Jan Strupczewski. "Europe seals new Greek bailout but doubts remain." *Reuters*, February 21, 2012, http://www.reuters.com/article/2012/02/21/us-greece-idUSTRE8120HI20120221

"Britain's emergency budget Ouch!" *The Economist*, June 22, 2010, http://www.economist.com/blogs/newsbook/2010/06/britains_emergency_budget?zid=295&ah=0bca374e65f2354d553956ea65f756e0

Brogan, Peter. "Getting to the CORE of the Chicago Teachers' Union transformation." *Studies in Social Justice*, 8:2 (2014), 145–164.

Buchanan, Rose Troup. "Almost 50% of referrals to food banks in the UK are due to 'issues with the welfare system.'" *The Independent*, December 9, 2014, http://www.independent.co.uk/news/uk/home-news/almost-50-of-referrals-to-food-banks-in-the-uk-are-due-to-issues-with-the-welfare-system-9910973.html

"Budget 2010: key points." *The Guardian*, June 22, 2010, http://www.theguardian.com/uk/2010/jun/22/budget-2010-key-points

"Budget 2012 at a glance: George Osborne's key points." *BBC News*, March 22, 2012, http://www.bbc.com/news/uk-politics-17449501

"Budget 2013 at a glance: George Osborne's key points." *BBC News*, March 20, 2013, http://www.bbc.com/news/uk-politics-21851965

"Budget 2015 'marks end of austerity' as welfare hikes, tax cuts announced." *RTÉ News*, October 14, 2014, http://www.rte.ie/news/budget/2014/1014/652098-budget-morning/

Buendía, Luis. "Crisis, austerity and labor reactions—Spain in the spotlight." *ZNet*, October 20, 2010, http://zcomm.org/znetarticle/crisis-austerity-and-labor-reactions-spain-in-the-spotlight-1st-part-by-luis-buend-a/

Bureau of Labor Statistics, "Table 2. Median weekly earnings of full-time wage and salary workers by union affiliation and selected characteristics." Bureau of Labor Statistics, 2015, http://www.bls.gov/news.release/union2.t02.htm

Bureau of Labor Statistics, "Table 4. Median weekly earnings of full-time wage and salary workers by union affiliation, occupation, and industry, 2013–2014 annual averages." Bureau of Labor Statistics, 2015, http://www.bls.gov/news.release/union2.t04.htm

Burke-Kennedy, Eoin. " 'Married or co-habiting women hit harder by austerity.' "*The Irish Times*, October 3, 2014, http://www.irishtimes.com/business/economy/married-or-co-habiting-women-hit-harder-by-austerity-1.1950132

Butler, Patrick, and Amelia Gentleman. "Benefit cuts putting 200,000 children in poverty must be stopped, experts say." *The Guardian*, March 27, 2013, http://www.theguardian.com/society/2013/mar/27/benefit-cuts-poverty-stopped-experts

"Call for emergency TUC meeting." *Express*, June 21, 2010, http://www.express.co.uk/news/uk/182086/Call-for-emergency-TUC-meeting

Cantin, Étienne. "The politics of austerity and the conservative offensive against US public sector unions, 2008–2012." *Relations Industrielles*, 67:4 (Fall 2012), 612–632

Carrell, Severin, Dan Milmo, Alan Travis, and Nick Hopkins, "Day of strikes as millions heed unions' call to fight pension cuts." *The Guardian*, November 30, 2011, http://www.theguardian.com/society/2011/nov/30/public-sector-workers-strike-uk

Cassidy, John. "By George, Britain's Austerity Experiment Didn't Work!" *The New Yorker*, December 5, 2013, http://www.newyorker.com/news/john-cassidy/by-george-britains-austerity-experiment-didnt-work

———. "The Reinhart and Rogoff controversy: A summing up." *The New Yorker*, April 26, 2013, http://www.newyorker.com/news/john-cassidy/the-reinhart-and-rogoff-controversy-a-summing-up

Castle, Stephen. "With details settled, a 2nd Greek bailout is formally approved." *The New York Times,* March 14, 2012, http://www.nytimes.com/2012/03/15/business/global/greece-gets-formal-approval-for-second-bailout.html

Centonze, Arthur L. "The Irish banking crisis." *Review of Business and Finance Studies*, 5:2 (2014), 85–108.

Cha, Ariana Eunjung. "Occupy movement evolves in Spain." *The Washington Post*, September 17, 2012, http://www.washingtonpost.com/business/economy/occupy-movement-evolves-in-spain/2012/09/17/92605a86-fb66-11e1-8adc-499661afe377_story.html

Choonara, Joseph. "The class struggles in Europe." International Socialism, 138, (2013), http://www.isj.org.uk/?id=883#138choonara52

Clement, Scott, and Aaron Blake, "Wisconsin recall: Union voters ≠ union households." *The Washington Post*, June 6, 2012, http://www.washingtonpost.com/blogs/the-fix/post/wisconsin-recall-union-voters--union-households/2012/06/06/gJQA3l6VHV_blog.html

Coalition for Health Funding. *Faces of Austerity: How Budget Cuts Hurt America's Health*, July (2014).

Cohen, Robin. "Transnational social movements: an assessment." Paper to the Transnational Communities Program, 19 June, 1998, http://aix1.uottawa.ca/~rroberge/cohen.pdf

Conde-Ruiz, J. Ignacio, and Carmen Marín, "The fiscal crisis in Spain," *Intereconomics* (2013), http://www.intereconomics.eu/archive/year/2013/1/austerity-measures-in-crisis-countries-results-and-impact-on-mid-term-development/

Cooper, Charlie. "Tough austerity measures in Greece leave nearly a million people with no access to healthcare, leading to soaring infant mortality, HIV infection and suicide." *The Independent*, February 21, 2014, http://www.independent.co.uk/news/world/europe/tough-austerity-measures-in-greece-leave-nearly-a-million-people-with-no-access-to-healthcare-leading-to-soaring-infant-mortality-hiv-infection-and-suicide-9142274.html

Coulter, Steve. "Insider lobbying: 'New Labour and the TUC.'"New European Trades Union Forum, February 27, 2014, http://blogs.lse.ac.uk/netuf/2014/02/27/insider-lobbying-new-labour-and-the-tuc/

Counihan, Patrick. "Irish Labour Party vote collapses in local and European elections." *Irish Central*, May 24, 2014, http://www.irishcentral.com/news/politics/Irish-Labour-Party-vote-collapses-in-local-and-European-elections.html?showAll=y

Cox, Laurence. "Why are the Irish not resisting austerity?" *Open Democracy*, October 11, 2013, https://www.opendemocracy.net/can-europe-make-it/laurence-cox/why-are-irish-not-resisting-austerity

Coy, Peter. "FAQ: Reinhart, Rogoff, and the Excel Error That Changed History." *Businessweek*, April 18, 2013, http://www.businessweek.com/articles/2013-04-18/faq-reinhart-rogoff-and-the-excel-error-that-changed-history

Crafts, Nicholas. "How housebuilding helped the economy recover: Britain in the 1930s." *The Guardian*, April 19, 2013, http://www.theguardian.com/housing-network/2013/apr/19/1930s-house-building-economic-recovery

Credit Suisse. *Global Wealth Report 2014.* (Zurich: Credit Suisse Research Institute, 2014).

Croucher, Shane. "UK Strikes: Number of Working Days Lost Rockets 78% in 2013." *International Business Times*, July 17, 2014, http://www.ibtimes.co.uk/uk-strikes-number-working-days-lost-rockets-78-2013-1457055

Culzac, Natasha. "Teachers' strike: Mass public sector walk-out as thousands protest against pay and working conditions." *The Independent*, July 10, 2014, http://www.independent.co.uk/news/uk/teachers-strike-mass-public-sector-walkout-as-thousands-protest-against-pay-and-working-conditions-9596547.html

"Daily Treasury Long Term Rate Data." *US Department of Treasury*, May 27, 2015, http://www.treasury.gov/resource-center/data-chart-center/interest-rates/Pages/TextView.aspx?data=longtermrateAll

DeSilver, Drew. "For most workers, real wages have barely budged for decades." *Pew Research Center*, October 9, 2014, http://www.pewresearch. org/fact-tank/2014/10/09/for-most-workers-real-wages-have-barely-budged-for-decades/

Dine, Philip. *State of the Unions*. (New York: McGraw Hill, 2008).

Dinerstein, Ana Cecilia, and Juan Pablo Ferrero. "The limits of participatory democracy: social movements and the displacement of disagreement in South America." *Working Paper. Centre for Development Studies*, (Bath: University of Bath, 2012).

Donadio, Rachel. "Supporters of Bailout Claim Victory in Greek Election." *The New York Times*, June 18, 2012, http://www.nytimes.com/2012/06/18/world/europe/greek-elections.html?pagewanted=all&_r=0

Douzinas, Costas. "Syriza can be the future for Greece, and for Europe too." *The Guardian*, June 3, 2014, http://www.theguardian.com/commentisfree/2014/jun/03/syriza-future-greece-europe-radical-left

Drum, Kevin. "How austerity wrecked the American economy." *Mother Jones*, September 23, 2013, http://www.motherjones.com/kevin-drum/2013/09/obama-austerity-wrecked-american-economy

Duncan, Hugo. "Top central banker Alan Greenspan praises Osborne's austerity measures as economic recovery continues to gather speed." *Daily Mail*, October 22, 2013, http://www.dailymail.co.uk/news/article-2471132/Banker-Alan-Greenspan-praises-George-Osbornes-austerity-measures.html

Durgan, Andy, and Joel Sans, ""No one represents us": the 15 May movement in the Spanish state." *International Socialism*, 132, October, 2011, http://www.isj.org.uk/?id=757

Eaton, George. "How Ukip is turning left on the economy," *The New Statesman*, April 22, 2014, http://www.newstatesman.com/politics/2014/04/how-ukip-turning-left-economy

"ECB threatened to cut off emergency funding for banks in 'secret' Nov 2010 letter." *Breaking News.ie*, November 6, 2014, http://www.breakingnews.ie/ireland/ecb-threatened-to-cut-off-emergency-funding-for-banks-in-secret-nov-2010-letter-649969.html

"Economy tracker: Unemployment." *BBC News*, November 12, 2014, http://www.bbc.co.uk/news/10604117

Eisenscher, Michael. "Is the secret to Labor's future in Its past?" *WorkingUSA* 5:4 (2002), 95–122.

"Election 2010." *BBC News*, 2010, http://news.bbc.co.uk/2/shared/election2010/results/

"Election 2015." *BBC News*, 2015, http://www.bbc.com/news/election/2015/results

Elliott, Larry, and Hélène Mulholland. "Budget 2010: VAT to rise to 20% as Osborne seeks to balance books by 2015." *The Guardian*, http://www.the-guardian.com/uk/2010/jun/22/budget-2010-vat-rise-osborne

Elola, Joseba. "Where did the 15-M movement go?" *El Pais*, May 9, 2012, http://elpais.com/elpais/2012/05/09/inenglish/1336575923_876352.html

"Employee Benefits in the United States—March 2014," *Bureau of Labor Statistics*, 2014, http://www.bls.gov/news.release/pdf/ebs2.pdf

Epstein, Barbara. "Anarchism and the Anti-Globalization Movement." *Monthly Review*, (September 2001), 1–14.

Erne, Ronald. "Let's accept a smaller slice of a shrinking cake. The Irish Congress of Trade Unions and Irish public sector unions in crisis." *Transfer: European Review of Labour and Research*, 19:3 (2013), 425–430.

Ertel, Manfred, and Christoph Schult. "Greek Roulette: What Would Syriza's Victory Mean for Europe?" *Der Spiegel*, January 5, 2015, http://www.spiegel.de/international/europe/aims-of-greek-politician-alexis-tsipras-remain-a-mystery-in-europe-a-1011288.html

"Europe and IMF Agree €110 Billion Financing Plan With Greece." *IMF Survey Magazine*, May 2, 2010, http://www.imf.org/external/pubs/ft/survey/so/2010/car050210a.htm

European Economic and Social Committee Workers' Group. *The Impact of Anti-Crisis Measures, and the Social and Employment Situation: Greece*, (2012), http://www.ictu.ie/download/pdf/greceen.pdf

"Eurozone approves massive Greece bail-out." *BBC News*, May 2, 2010, http://news.bbc.co.uk/2/hi/business/8656649.stm

"Europe's most earnest protesters." *The Economist*, July 14, 2011, http://www.economist.com/node/18959259

Evans, Geoffrey, and Jon Mellon. "Working class votes and Conservative losses: solving the UKIP puzzle." The London School of Economics and Political Science, April 30, 2015, http://blogs.lse.ac.uk/generalelection/working-class-votes-and-conservative-losses-solving-the-ukip-puzzle/

Evans-Pritchard, Ambrose. "Britain to have worst 2014 trade deficit in industrial world on EU forecasts." *The Telegraph*, November 5, 2013, http://www.telegraph.co.uk/finance/economics/10427783/Britain-to-have-worst-2014-trade-deficit-in-industrial-world-on-EU-forecasts.html

"Executive Order 13531—National Commission on Fiscal Responsibility and Reform." *Office of the Press Secretary: White House*, February 18, 2010, http://www.whitehouse.gov/the-press-office/executive-order-national-commission-fiscal-responsibility-and-reform

Faiola, Anthony. "Ireland agrees to $90 billion bailout terms." *The Washington Post*, November 28, 2010, http://www.washingtonpost.com/wp-dyn/content/article/2010/11/28/AR2010112804133.html

———. "Irish government, seeking bailout, unveils $20 billion in spending cuts, taxes." *The Washington Post*, November 24, 2010, http://www.washingtonpost.com/wp-dyn/content/article/2010/11/24/AR2010112401510.html

Fantasia, Rick, and Kim Voss. *Hard Work* (Berkeley: University of California Press, 2004).

Feurer, Rosemary. "William Senter, the UE, and Civic Unionism in St. Louis." In *The CIO's Left-Led Unions*, edited by Steve Rosswurm, 95–117 (New Brunswick, NJ: Rutgers University Press, 1992).

Filippelli Ronald L., and Mark D. McColloch, *Cold War in the Working Class: The Rise and Decline of the United Electrical Workers*. (Albany, NY: State University of New York, 1995).

"Financial Assistance to Greece." *European Commission*, October 20, 2014, http://ec.europa.eu/economy_finance/assistance_eu_ms/greek_loan_facility/

Finn, Christina. "ASTI accepts latest Haddington Road Agreement." *The Journal*, December 19, 2013, http://www.thejournal.ie/asti-accept-haddington-road-agreement-1232561-Dec2013/

Fishman, Nina. "The Union Makes us Strong." *TUC Online*, n.d. http://www.unionhistory.info/timeline/1960_2000.php

Friedman, Thomas L. "Greece's newest odyssey." *The New York Times*, May 12, 2010, http://www.nytimes.com/2010/05/12/opinion/12friedman.html

"Full Page Ad." *CATO Institute*, January 9, 2009, www.cato.org/spccial/stimulus09/cato_stimulus.pdf

Gago, Angie. "Spanish trade unions must change with the times if they are to offer a coherent voice against austerity policies." *The London School of Economics and Political Science*, August (2013), http://blogs.lse.ac.uk/europpblog/2013/08/19/spanish-trade-unions-must-change-with-the-times-if-they-are-to-offer-a-coherent-voice-against-austerity-policies/

————. "Trade unions' strategies and austerity politics in Southern Europe: The role of Labour in Spain, Italy and Portugal vis-à-vis austerity measures." Paper prepared for the ECPR General Conference 2014, Glasgow Panel: Anti-Austerity Protest in Southern Europe Section: Reshaping State and Society in Southern Europe 3–6 September 2014, University of Glasgow.

Galluzzo, Mauro. "Anti-cuts march: 500,000 protest against cuts." *Express*, March 26, 2011, http://www.express.co.uk/news/uk/236958/Anti-cuts-march-500-000-protest-against-cuts

Gambino, Lauren. "Chicago lays off 1,150 teachers and school staff as enrolment dwindles." *The Guardian*, June 28, 2014, http://www.theguardian.com/world/2014/jun/28/chicago-schools-teacher-layoffs-rahm-emanuel-union

"GDP growth (annual %)." *World Bank*, 2014, http://data.worldbank.org/indicator/NY.GDP.MKTP.KD.ZG

Gee, Tim. "Occupy one year on: What is the financial system's achilles heel?" *The Guardian*, February 28, 2013, http://www.theguardian.com/commentisfree/2013/feb/28/occupy-one-year-on

Gelderloos, Peter. "Spain fights austerity." April 3, 2012, http://www.counterpunch.org/2012/04/03/spain-fights-austerity/

————. "Spanish Revolution at a Crossroads." *Counterpunch*, June 7, 2011, http://www.counterpunch.org/2011/06/07/spanish-revolution-at-a-crossroads/

Gilbert, Craig. "State posts largest percentage job loss in U.S. over past year." *Milwaukee Journal Sentinel*, April 24, 2012, http://www.jsonline.com/business/state-posts-largest-percentage-job-loss-in-us-over-past-year-report-shows-ib54utt-148694855.html

Gilbert, Mark. "Britain's austerity finally leads to economic growth." *Bloomberg*, May 1, 2014, http://www.bloomberg.com/bw/articles/2014-05-01/britains-austerity-finally-leads-to-economic-growth

Giles, Chris. "Poor to be hit most by service cuts." *Financial Times*, June 23, 2010, http://www.ft.com/intl/cms/s/0/47b05ac2-7efe-11df-8398-00144feabdc0.html#axzz3KsPKGHFC

Gill, Stephen. "Finance, production and Panopticism: Inequality, risk and resistance in an era of disciplinary neo-liberalism." In *Globalization, Democratization and Multilateralism* edited by Stephen Gill, 51–76 (NY: St. Martin's Press, 1997).

———. "Globalisation, Market Civilisation, and Disciplinary Neoliberalism" *Millennium*, 24:3 (1995), 99–423.

———. "Knowledge, politics, and neo-liberal political economy." In *Political Economy and the Changing Global Order* edited by Richard Stubbs and Geoffrey Underhill, 2nd edition, 48–59, (Canada: Oxford University Press, 2000)

———. "Market civilization, new constitutionalism, and world order." In *New Constitutionalism and World Order*, edited by Stephen Gill and A. Claire Cutler, 29–44 (Cambridge: Cambridge University Press, 2014).

———. "Neo-liberalism and the shift towards a US-centred transnational hegemony.' In *Restructuring Hegemony in the Global Political Economy*, edited by Henk Overbeek, 246–282 (London: Routledge, 1993).

———. "Structural change and global political economy: Globalizing elites and the emerging world order. In *Global Transformation*, edited by Y. Sakamoto, 169–199 (Japan: United Nations University 1994).

Gill, Stephen, and David Law, "Global hegemony and the structural power of capital,' *International Studies Quarterly*, 33:4 (1989), 475–499.

Gongloff, Mark. "Janet Yellen: Rising income inequality could seriously harm the U.S. economy," *The Huffington Post*, October 17, 2014, http://www.huffingtonpost.com/2014/10/17/janet-yellen-inequality_n_6002774.html

———. "U.S. creates 248,000 jobs in September; unemployment rate falls to 5.9%." *The Huffington Post*, October 3, 2014, http://www.huffingtonpost.com/2014/10/03/september-jobs-report-unemployment-rate_n_5922146.html

Gould, Elise, and Will Kimball. "'Right-to-Work' states still have lower wages." *Economic Policy Institute*, April 22, 2015, http://www.epi.org/publication/right-to-work-states-have-lower-wages

"Greece GDP." *Trading Economics*, 2015, http://www.tradingeconomics.com/greece/gdp

"Greece GDP Annual Growth Rate." *Trading Economics*, 2015, http://www.tradingeconomics.com/greece/gdp-growth-annual

Greenhouse, Steven. "Wisconsin's legacy for unions." *The New York Times*, February 22, 2014, http://www.nytimes.com/2014/02/23/business/wisconsins-legacy-for-unions.html

Hancox, Dan. "Podemos: The Radical Party turning Spanish politics on its head." *Newsweek*, October 31, 2014, http://www.newsweek.com/2014/10/31/podemosradical-party-turning-spanish-politics-head-279018.html

Hardiman, Niamh, and Aidan Regan. "The politics of austerity in Ireland." *Intereconomics* (2013), http://www.intereconomics.eu/archive/year/2013/1/austerity-measures-in-crisis-countries-results-and-impact-on-mid-term-development/

Harissis, George. "Unions in the firing line." *The Institute of Employment Rights*, August 22, 2014, http://www.ier.org.uk/blog/unions-firing-line

Hedgecoe, Guy. "Has the party ended for Podemos?" *Politico*, December 4, 2015, http://www.politico.eu/article/has-the-party-ended-for-podemos-spain-syriza-general-elections/

Helleiner, Eric. "Freeing money: Why have states been more willing to liberalize capital controls than trade barriers." *Policy Science*, 27:4 (1994), 299–318.

Henwood, Doug. "Walker's victory, un-sugar-coated." *LBO News from Doug Henwood*, June 6, 2012, http://lbo-news.com/2012/06/06/walkers-victory-un-sugar-coated/

Hicks, Josh. "Obama gives federal workers a 2015 pay raise." *The Washington Post*, December, 19, 2014, http://www.washingtonpost.com/blogs/federal-eye/wp/2014/12/19/obama-gives-federal-workers-a-2015-pay-raise/

Hills, Sally, and Ryland Thomas. "The UK recession in context—what do three centuries of data tell us?" *Bank of England*, http://www.bankofengland.co.uk/publications/Documents/quarterlybulletin/qb100403.pdf

Hirsch Barry T., and David A. Macpherson. "Union membership, coverage, density and employment by state, 2011." *Unionstats.com*, 2012, http://unionstats.gsu.edu/State_U_2011.htm

———. "Union membership, coverage, density and employment by state, 2014," *Unionstats.com*, 2015, http://unionstats.gsu.edu/State_U_2014.htm

Hirschsohn, Philip. "From grassroots democracy to national mobilization: COSATU as a model of social movement unionism." *Economic and Industrial Democracy*, 19 (1988): 633–666.

Hoggett, Paul, Hen Wilkinson, and Pheobe Beedell, "Fairness and the politics of resentment," *Journal of Social Policy*, 42:3 (2013), 567–585.

Hood, Joel. "Chicago Teachers Union gets a new chance to contest 2010 firings," *Chicago Tribune*, February 16, 2011, http://articles.chicagotribune.com/2011-02-16/news/ct-met-teacher-firings-0217-20110216_1_chicago-teachers-union-cps-firings

"How a union saved 1500 jobs, a $2,000,000 payroll and the business they create for St. Louis," March 1940, pp. 5–6, *United Electrical, Radio and Machine Workers of America Archive [UEA]*, University of Pittsburgh, Box 1430, FF6.

Hoxie, Robert. *Trade Unionism in the United States*. 2nd edition, (New York: Appleton, Century, Crofts Inc., 1966).

Hurd, Richard W. "Contesting the dinosaur image: The labor movement's search for a future," *Labor Studies Journal* 22:4 (Winter 1998), 5–30.

Hutton, Will. "Inequality has become a challenge to us as moral beings." *The Guardian*, January 25, 2015, http://www.theguardian.com/books/2015/jan/25/inequality-has-become-challenge-how-good-we-can-be-extract-will-hutton

IMF. "Greece: Ex post evaluation of exceptional access under the 2010 stand-by arrangement." *IMF Country Report No. 13/156* (June 2013).

"Ireland Budget: More austerity measures." *Sky News*, December 5, 2012, http://news.sky.com/story/1021182/ireland-budget-more-austerity-measures

"Ireland has the highest birth, lowest death and greatest emigration rates in Europe." *The Journal*, November 21, 2013, http://www.thejournal.ie/emigration-figures-ireland-1185157-Nov2013/

"Ireland unemployment rate." *Trading Economics*, 2014, http://www.tradingeconomics.com/ireland/unemployment-rate

"Ireland's 'final austerity budget' unveiled." *Sky News*, October 15, 2013, http://news.sky.com/story/1154987/irelands-final-austerity-budget-unveiled

"Irish healthcare suffers most in Europe from austerity." *Breaking News.ie*, November 21, 2014, http://www.breakingnews.ie/ireland/irish-healthcare-suffers-most-in-europe-from-austerity-651885.html

"Irish water: Domestic water charges scheme to begin." *BBC News*, September 30, 2014, http://www.bbc.com/news/world-europe-29423564

Irwin, Neil. *The Alchemists: Three Central Bankers and a World on Fire*. (NY: The Penguin Press, 2013) Kindle Edition.

"Issue of the Week: Walker's austerity agenda is killing job creation." *Express Milwaukee*, March 28, 2014, http://expressmilwaukee.com/article-23007-issue-of-the-week:-walker%E2%80%99s-austerity-agenda-is-killing-job-creation-|-expresso-|-shepherd-express.html

Jonas, Andrew E.G. "Investigating the Local-Global Paradox," in *Organizing the Landscape: Geographical Perspectives on Labor Unionism*, edited by Andrew Herod, 325–350, (London: University of Minnesota Press, 1998).

———. "Labor and Community in the Deindustrialization of Urban America." *Journal of Urban Affairs*, 17:2 (1995), 183–199.

Jones, Owen. "It's socialism for the rich and capitalism for the rest of us in Britain." *The Guardian*, August 29, 2014, http://www.theguardian.com/books/2014/aug/29/socialism-for-the-rich

———. "Viva Podemos: the left shows it can adapt and thrive in a crisis." *The Guardian*, November 16, 2014, http://www.theguardian.com/commentisfree/2014/nov/16/podemos-left-crisis-ukip-anti-immigrant

Jones, Tim. "Republican whipping-boy Illinois beats Wisconsin on jobs." *Bloomberg*, April 20, 2012, http://www.bloomberg.com/news/2012-04-20/republican-whipping-boy-illinois-beats-wisconsin-on-jobs.html

Kamenetz, Anya. "These people can make student loans disappear." *NPR*, September 17, 2014, http://www.npr.org/blogs/ed/2014/09/17/348036877/these-people-can-make-student-loans-disappear

Kaplan, David. "The Chicago teachers' strike and beyond." *Monthly Review*, 65: 2 (June 2013), http://monthlyreview.org/2013/06/01/the-chicago-teachers-strike-and-beyond/

Kassam, Ashifa. "Spain's politicians distance themselves from euro crisis: 'This isn't Greece.'" *The Guardian*, July 7, 2015, http://www.theguardian.com/world/2015/jul/06/spain-politicians-euro-crisis-greece-podemos

Kaufman, Dan. "Scott Walker and the Fate of the Union," *The New York Times*, June 12, 2015, http://www.nytimes.com/2015/06/14/magazine/scott-walker-and-the-fate-of-the-union.html

Kaufmann, Eric. "The 'shy' English nationalists who won it for the Tories and flummoxed the pollsters." The London School of Economics and Political Science, May 12, 2015, http://blogs.lse.ac.uk/generalelection/the-shy-eng-lish-nationalists-who-won-it-for-the-tories-and-flummoxed-the-pollsters/

Kelland, Kate. "Spanish austerity cuts put lives at risk, study finds." *Reuters*, June 13, 2013, http://www.reuters.com/article/2013/06/13/us-austerity-spain-idUSBRE95C0DB20130613

Kenny, Ciara. "Emigration of Irish nationals falls 20% in year to April." *The Irish Times*, August 26, 2014, http://www.irishtimes.com/news/social-affairs/emigration-of-irish-nationals-falls-20-in-year-to-april-1.1908275

Kertscher, Tom. "Under Scott Walker, Wisconsin lags U.S. in wage, job growth, 'Meet the Press' host Chuck Todd says." *Politifact*, November 28, 2014, http://www.politifact.com/wisconsin/statements/2014/nov/28/chuck-todd/under-scott-walker-wisconsin-lags-us-wage-job-grow/

Kinsella, Stephen. "Is Ireland really the role model for austerity?" *Cambridge Journal of Economics* 36:1 (2012), 223–235.

Kirkup, James. "Osborne: We've saved the economy and proved Labour wrong," *The Telegraph*, September 9, 2013, http://www.telegraph.co.uk/news/politics/georgeosborne/10295060/Osborne-Weve-saved-the-economy-and-proved-Labour-wrong.html

Klein, Erza. "What is actually being proposed in Wisconsin?" *The Washington Post*, February 18, 2011, http://voices.washingtonpost.com/ezra-klein/2011/02/what_is_actually_being_propose.html

Kochhar, Rakesh, and Richard Fry. "Wealth inequality has widened along racial, ethnic lines since end of Great Recession." *Pew Research Center*, December 12, 2014, http://www.pewresearch.org/fact-tank/2014/12/12/racial-wealth-gaps-great-recession/

Konzelmann, Sue. "The economics of austerity," *Centre for Business Research*, University of Cambridge Working Paper No. 434 (June 2012), 1–38.

Koutantou, Angeliki. "Greek PM Samaras vows tax cuts as leftists hold poll lead." *Reuters*, January 10, 2015, http://www.reuters.com/article/2015/01/10/us-greece-election-samaras-idUSKBN0KJ0H520150110

Kroll, Andy. "What's happening in Wisconsin explained." *Mother Jones*, March 17, 2011, http://www.motherjones.com/mojo/2011/02/whats-happening-wisconsin-explained

————. "Wisconsin Gov. Scott Walker: Funded by the Koch Bros." *Mother Jones*, February 18, 2011, http://www.motherjones.com/mojo/2011/02/wisconsin-scott-walker-koch-brothers

Krugman, Paul. "American austerity, charted yet again." *The New York Times*, March 1, 2014, http://krugman.blogs.nytimes.com/2014/03/01/american-austerity-charted-yet-again/?_r=1

————. *End This Depression Now!* (London and New York: W.W. Norton & Company, 2013) Kindle Edition.

————. "How the case for austerity has crumbled." *The New York Review of Books*, June 6 (2013), http://www.nybooks.com/articles/archives/2013/jun/06/how-case-austerity-has-crumbled/?pagination=false

————. "Introduction to *The General Theory of Employment, Interest, and Money*, by John Maynard Keynes," 2000, http://www.pkarchive.org/economy/GeneralTheoryKeynesIntro.html

Labonte, Marc, and Mindy R. Levit. "Congressional Research Service: The Budget Control Act of 2011: Effects on spending levels and the budget deficit." *Council on Foreign Relations*, October 5, 2011, http://www.cfr.org/united-states/congressional-research-service-budget-control-act-2011-effects-spending-levels-budget-deficit/p26369

"Labour won't reverse Tory public spending cuts, Miliband will announce." *Huffington Post*, June 22, 2013, http://www.huffingtonpost.co.uk/2013/06/21/labour-spending-cuts-hars_n_3480442.html

Lanchester, John. "Let's call it failure." *London Review of Books*, 35:1 (January 3, 2013), http://www.lrb.co.uk/v35/n01/john-lanchester/lets-call-it-failure

Landon, Jr., Thomas. "Money troubles take personal toll in Greece." May 15, 2011, http://www.nytimes.com/2011/05/16/business/global/16drachma.html?_r=3&pagewanted=all&

Lane, Philip R. "The European sovereign debt crisis," *Journal of Economic Perspective*, 26:3 (2012), 49–68.

Lee-Murphy, Michael. "Ireland's Resurgent Left." *Jacobin*, January 2015, https://www.jacobinmag.com/2015/01/ireland-water-charges-sinn-fein/

"Leftist Syriza wins Greek EU poll, requests early general election." *Euractiv*, May 26, 2014, http://www.euractiv.com/sections/eu-elections-2014/leftist-syriza-wins-greek-eu-poll-requests-early-general-election-302396

"Long-term profile of Gross Domestic Product (GDP) in the UK." *Office for National Statistics*, August 23, 2013, http://www.ons.gov.uk/ons/rel/elmr/explaining-economic-statistics/long-term-profile-of-gdp-in-the-uk/sty-long-term-profile-of-gdp.html

Luhby, Tami. "Gov. Scott Walker unveils Wisconsin budget." *CNN*, March 1, 2011, http://money.cnn.com/2011/03/01/news/economy/wisconsin_budget_walker/

Lunney, Kellie. "Obama signs off on fed pay freeze." *Government Executive*, March 26, 2013, http://www.govexec.com/pay-benefits/2013/03/obama-signs-fed-pay-freeze/62103/

Lyddon, Dave. "Industrial relations." *TUC Online*, n.d. http://www.unionhistory.info/timeline/1960_2000_7.php

———. "The 1984–85 miners' strike." *TUC Online*, n.d. http://www.unionhistory.info/timeline/1960_2000_Narr_Display_2.php?Where=NarTitle+contains+%27The+1984-85+Miners+Strike%27+

———. "The Union makes us strong." *TUC Online*, n.d. http://www.unionhistory.info/timeline/1960_2000_Narr_Display.php?Where=NarTitle+contains+%27Anti-Union+Legislation%3A+1980-2000%27+

Mann, Keith. "Resistance to Neo-Liberalism: France, Greece, Spain, and the US." *Perspectives on Global Development and Technology*, 11 (2012), 182–191.

Marx, Anthony W. "South African Black trade unions as an emerging working-class movement." *The Journal of Modern African Studies*, 27:3 (1989), 383–400.

Mason, Paul. "A snapshot of the 26 March demo." *BBC News*, March 26, 2011, http://www.bbc.co.uk/blogs/legacy/newsnight/paulmason/2011/03/a_snapshot_of_the_26_march_dem.html

———. "'Hope begins today': the inside story of Syriza's rise to power." *The Guardian*, January 29, 2015, http://www.theguardian.com/world/2015/jan/28/greek-people-wrote-history-how-syriza-rose-to-power

Mason, Rowena. "Clegg backs Osborne's timetable for eliminating UK's structural deficit." *The Guardian*, February 11, 2014, http://www.theguardian.com/politics/2014/feb/10/clegg-backs-osborne-timetable-eliminate-uk-structural-deficit

"Massive Montreal rally ends with police clashes." *CBC News*, May 22, 2012, http://www.cbc.ca/news/canada/montreal/massive-montreal-rally-ends-with-police-clashes-1.1138111

"Massive student tuition march paralyzes Montreal." *CBC News*, March 22, 2011 http://www.cbc.ca/news/canada/montreal/massive-student-tuition-march-paralyzes-montreal-1.1165575

Matles James J., and James Higgins. *Them and Us: Struggles of a Rank-and-File Union.* (NJ: Prentice-Hall, 1995),

McCluskey, Len. "Mandelson is wrong: Labour can't survive without the unions." *The Guardian*, May 13, 2015, http://www.theguardian.com/commentisfree/2015/may/13/labour-survive-unite-unions-peter-mandelson

McDonald, Henry. "Ireland budget imposes more austerity." *The Guardian*, December 5, 2012, http://www.theguardian.com/world/2012/dec/05/ireland-austerity-budget

McKittrick, David. "Election results 2014: Sinn Fein profits as voters reject austerity policies." *The Independent*, May 26, 2014, http://www.independent.co.uk/news/uk/politics/election-results-2014-sinn-fein-profits-as-voters-reject-austerity-policies-9434210.html

Mejia, Paula. "Occupy Wall Street offshoot Rolling Jubilee wants to pay off your student debt." *Newsweek*, September 17, 2014, http://www.newsweek.com/occupy-wall-street-offshoot-rolling-jubilee-wants-pay-your-student-debt-271273

Mercille, Julien. "Ireland under austerity." *Counterpunch*, April 3, 2014, http://www.counterpunch.org/2014/04/03/ireland-under-austerity-2/

"Mexico external debt." *Index Mundi*, http://www.indexmundi.com/mexico/debt_external.html

Michael-Matsas, Savas. "Greece at the boiling point." *Critique*, 41:3 (2013), 437–443.

"Millions Spent on Wisconsin Recall Election." *The New York Times*, June 4, 2012, http://www.nytimes.com/interactive/2012/06/04/us/politics/money-spent-on-wisconsin-recall-election.html?_r=0

Milmo, Dan, and Jessica Shepherd, "Public sector workers prepare to strike over cuts and pension reforms." *The Guardian*, May 10, 2012, http://www.theguardian.com/society/2012/may/09/public-sector-workers-strike-

Milne, Seumas. "This strike could start to turn the tide of a generation." *The Guardian*, December 1, 2011, http://www.theguardian.com/commentisfree/2011/nov/30/strike-turns-tide-of-generation

Milonas, Ilias. "The New Programme of SYRIZA." *The Socialist Network*, December 27, 2014, http://socialistnetwork.org/the-new-programme-of-syriza/

Minder, Raphael. "Saying no to austerity, Spain unveils tax cuts." *The New York Times*, June 21, 2014, http://www.nytimes.com/2014/06/21/business/international/spain-stepping-back-from-austerity-plans-to-cut-taxes.html?_r=0

Monastiriotis, Vassilis. "A very Greek crisis," *Intereconomics*, (2013), http://www.intereconomics.eu/archive/year/2013/1/austerity-measures-in-crisis-countries-results-and-impact-on-mid-term-development/

Montopoli, Brian. "Scott Walker wins Wisconsin recall election." *CBS News*, June 6, 2012, http://www.cbsnews.com/news/scott-walker-wins-wisconsin-recall-election/

"Montreal protesters defy demo law and clash with police." *CBC News*, May 21, 2012, http://www.cbc.ca/news/canada/montreal/montreal-protesters-defy-demo-law-and-clash-with-police-1.1279274

Moody, Kim. *From Welfare State to Real Estate*. (New York: The New Press, 2007).

———. *Workers in a Lean World* (London and NY: Verso, 1997).

Moody, Kim, and Charles Post, "The Politics of US Labor: Paralysis and Possibilities" in *Socialist Register*, edited by Leo Panitch and Greg Albo. (London: Merlin Press, 2014): 295–317.

Morris, Nigel. "Benefit cuts sends number of food bank users soaring." *The Independent*, July 11, 2013, http://www.independent.co.uk/news/uk/politics/benefit-cuts-sends-number-of-food-bank-users-soaring-8701367.html

———. "Nigel Farage's suggestion of a privatised NHS flares tensions within Ukip," *The Independent*, January 21, 2015, http://www.independent.co.uk/news/uk/politics/farages-suggestion-of-a-privatised-nhs-flares-tensions-within-ukip-9991340.html

Mulhern, Francis. "Towards 2000, or News From You-Know-Where," *New Left Review*, 148, November-December (1984): 5–30.

Mulholland, Hélène. "David Cameron admits day of action was 'obviously a big strike.'" *The Guardian*, December 1, 2011, http://www.theguardian.com/society/2011/dec/01/david-cameron-obviously-big-strike?newsfeed=true

Murray, Patty. "Ten facts you may not know about the Federal Budget," *Senate Budget Committee*, 2014, http://www.budget.senate.gov/democratic/public/index.cfm/blog?ID=151019c5-2655-4530-8e6b-c7455de71dba

Nagin, Rick. "Nationwide rallies against austerity." *People's World*, January 31, 2013, http://peoplesworld.org/nationwide-rallies-against-austerity/

The National Commission on Fiscal Responsibility and Reform, "The moment of truth." *The White House*, December 2010, http://momentoftruthproject.org/sites/default/files/TheMomentofTruth12_1_2010.pdf

Nellas, Demertis, and Elena Becatoros. "Greek election results: New Democracy wins." *The World Post*, June 16, 2012, http://www.huffingtonpost.com/2012/06/17/greek-election-results-new-democracy-wins_n_1603971.html

Nelson, Fraser. "We'll balance the books!! (By 2020) George Osborne speech analysis," *The Spectator*, http://blogs.spectator.co.uk/coffeehouse/2013/09/tory-conference-2013-well-balance-the-books-by-2020-george-osbornes-speech-analysis/

"Nonunion Workers' Pay Lower." *AFL-CIO*, 2014, http://www.aflcio.org/Learn-About-Unions/What-Unions-Do/The-Union-Difference/Nonunion-Workers-Pay-Lower

Norton, Quinn. "A Eulogy for #Occupy." *Wired*, December 12, 2012, http://www.wired.com/2012/12/a-eulogy-for-occupy/all/

Offe, Claus. "Reflections on the institutional self-transformation of movement politics: A tentative stage mode." In *Challenging the Political Order*, edited by Russell J. Dalton and Manfred Kuechler, 232–250 (NY: Oxford University Press, 1990).

Ouziel, Pablo. "Spain's 'Indignant Ones.'" *Common Dreams*, June 15, 2011, http://www.commondreams.org/views/2011/06/15/spains-indignant-ones

Owen, Paul. "Budget 2013—the key points." *The Guardian*, March 20, 2013, http://www.theguardian.com/uk/2013/mar/20/budget-2013-key-points-live

Papachristou, Harry. "Factbox: Greek austerity and reform measures," *Reuters*, February 19, 2012, http://www.reuters.com/article/2012/02/19/us-greece-austerity-idUSTRE81I05T20120219

Pashkoff, Susan. "Women and austerity in Britain." *New Politics*, Winter (2014), http://newpol.org/content/women-and-austerity-britain

Phillips, Matt. "American families are stuck in a lost quarter century." *Quartz*, September 16, 2014, http://qz.com/265980/american-families-are-stuck-in-a-lost-quarter-century/

Pianin, Eric. "The Surprising fact of hunger in America." *The Fiscal Times*, December 19, 2014, http://www.thefiscaltimes.com/2014/12/19/Surprising-Fact-Hunger-America

Poinasamy, Krisnah. *The True Cost of Austerity and Inequality*. (Oxford: Oxfam GB for Oxfam International. September 2013), http://www.oxfam.org/sites/ www.oxfam.org/files/cs-true-cost-austerity-inequality-uk-120913-en.pdf

"Policies for People." *UKIP website*, n.d, http://www.ukip.org/policies_for_people

Pollin, Robert. "Austerity economics and the struggle for the soul of US capitalism." *Social Research*, 80: 3 (2013), 749–780.

Pollin, Robert, and Michael Ash. "Debt and growth: A response to Reinhart and Rogoff." *The New York Times*, April 29, 2013, http://www.nytimes. com/2013/04/30/opinion/debt-and-growth-a-response-to-reinhart-and-rogoff.html?_r=0

Power, Séamus A., and David Nussbaum,."The Fightin' Irish? Not when it comes to recession and austerity." *The Guardian*, July 24, 2014, http://www.theguardian.com/science/head-quarters/2014/jul/24/the-fightin-irish-not-when-it-comes-to-recession-and-austerity

Proyect, Louis. "The rise of Podemos." *Counterpunch*, December 12–14, 2014, http://www.counterpunch.org/2014/12/12/the-rise-of-podemos/

"Public sector pensions: Most unions agree some changes." *BBC News*, December 19, 2011, http://www.bbc.co.uk/news/business-16243824

"Quebec offers to stretch tuition hike over 7 years." *CBC News*, April 27, 2012, http://www.cbc.ca/news/canada/montreal/quebec-offers-to-stretch-tuition-hike-over-7-years-1.1209004

"Quebec students stage massive tuition fee protest." *CBC News*, November 10, 2011, http://www.cbc.ca/news/canada/montreal/quebec-students-stage-massive-tuition-fee-protest-1.1044340

"Quebec student strike grows." *CBC News*, February 20, 2012, http://www.cbc.ca/ news/canada/montreal/quebec-student-strike-grows-1.1278364

Rainsford, Sarah. "Spain's 'Indignants' lead international protest day." *BBC News*, October 14, 2011, http://www.bbc.com/news/world-europe-15315270

Reilly, Gavan. "Here's what's contained in the new 'Haddington Road' public pay deal." *The Journal*, May 23, 2013, http://www.thejournal.ie/ haddington-road-agreement-922129-May2013/

Reinhardt, Carmen, and Kenneth Rogoff. "Growth in a time of debt." *National Bureau of Economic Research* working paper 15639, Cambridge, MA, January (2010), http://www.nber.org/papers/w15639.pdf

"Reliance on austerity is counterproductive, says former IMF mission chief." *RTÉ News*, April 11, 2013, http://www.rte.ie/news/business/2013/0411/380836-too-much-austerity-in-bailout-imf-mission-chief/

Rickman, Dina. "More than 100 mentally ill people a day have their benefits sanctioned." *The Independent*, January 21, 2015, http://i100.independent. co.uk/article/more-than-100-mentally-ill-people-a-day-have-their-benefits-sanctioned--gky3O8Nmsl

" 'Right to Work' laws: Get the facts." *Minnesota AFL-CIO*, n.d., http://www. mnaflcio.org/news/right-work-laws-get-facts

Rigney, Peter. *The Impact of Anti-crisis Measures and the Social and Employment Situation: Ireland*. (Dublin: European Economic and Social Committee

Workers' Group, 2012), http://www.ictu.ie/download/pdf/impact_of_austerity_on_ireland_eesc_paper.pdf

Robinson, Ian. "Does neoliberal restructuring promote social movement unionism? U.S. developments in comparative perspective." In *Unions in a Globalized Environment*, edited by Bruce Nissen, 189–235. (Armonk, NY: M.E. Sharpe. 2002).

Robson, Tony. "UK: TUC moves to sell out fight against public sector pension cuts." *World Socialist Web Site*, December 22, 2011, http://www.wsws.org/en/articles/2011/12/tucp-d22.html

Rogers, Simon. "Major UK demonstrations and protests listed: which one was biggest?" *The Guardian*, March 28, 2011, http://www.theguardian.com/news/datablog/2011/mar/28/demonstrations-protests-uk-list

Rosenfeld, Jesse. "Quebec students spark mass protests against austerity." *The Nation*, June 12, 2012, http://www.thenation.com/article/168355/quebec-students-spark-mass-protests-against-austerity#

Rüdig, Wolfgang, and Georgios Karyotis, "Who protests in Greece? Mass opposition to austerity." *British Journal of Political Science*, 44:3 (2014), 487–513.

Sachs, Jeffrey. "Time to plan for post-Keynesian era," *The Financial Times*, June 7, 2010, http://www.ft.com/intl/cms/s/0/e7909286-726b-11df-9f82-00144feabdc0.html#axzz3KghUVntJ

Saez, Emmanuel, and Gabriel Zucman. "Exploding wealth inequality in the United States." *Washington Center for Equitable Growth*, October 20, 2014, http://equitablegrowth.org/research/exploding-wealth-inequality-united-states/

Samuels, Robert. "Walker's anti-union law has labor reeling in Wisconsin." *The Washington Post*, February 22, 2015, http://www.washingtonpost.com/politics/in-wisconsin-walkers-anti-union-law-has-crippled-labor-movement/2015/02/22/1eb3ef82-b6f1-11e4-aa05-1ce812b3fdd2_story.html

"Sarah Ahmed Quotes." *Goodreads*, n.d. http://www.goodreads.com/author/quotes/11036.Sara_Ahmed

Saunders, Lee A. "Scott Walker's austerity plan: Turning Wisconsin into the new Greece." *The Huffington Post*, May 23, 2013, http://www.huffingtonpost.com/lee-a-saunders/scott-walker-austerity_b_3326111.html

Schiavone, Michael. "Moody's account of social movement unionism: An analysis." *Critical Sociology*, 33 (March 2007), 279–309.

———. "Social movement unionism and the UE," *The Flinders Journal of History and Politics*, 23 (2006), 57–83.

———. "Social movement unions and political parties (in South Africa and the Philippines): A win-win situation?" *African and Asian Studies*, 6 (2007), 373–393.

———. *Sports and Labor in the United States*. (Albany, NY: SUNY Press, 2015).

———. *Unions in Crisis? The Future of Organized Labor in America*, (Westport, CT: Praeger, 2008).

Schneider, Howard. "An amazing mea culpa from the IMF's chief econo-mist on austerity." *The Washington Post*, January 3, 2013, http://www.washingtonpost.com/blogs/wonkblog/wp/2013/01/03/an-amazing-mea-culpa-from-the-imfs-chief-economist-on-austerity/

Schwartz, Mattathias. "Pre-occupied." *The New Yorker*, November 28, 2011, http://www.newyorker.com/magazine/2011/11/28/pre-occupied

Seymour, Richard. *Against Austerity: How We Can Fix the Crisis They Made* (London and New York Pluto Press, 2014). Kindle Edition.

———. "How to protest in the age of austerity." *The Guardian*, October 22, 2013, http://www.theguardian.com/commentisfree/2013/oct/22/how-to-protest-austerity-left-social-movements-union

Sharlet, Jeff. "Inside Occupy Wall Street." *Rolling Stone*, November 10, 2011, http://www.rollingstone.com/politics/news/occupy-wall-street-welcome-to-the-occupation-20111110

Sheahan, Fionnan, and John Downing. "Sinn Fein backs austerity in North and rejects it in South.'"*Irish Independent*, February 8, 2014, http://www.independent.ie/irish-news/politics/sinn-fein-backs-austerity-in-north-and-rejects-it-in-south-29990949.html

Smith, Amelia. "Radical Spanish Party Podemos lead polls for first time." *Newsweek*, November 3, 2014, http://www.newsweek.com/radical-spanish-party-podemos-lead-polls-first-time-281699

Smith, Helena. "Greek PM Samaras forced into U-turn as Syriza closes in on election victory." *The Guardian*, January 11, 2015, http://www.theguardian.com/world/2015/jan/10/greece-election-u-turn-antonis-samaras-syriza

———. "The future has begun, says leftist Alexis Tsipras as he scents power in Greece." *The Guardian*, December 30, 2014, http://www.theguardian.com/world/2014/dec/29/syriza-leading-polls-future-begun-alexis-tsipras-greece;

Smith, Helena, Emma Graham-Harrison, Ben Quinn, Heather Stewart, and Graeme Wearden, "Greek MPs pass austerity bill as Athens police clash with protest-ers." *The Guardian*, July 16, 2015, http://www.theguardian.com/world/2015/jul/15/greek-mps-pass-austerity-bill-as-athens-police-clash-with-protesters

Smith, Helena, and Ian Traynor, "Greek PM Alexis Tsipras unveils cabinet of mavericks and visionaries." *The Guardian*, January 28, 2015, http://www.theguardian.com/world/2015/jan/27/greece-alexis-tsipras-syriza-cabinet

Smith, Helena, and Jill Treanor. "Greece plunged into crisis as failure to elect pres-ident sets up snap election." *The Guardian*, December 30, 2014, http://www.theguardian.com/world/2014/dec/29/greece-crisis-president-snap-election

"Spain." *Center for Economic and Social Rights*, January 2015, http://www.cesr.org/downloads/FACTSHEET_Spain_2015_web.pdf

"Spain budget imposes further austerity measures." *BBC News*, September 27, 2012, http://www.bbc.com/news/business-19733995

"Spain's debt-to-GDP ratio to top 100% in 2015." *RTÉ News*, September 30, 2014, http://www.rte.ie/news/business/2014/0930/649073-spain-gdp-2015/

"Spain GDP Growth Rate." *Trading Economics*, http://www.tradingeconomics. com/spain/gdp-growth

"Spain Government Debt to GDP." Trading Economics, http://www.tradingeconomics.com/spain/government-debt-to-gdp

"Spain's Reform Example." *The Wall Street Journal*, October 29, 2014, http://online. wsj.com/articles/spains-reform-example-1414539336

"Spain Unemployment Rate." *Trading Economics*, http://www.tradingeconomics. com/spain/unemployment-rate

Spear, Michael. "In the Shadows of the 1970s Fiscal Crisis: New York City's Municipal Unions in the Twenty-First Century," *WorkingUSA*, September (2010): 351–366.

Stein, Jason, Patrick Marley, and Lee Bergquist, "Walker's budget cuts would touch most Wisconsinites." *Milwaukee Journal Sentinel*, March 1, 2011, http:// www.jsonline.com/news/statepolitics/117154428.html

Stepan-Norris, Judith, and Maurice Zeitlin. "Union democracy, radical leadership, and the hegemony of capital." *American Sociological Review*, 60: 6 (December 1995), 829–50.

Stevenson, Alex. " 'God' denies coalition meddling." *Politics.co.uk*, October 28, 2010, http://www.politics.co.uk/news/2010/10/28/god-denies-coalition-meddling

Stevis, Matina, and Ian Talley. "IMF concedes it made mistakes on Greece." *The Wall Street Journal*, June 5, 2013, http://online.wsj.com/articles/SB1000142 4127887324299104578527202781667088

Summers, Deborah. "David Cameron warns of 'new age of austerity.' " *The Guardian*, April 26, 2009, http://www.theguardian.com/politics/2009/apr/26/ david-cameron-conservative-economic-policy1

Summers, Larry. "Britain's economic growth is not a sign that austerity works." *The Washington Post*, May 4, 2014, http://www.washingtonpost.com/opinions/ britains-economic-growth-is-not-a-sign-that-austerity-works/2014/05/04/2 6b345e8-d204-11e3-937f-d3026234b51c_story.html

Swinney, Dan. "Strategic lessons for labor from Candyland," *New Labor Forum* 55 (Fall/Winter 1999).

Taylor, Matthew, Rowena Mason, Helena Horton, and Rebecca Maguire, "Public-sector strikes: hundreds of thousands join rallies in pay protest." *The Guardian*, July 11, 2014, http://www.theguardian.com/society/2014/jul/10/ public-sector-strikes-rallies-francis-maude-frances-ogrady

"Teaching unions accept pension deal." *The Guardian*, January 31, 2012, http://www.theguardian.com/society/2012/jan/30/association-teachers-accepts-pension-reforms

"Tenure rights restored in Chicago." *Chicago Teachers Union*, March 29, 2011, http://www.ctunet.com/blog/appeals-court-orders-board-to-recall-unlawfully-fired-teachers

"There could be trouble ahead." *The Economist*, December 10, 2011, http://www.economist.com/node/21541388

"Timeline: Spain's economic crisis." *Reuters*, December 30, 2011, http://www.reuters. com/article/2011/12/30/us-spain-cuts-economy-idUSTRE7BT0RL20111230

Townsend, Mark. "Five million votes, two seats: Smaller parties demand a change in the rules." *The Guardian*, May 9, 2015, http://www.theguardian.com/ politics/2015/may/09/margate-ukip-greens-electoral-reform-farage

Townsend, Mark, Tracy McVeigh, Jamie Doward, and David Sharrock. "Anti-cuts march draws hundreds of thousands as police battle rioters." *The Guardian*, March 27, 2011, http://www.theguardian.com/society/2011/mar/26/ anti-cuts-march-police-rioters

"Trade Union membership 2014." *Department for Business, Innovation & Skills*, June 2015, https://www.gov.uk/government/statistics/trade-union-statistics-2014

"Trade Union responses to the emergency budget." *Trade Union Solidarity*, June 22, 2010, http://solidaritymagazine.org/2010/06/trade-union-responses-to-the-emergency-budget/

Traynor, Ian. Tsipras's shock call for vote on Greek bailout sets day of destiny for Europe." *The Guardian*, June 28, 2015, http://www.theguardian.com/ world/2015/jun/27/greece-bailout-referendum-ramps-up-eurozone-crisis

Traynor, Ian, John Hooper, and Helena Smith. "Greek referendum no vote signals huge challenge to eurozone leaders." July 6, 2015, http://www. theguardian.com/business/2015/jul/05/greek-referendum-no-vote-signals-huge-challenge-to-eurozone-leaders

Traynor, Ian, and Jennifer Rankin. "Greek failure to make IMF payment deals historic blow to Eurozone." *The Guardian*, July 1, 2015, http://www.theguardian.com/ world/2015/jun/30/eurozone-emergency-greece-without-financial-lifeline

Traynor, Ian, Jennifer Rankin, and Helena Smith, "Greek crisis: surrender fiscal sovereignty in return for bailout, Merkel tells Tsipras," *The Guardian*, July 13, 2015, http://www.theguardian.com/business/2015/jul/12/greek-crisis-surrender-fiscal-sovereignty-in-return-for-bailout-merkel-tells-tsipras

Traynor, Ian, and Helena Smith. "Syriza's historic win puts Greece on collision course with Europe." *The Guardian*, January 26, 2015, http://www.theguardian.com/ world/2015/jan/25/syriza-historic-win-greece-european-union-austerity

Tremlett, Giles. "Spain: the pain of austerity deepens." *The Guardian*, January 1, 2013, http://www.theguardian.com/world/2013/jan/01/spain-pain-austerity-deepens

Trichet, Jean-Claude. "Stimulate no more—it is now time for all to tighten." *The Financial Times*, July 22, 2010, http://www.ft.com/intl/cms/s/0/1b3ae97e-95c6-11df-b5ad-00144feab49a.html#axzz1rw5D7xpm

"The true cost of austerity and inequality." *Oxfam*, September 2013, https://www. oxfamireland.org/sites/default/files/upload/pdfs/austerity-ireland-case-study.pdf

Trumka, Richard. "Austerity only weakens the economy." *The Hill*, March 19, 2013, http://thehill.com/special-reports/jobs-and-the-economy-march-2013/ 289143-austerity-only-weakens-the-economy

"Tuition hike angers Quebec students." *CBC News*, March 18, 2011, http://www.cbc.ca/news/canada/montreal/tuition-hike-angers-quebec-students-1.990024

Tufts, Steven, and Mark P. Thomas. "Populist Unionism Confronts Austerity in Canada." *Labor Studies Journal*, 39:1 (2014), 60–82.

Turner, Lowell. "Reviving the labor movement: A comparative perspective" [Electronic version], *Cornell University, ILR School site*, 2003, http://digitalcommons.ilr.cornell.edu/articles/756/

UE News, August 5, 1944.

———. January 15, 1993.

———. February 4, 1994.

Uetricht, Micah. "Strike for America: The CTU and the Democrats." *Jacobin*, December 2012, https://www.jacobinmag.com/2012/12/ctu-and-dems/

"UK economy 'faces crisis' warns former IMF cconomist." *BBC News*, February 7, 21010, http://news.bbc.co.uk/2/hi/8503090.stm

"UK to dodge Greek fate with tough budget—Osborne." *Reuters*, June 20, 2010, http://uk.reuters.com/article/2010/06/20/uk-britain-osborne-budget-idUKTRE65J0UX20100620

"UK wages rise more than expected, unemployment rate stays unchanged." *Reuters*, November 12, 2014, http://uk.reuters.com/article/2014/11/12/uk-britain-jobs-idUKKCN0IW0VJ20141112

Umhoefer, Dave. "Gov. Scott Walker says he asked unions for concessions and they refused." *PolitiFact Wisconsin*, September 16, 2011, http://www.politifact.com/wisconsin/statements/2011/sep/16/scott-walker/gov-scott-walker-says-he-asked-unions-concessions-/

"Unemployment rate by sex and age groups—monthly average, %." *Eurostat*, November 18, 2014, http://appsso.eurostat.ec.europa.eu/nui/show.do?dataset=une_rt_m&lang=en

"The Union Advantage." *TUC*, 2014, http://strongerunions.org/wp-content/uploads/2014/09/TUC_UnionADV_A5_16pp_FINAL-LO1.pdf

"The Union Difference." *AFL-CIO*, 2014, http://www.aflcio.org/content/download/144451/3726001/version/1/file/UnionDifference_Mar2014.pdf

"Union membership in Wisconsin—2014." *Bureau of Labor Statistics*, 2015, http://www.bls.gov/regions/midwest/news-release/unionmembership_wisconsin.htm

"United Kingdom Government debt to GDP, 1980–2014." *Trading Economics*, 2014, http://www.tradingeconomics.com/united-kingdom/government-debt-to-gdp

"United States Government debt to GDP." *Trading Economics*, 2014, http://www.tradingeconomics.com/united-states/government-debt-to-gdp

"United States unemployment rate." *Trading Economics*, 2014, http://www.tradingeconomics.com/united-states/unemployment-rate

"UPDATE: Sigma Dos poll shows Ciudadanos second behind PP." *The Spain Report*, November 19, 2015, https://www.thespainreport.com/newsitems/329-151119215346-update-sigma-dos-poll-shows-ciudadanos-second-behind-pp

van Stekelenburg, Jacquelien. "The Occupy Movement: Product of this time." *Local/Global Encounters*, 55:2 (2012), 224–231.

Vogiatzoglou, Markos. "Trade unions in Greece: Protest and social movements in the context of austerity politics," 4–6. Translated from Markos Vogiatzoglou," Die griechische Gewerkschaftsbewegung: Protestund Sozialbewegungen im Kontext der Austeritätspolitik," *WSI-Mitteilungen*, 2014.

Voskeritsian, Horen. "Whither Greek trade unionism?" *Better Together*, July (2013): 1–5.

Walker, Kirsty. "Vince Cable admits previously opposing VAT rise to 'score points.'"*Daily Mail*, June 28, 2010, http://www.dailymail.co.uk/news/article-1290176/Vince-Cable-admits-previously-opposing-VAT-score-points.html#ixzz3KlAO6gtg

Wahl, Asbjørn. "Political and ideological crisis in an increasingly more authoritarian European Union," *Monthly Review*, 65:8 (2014), http://monthlyreview.org/2014/01/01/european-labor/

Waldron, Travis. "11 republicans who cited a faulty study to push for drastic spending cuts." *Think Progress*, April 16, 2013, http://thinkprogress.org/economy/2013/04/16/1875541/11-republicans-who-cited-a-flawed-study-to-push-for-drastic-spending-cuts/

Walker, Jonathan. "'Abandon austerity and borrow' North East Labour MPs urge Ed Miliband." *Chronicle Live*, January 28, 2015, http://www.chroniclelive.co.uk/news/north-east-news/abandon-austerity-borrow-north-east-8526379

Wearden, Graeme. "Greece bailout agreement: key points." *The Guardian*, July 14, 2015, http://www.theguardian.com/business/2015/jul/13/greece-bailout-agreement-key-points-grexit

———. "Ireland austerity budget announced as markets cling to debt ceiling deal hopes—as it happened." *The Guardian*, October 16, 2013, http://www.theguardian.com/business/2013/oct/15/us-debt-ceiling-deal-hopes-push-markets-higher-live

Werdigier, Julia. "Its growth slowing, Britain extends austerity measures." *The New York Times*, November 29, 2011, http://www.nytimes.com/2011/11/30/business/global/britain-lowers-economic-growth-forecast.html?_r=0

"What is austerity?" *The Economist*, May 20, 2015, http://www.economist.com/blogs/buttonwood/2015/05/fiscal-policy

"What most people don't understand about the Wisconsin Budget Repair Bill." *Daily Kos*, February 17, 2011, http://www.dailykos.com/story/2011/02/18/946466/-What-Most-People-Don-t-Understand-About-the-Wisconsin-Budget-Repair-Bill-Updated#

"What we stand for." *UKIP website*, n.d, http://www.ukip.org/issues

Whitaker, Andrew. "Labour will keep austerity, says Miliband." *The Scotsman*, February 11, 2014, http://www.scotsman.com/news/uk/labour-will-keep-austerity-says-miliband-1-3300839

White, Michael. "Public sector strikers clean up after giving dressing down to government." *The Guardian*, June 30, 2011, http://www.theguardian.com/society/2011/jun/30/public-sector-pensions-policy

Wigmore, Tim. "20 seats with the lowest turnout show Labour voters drifting to Ukip—or not voting at all." *New Statesman*, May 13, 2015, http://www.

newstatesman.com/politics/2015/05/20-seats-lowest-turnout-show-labour-voters-drifting-ukip-or-not-voting-all

Williamson, John. "A short history of the Washington Consensus," paper commissioned by Fundación CIDOB for the conference "From the Washington Consensus towards a New Global Governance," Barcelona, September 24–25 (2004).

Wintour, Patrick. "Strikes a mistake, insists Ed Miliband—but signs of dissent in shadow cabinet." *The Guardian*, June 27, 2011, http://www.theguardian.com/politics/2011/jun/26/strikes-mistake-miliband-dissent-cabinet

Wintour, Patrick, and Allegra Stratton, "Ed Miliband sets out reform agenda and says: Labour cannot go on like this." *The Guardian*, June 25, 2011, http://www.theguardian.com/politics/2011/jun/24/labour-ed-miliband-reform

Woodruff, Betsy. "Wisconsin three-peat," *Slate*, November 5, 2014, http://www.slate.com/articles/news_and_politics/politics/2014/11/scott_walker_wins_wisconsin_again_why_the_conservative_governor_won_again.html

Woolls, Daniel, and Ciaran Giles. "Spain's austerity plan aims to shave $79 billion off the state budget." *The Huffington Post*, September 10, 2012, http://www.huffingtonpost.com/2012/07/11/spain-austerity-plan_n_1664443.html

Wren-Lewis, Simon. "How much has austerity cost (so far)?" *Mainly Macro*, July 21, 2013, http://mainlymacro.blogspot.com.au/2013/07/how-much-has-austerity-cost-so-far.html

———. "Recovery rhetoric and reality." *Mainly Macro*, April 29, 2014, http://mainlymacro.blogspot.com.au/2014/04/recovery-rhetoric-and-reality.html

Wright, Oliver. "Tory attitudes to poverty under fire amid benefit sanctions and Baroness Jenkin comment that poor 'don't know how to cook.'" *The Independent*, December 9, 2014, http://www.independent.co.uk/news/uk/politics/tory-attitudes-to-poverty-under-fire-amid-benefit-sanctions-and-baroness-jenkin-comment-that-poor-dont-know-how-to-cook-9911580.html

Yates, Michael D. "Does the U.S. labor movement have a future?" *Monthly Review*, 48:9 (1997), 1–18.

———. "Occupy Wall Street and the significance of political slogans." *Counterpunch*, February 27, 2013, http://www.counterpunch.org/2013/02/27/occupy-wall-street-and-the-significance-of-political-slogans/

Zelizer, Julian. "How labor unions and Democrats fell out of love." CNN, August 31, 2014, http://edition.cnn.com/2014/08/31/opinion/zelizer-labor-democrats/

Zieger, Robert H. *The CIO 1935–1955*. (Chapel Hill and London: University of North Carolina Press, 1995).

Zogby, John. "Demography of hunger in America in 2014." *Forbes*, December 17, 2014, http://www.forbes.com/sites/johnzogby/2014/12/17/the-demography-of-hunger-in-america-2014-2/

Zuckerman, Mortimer B. "Mort Zuckerman: The jobs picture is far worse than it looks." *US News & World Report*, February 28, 2013, http://www.usnews.com/opinion/mzuckerman/articles/2013/02/28/mort-zuckerman-the-jobs-picture-is-far-worse-than-it-looks

Index